PICTURING ADDITION

From Models to Symbols

Robert Madell
Elizabeth Larkin Stahl
Village Community School
New York City

Project Editor: Virginia Thompson

P. O. Box 10328
Palo Alto, California 94303
Printed in U.S.A.

1.081.8

ISBN:0-88488-072-9

TABLE OF CONTENTS

NOTES FROM THE AUTHORS

When we first started working on these materials, we already were using a program of individual instruction with Base 10 blocks. We needed paper and pencil activities that would preserve the advantages of that program. But what we did not realize at the time was that we would eventually create something more than an effective supplement to our block program. It was only in the process of writing and then using our sheets that we began to see how they could be expanded to help children make the transition to the more abstract work that they would find in standard elementary arithmetic texts.

This series of books is a compilation of what we felt were our most successful materials. All of the materials have been used in grades K–3 at the Village Community School in New York City, as well as in other parts of the country. We are pleased with the results and hope that you will be.

Supplementing the Base 10 Blocks

Perhaps the best way for us to introduce you to the features of this material is by referring you to our original goal. We wanted to preserve the advantages of our program with Base 10 blocks. As we analyzed our methods of instruction, we saw two features that we especially wanted to build into our activity sheets.

1) With blocks, the Base 10 system of numeration can be represented concretely by the child. For example, the number that is represented in abstract symbols as "123" can be concretely represented as 1 flat (hundred), 2 longs (tens), and 3 units (ones). The child can actually hold this representative in his or her hands and see the relationships between the ones, tens, and hundreds.

2) With blocks, no matter what the type of arithmetic problem, the teacher can indicate, and the child can actually carry out, the action that the problem implies. For example, the action of joining collections of objects that is associated with addition can be carried out *physically* by the child using the blocks.

We believed (and still do) that it was because the Base 10 blocks were giving our students the ability to represent physically both the system of numeration and the action necessary to solve a problem, that they were working happily at problems and even finding sophisticated ways to solve them. For example, consider the problem 342 ÷ 3. In this abstract form, it would be completely inappropriate for young children. However, when it was presented as:

Share 342 ice cream cones among 3 children.
How many will they each get?

we found that it could be solved after only little instruction in the use of Base 10 blocks. Our children would simply take 3 flats, 4 longs, and 2 units (representing the number concretely) and distribute the collection into 3 equivalent piles (performing a physical action). The necessary exchange of one of the longs for ten units did not stand in their way.

As a consequence of this analysis, we wrote activity pages in which the system of numeration was represented in a semi-concrete fashion and in which the necessary actions (such as joining for addition) were strongly suggested. Furthermore, in some sense, we wanted the child to be able to act physically, even if only with pictures on a piece of paper. This was accomplished as follows.

First we adopted a system which uses to represent one thousand, to represent one hundred, to represent ten, and ● to represent one. These symbols are abstractions from real Base 10 blocks, but they are far more concrete than numerals. We were very pleased with the ease with which even very young children mastered the notation. The symbols seemed nearly as real to the children as the blocks themselves. Somewhat surprisingly, we did not find it necessary to make extensive use of more concrete representations like those pictured below.

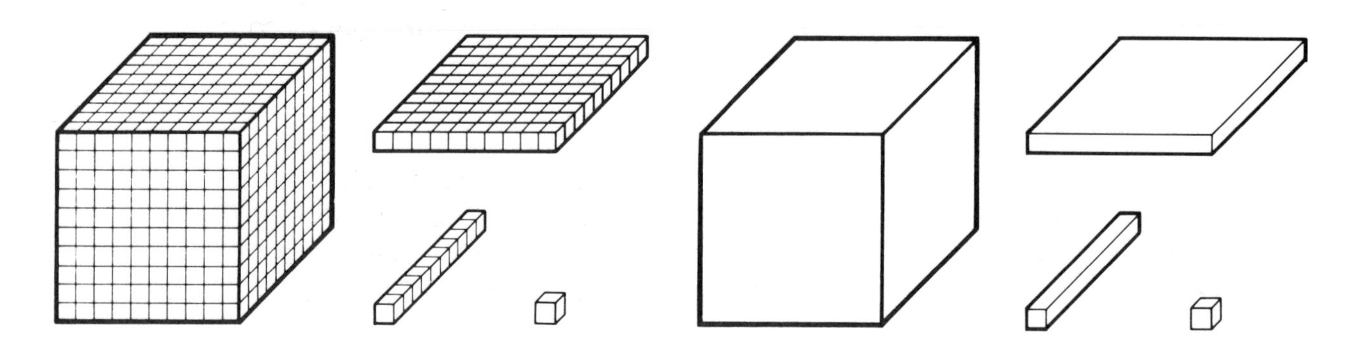

Then we sought problem formats that would make the actions required to solve the problems as clear as possible. The result was formats like this

Share. Give each can the same.

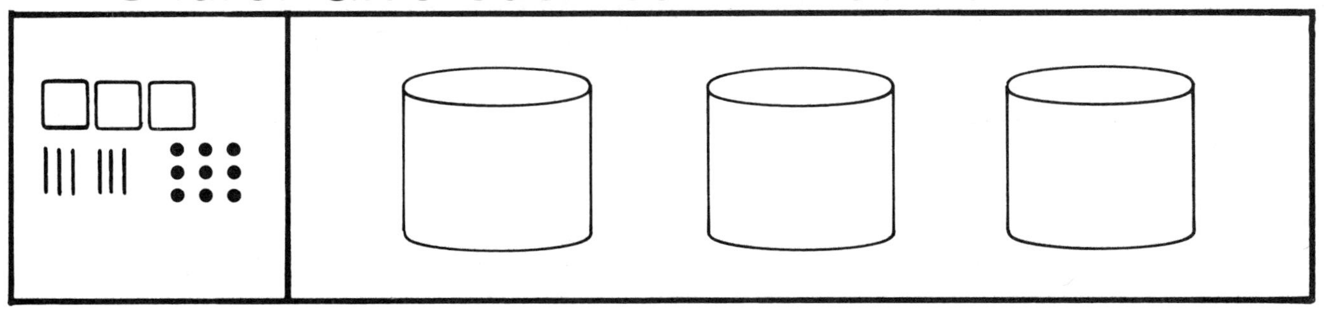

and this.

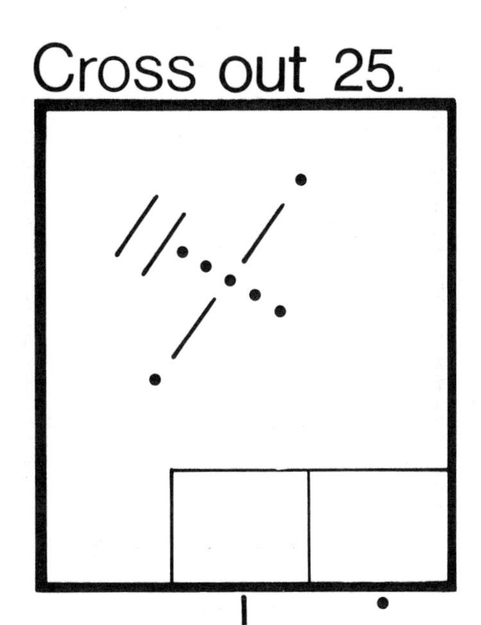

These formats are good examples of what we tried to achieve. For in each case, the numbers that are to be acted on are represented semi-concretely, the action that is required is strongly suggested, and there is room for the child to act physically. In the division problem the symbols can be distributed

Share. Give each can the same.

and in the subtraction problem they can be crossed out.

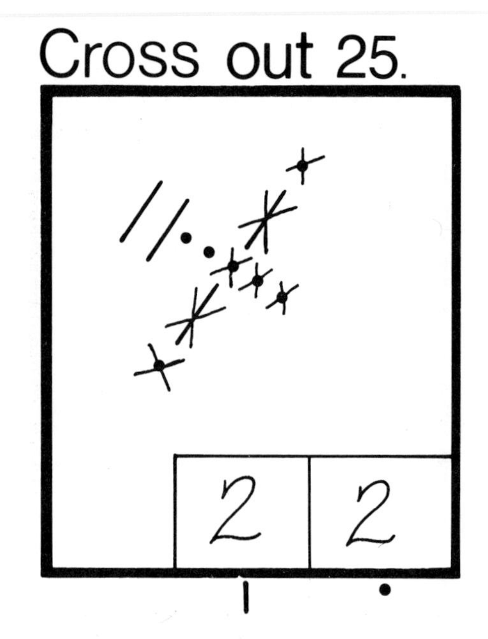
Cross out 25.
2
2

When we tried problems like these with our students, we found that the theory held up. The children attacked the problems freely and intelligently as they had done with the blocks themselves. That is not to say they never got confused or stuck, or that they never used inefficient reasoning processes. But, it is to say that the problems made sense to them. They understood them and approached them as puzzles to be solved rather than as routine exercises.

Making the Transition from Blocks to Numerals

As we were using these original sheets, we realized that we had built into them work that would surely help children *beyond* what the Base 10 blocks alone could do. On virtually all of our pages the children were required to use numerals in some way, primarily to record answers. We believed that this act of recording with numerals was bound to help the children establish a connection between the semi-concrete symbols ⧉ , □ , | and ● and abstract numerals. But we wanted more emphasis on this association. Thus, we set about producing two new kinds of activity sheets.

In the first place, we created some activities that did not involve the operations of addition, subtraction, multiplication, or division at all, but rather, only required the children to count and record. Below is a typical example.

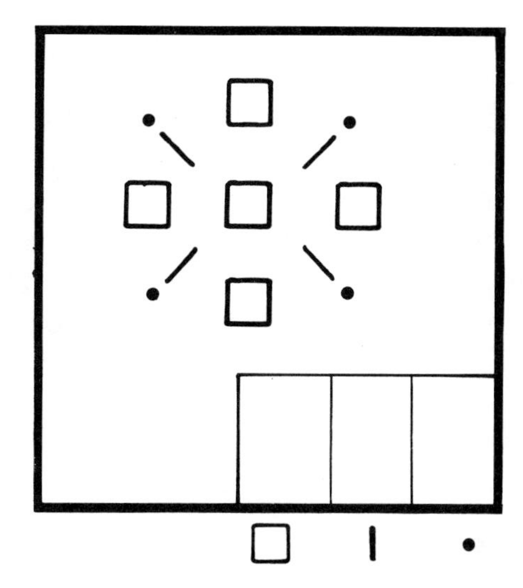

We hoped that by narrowing the task in this way, the children's attention would be focused on the nature and use of numerals. Problems of this type now make up the Numeration book.

Then, we went further. We felt it necessary to prepare children to *use* numerals—to *act* on them—in the same way in which they had acted on Base 10 blocks. We felt that since standard arithmetic texts presented problems like $\begin{array}{r}34\\+23\\\hline\end{array}$ and $\begin{array}{r}48\\-21\\\hline\end{array}$, we also would have to present problems using numerals. But we still wanted to maintain some sense of concreteness in our activities. Among the many activities that we tried, one of the most successful for addition is shown below.

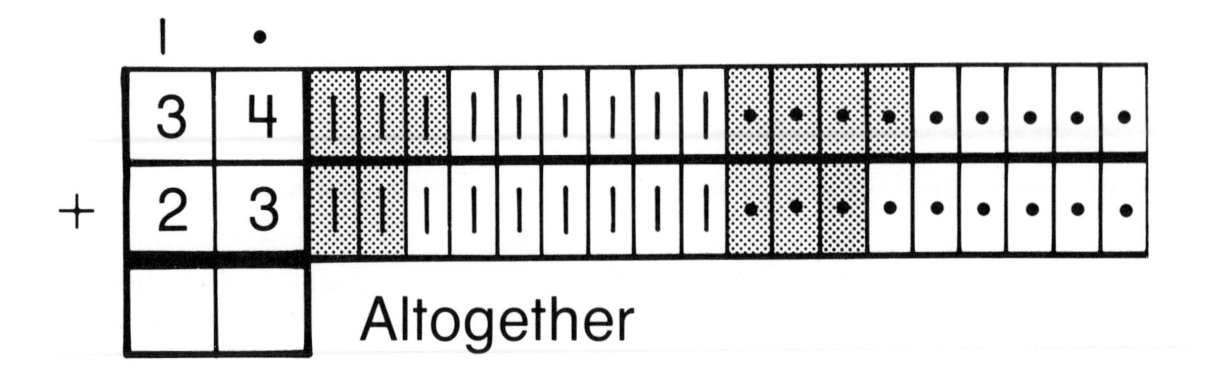

This format, while making the semi-concrete symbols for ten and one available, seems in practice to discourage their use. We suggested to our students that they shade in 3 tens and 4 ones in the top row and 2 tens and 3 ones in the bottom before finding the sum. But as time went on, many discovered that the sum could be found without that extra work. They *imagined* that they had done the shading and then used that imagery to do the necessary computation. They had been led to acting on numerals.

In this format,

Give away 21.

48

children are confronted with numerals *only.* But nevertheless, they find it more real than the corresponding $\begin{array}{r}48\\-21\\\hline\end{array}$. Eventually they are able to visualize the 4 tens and 8 ones inside the jar and then imagine the process of giving away 21.

Making the Transition from Action to Operation

Just as we saw the need to prepare children to give up their dependence on a concrete presentation of number, we saw also the need to prepare them to solve problems without the assistance of suggested action. They needed to learn what actions the symbols +, −, ×, and ÷ imply and to become familiar with their use in standard horizontal and vertical formats. Once again, rather than simply presenting problems like 143 + 221 = and $\begin{array}{r}47\\-23\\\hline\end{array}$ we tried to preserve some of the concreteness of our original work. The results were problems like these.

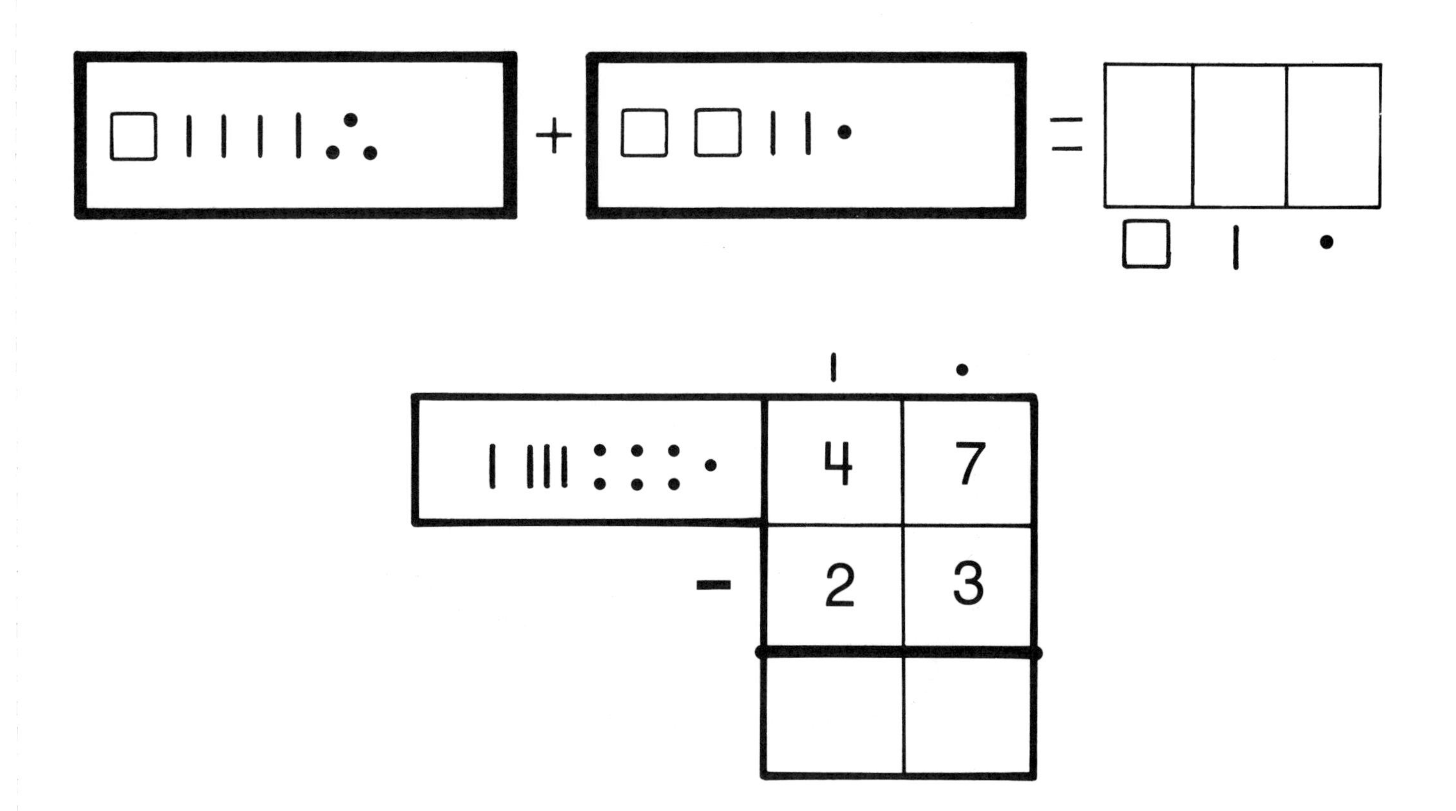

They have relatively familiar formats and use the standard operational symbols. They retain, on the other hand, the semi-concrete representation of number. We felt then, and still do, that the conventional representations should be approached very slowly. Symbols can acquire meaning only gradually. Their premature use can lead only to meaningless manipulation.

Making the Transition from Counting to Using Algorithms

We tried our new ideas with students who had made sufficient progress through the original sheets. Once again we were pleased with the results. The children continued to work intelligently, but now they could use numerals and operational symbols like + and − . They continued to produce more and more sophisticated methods of solution. But there was one thing that they did not yet do. They did not solve these problems with the standard algorithms. Thus, once again we decided to expand our materials. We wanted our students to learn the conventional computational procedures. This requires a little explanation.

When we started with our most basic sheets with semi-concrete symbols and implied action, we taught the children to solve the problems by counting. For example, in this problem

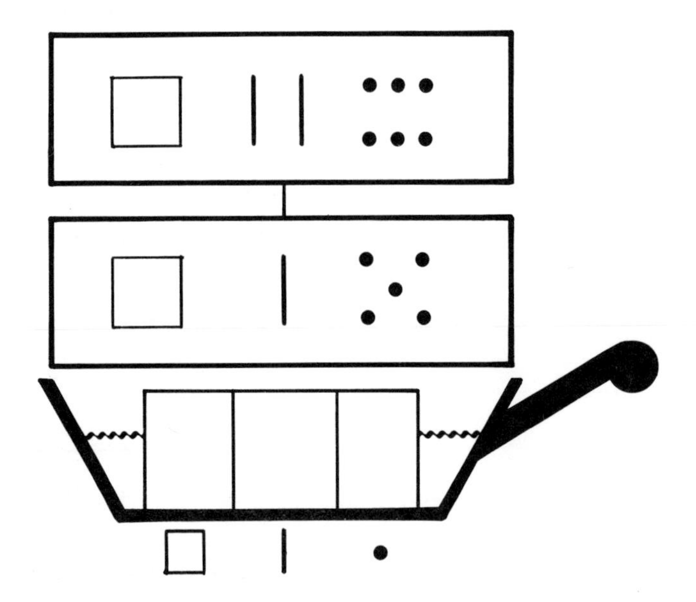

we had them count, 100, 200, 210, 220, 230, 231, 232, 233, 234, 235, 236, 237, 238, 239, 240, 241. Once we had introduced this basic counting method, the children began, at different rates, and quite on their own, to use more mature methods of solution. For example, some discovered that in this problem they could avoid the difficult jump from 239 to 240. These children would begin by counting out 10 of the ones, circling them, and replacing them by a ten.

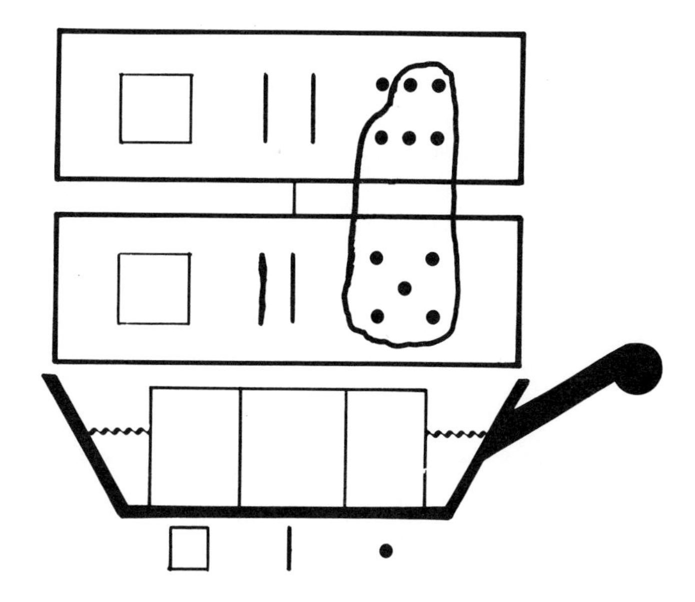

Having done so they would count, 100, 200, 210, 220, 230, 240, 241. Others learned to make use of just the recording process and didn't really count at all. Having made the same exchange as indicated above, these children simply wrote 2 for the 2 flats, 4 for the 4 longs, and 1 for the single unit. Still others would count, 100, 200 (record the 2), 10, 20, 30 (record the 3), 1, 2, 3, 4, 5, 6, 7, 8, 9, 10, 11 (erase the 3, replace it by 4, record 1 in the ones' column).

Recognizing that we could not completely control children's processes, we instead encouraged the children to do what they seemed to do naturally —search out better and better methods. Our most common response to any written work was "How did you do it?" We had the children compare their methods with one anothers'. We suggested methods of our own. We did all we could to support this kind of growth. Only when we were well satisfied that this period of searching had ended did we decide to go forward with formal instruction in the standard algorithms.

For that purpose we wrote a sequence of material for each algorithm, designed in each case to help the children bridge the gap from their own processes to that of the standard procedure. That material is included in the Addition and Subtraction books and for the most part we believe it speaks for itself. However, unlike all our other materials, these pages should be used in the order in which they appear. Also, they should be followed up with a routine program of regular computational practice. Beyond that, only one point requires further explanation.

Before we gave our children specific instruction in the algorithms, we found, almost universally, that they preferred to work both addition and subtraction problems from left to right. (You may have noticed that in the examples we gave above.) To help the children overcome this tendency, the beginning pages of each of the algorithm chapters were written to emphasize the finding of just the ones. That is why, as in the example below,

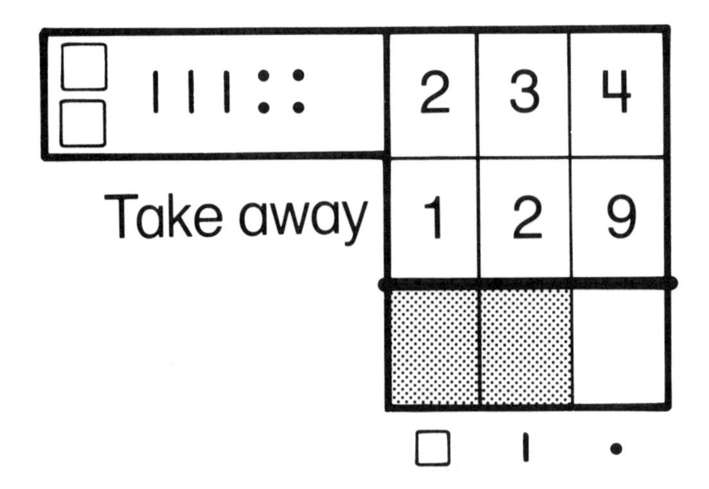

the other columns are shaded in. We felt that the students needed a little introduction before we demanded that they "Work from the right." As you work with your students on these pages, watch carefully the processes that they use. If they have difficulty in finding the ones (without first finding the tens and hundreds), they are not yet ready to work from the right and should be allowed to continue to use their own methods.

In conclusion, we hope that your students, with the help of these books, become terrific problem solvers, even with problems that use numerals and the operational symbols. When this is accomplished, we hope that they use the sections on the addition and subtraction algorithms to learn them in meaningful and therefore exciting ways.

We hope that you also enjoy the books. We do. In using them we have learned a lot about arithmetic and a lot about children. We hope that you also will feel this way. If you have any questions, comments, or suggestions, please write to us. It will help our own thinking, and therefore our teaching, to hear from you.

Rob Madell
Liz Stahl

NOTES ON USING THE BOOKS

1) For your convenience, each of the pages in Chapters 2, 4, and 6 of each of the three books has been coded to indicate the most difficult type of trading or regrouping that the problems on that particular page require. For addition and numeration:

O indicates that regrouping of *ones* to tens is required;
T indicates that regrouping of *tens* to hundreds is required;
H indicates that regrouping of *hundreds* to thousands is required.

For subtraction:

O indicates that regrouping of tens to *ones* is required;
T indicates that regrouping of hundreds to *tens* is required;
H indicates that regrouping of thousands to *hundreds* is required.

A given page may also be coded by a combination of these letters. For example, the appearance of "T and O" on an addition page indicates that the most difficult problems on that page require a regrouping of both *tens* to hundreds and *ones* to tens. The notation "T or O" on an addition page indicates that some of the problems require a regrouping of *tens* to hundreds and some require a regrouping of *ones* to tens, but none of the problems require both exchanges.

2) On many pages, the answer spaces are divided and labeled as shown

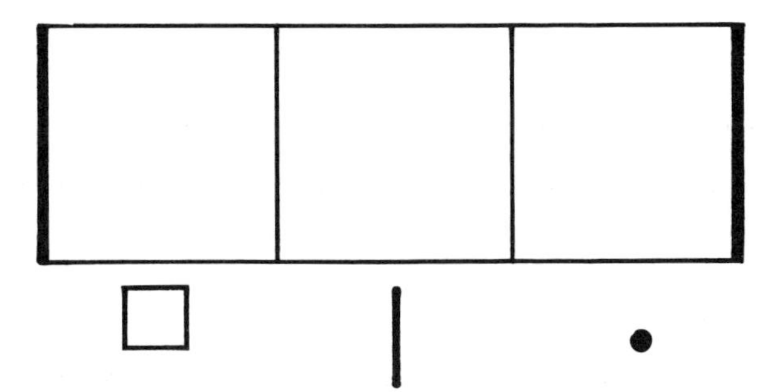

to help the children learn the recording process. On any such page that also requires regrouping, the direction "Trade if necessary" is given. That instruction is dropped from those more difficult pages on which the answer spaces are no longer divided.

3) As indicated in the NOTES FROM THE AUTHORS, the Addition and Subtraction books each have a chapter to assist in teaching the respective algorithms. In place of the algorithm chapter, the Numeration book has four pages of activities for each the four arithmetic operations. For each operation, each of the four sheets represents a different level of difficulty. One blank format sheet has also been included for each operation for you to use to make up problems of your own choosing.

4) The last chapter of all three books consists of blank pages of several of the formats. These are included so that you will be able to make your own problems in areas where your students need more work.

Combine and record.

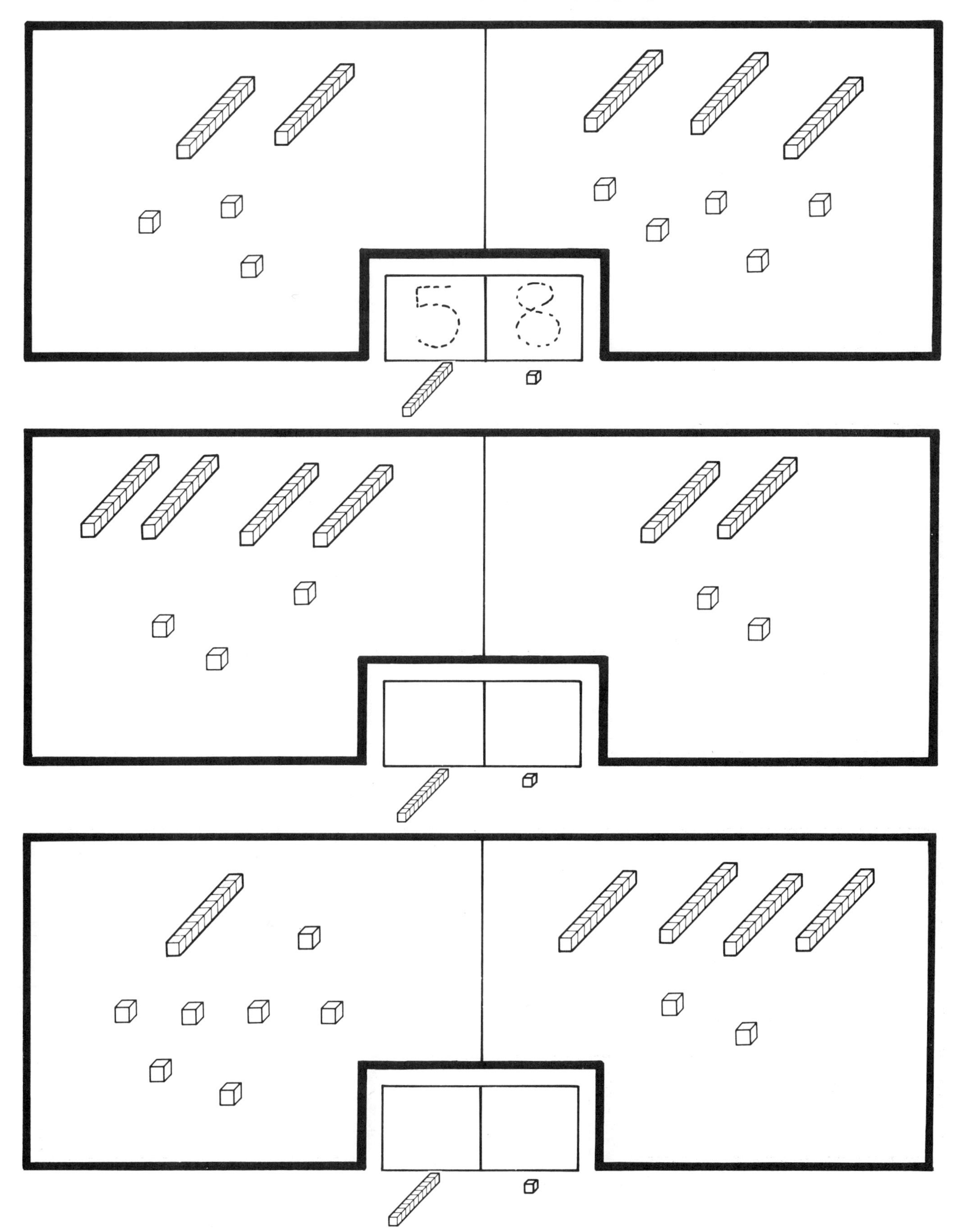

Combine and record.

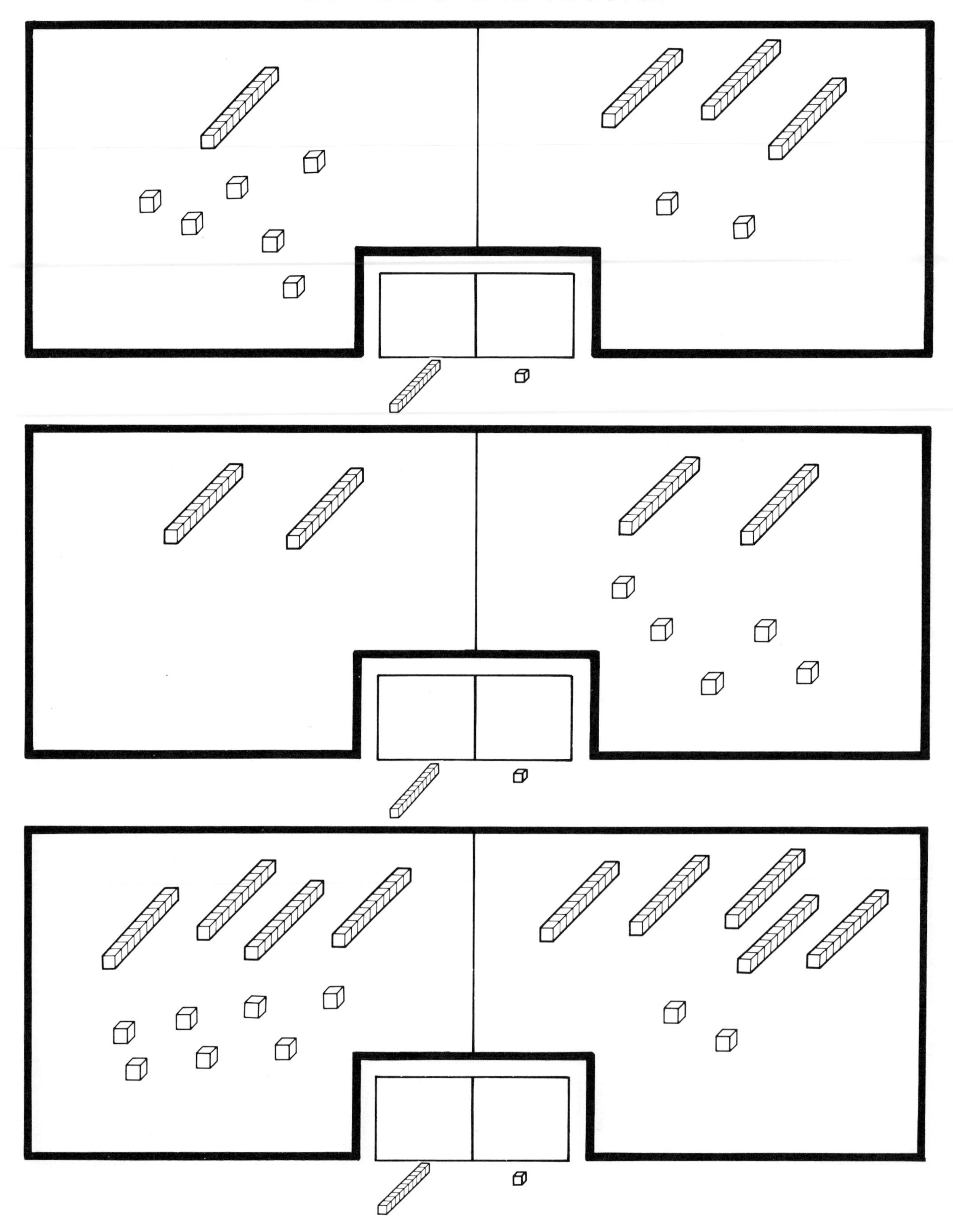

Combine and record.

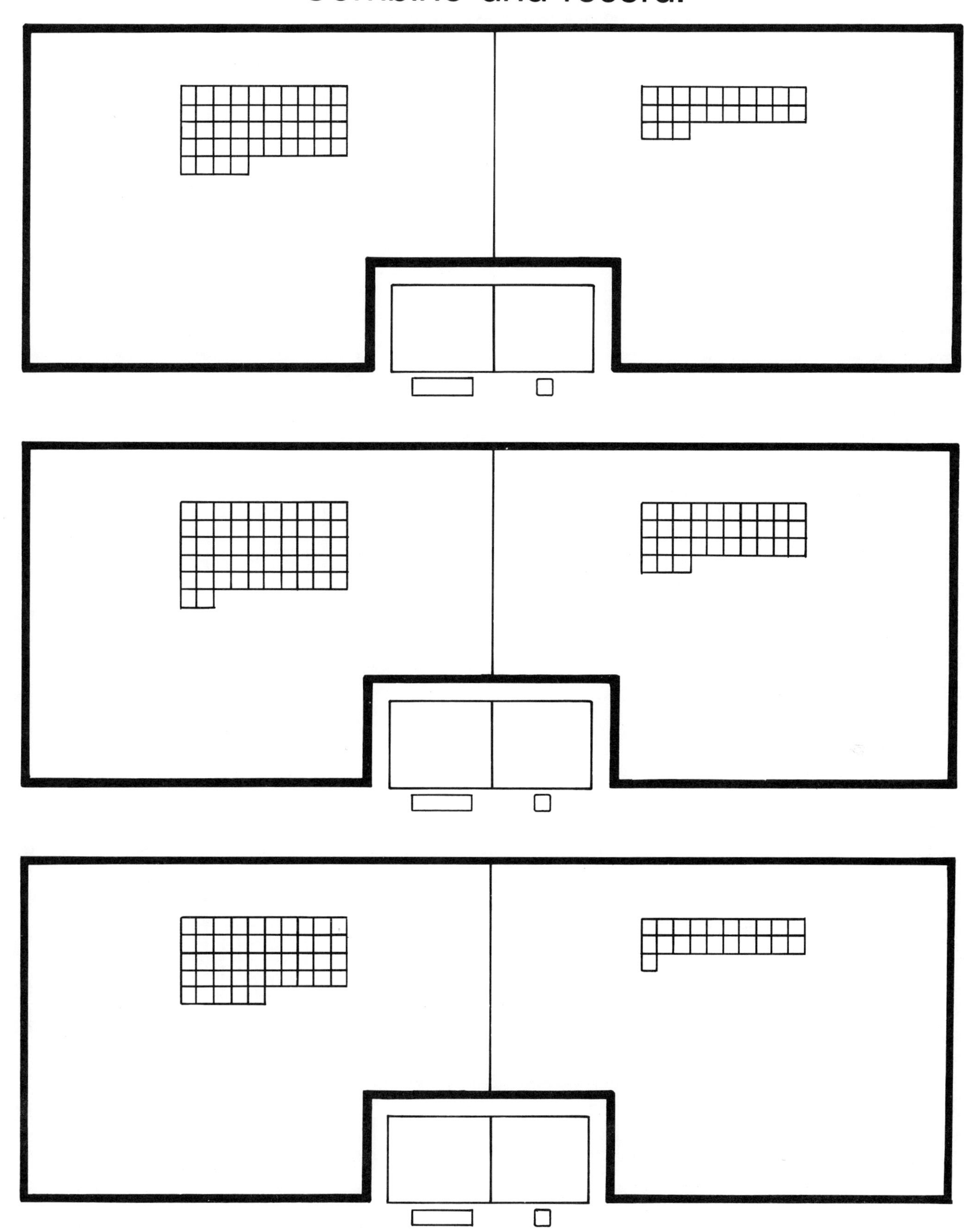

Combine and record.

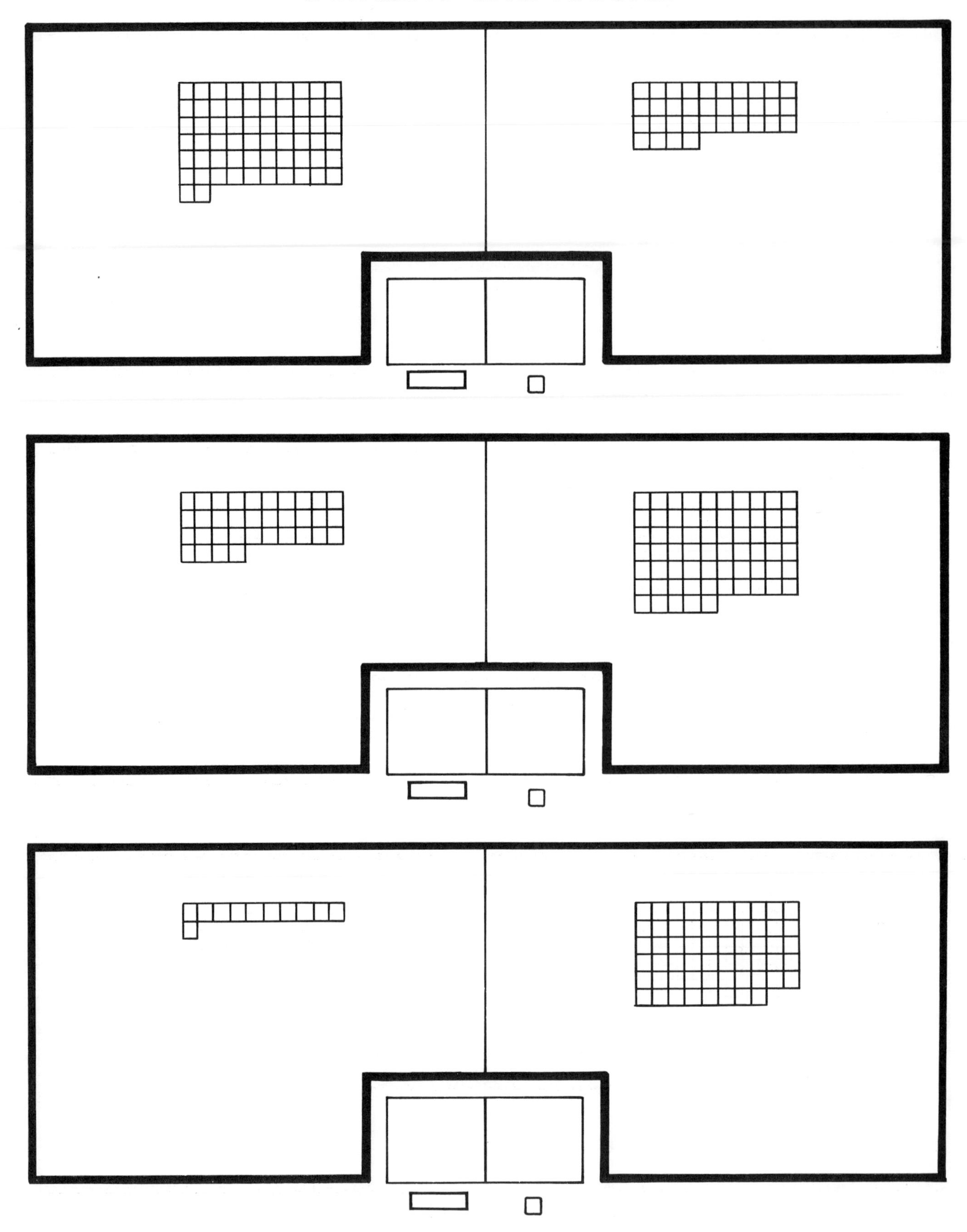

Combine and record.

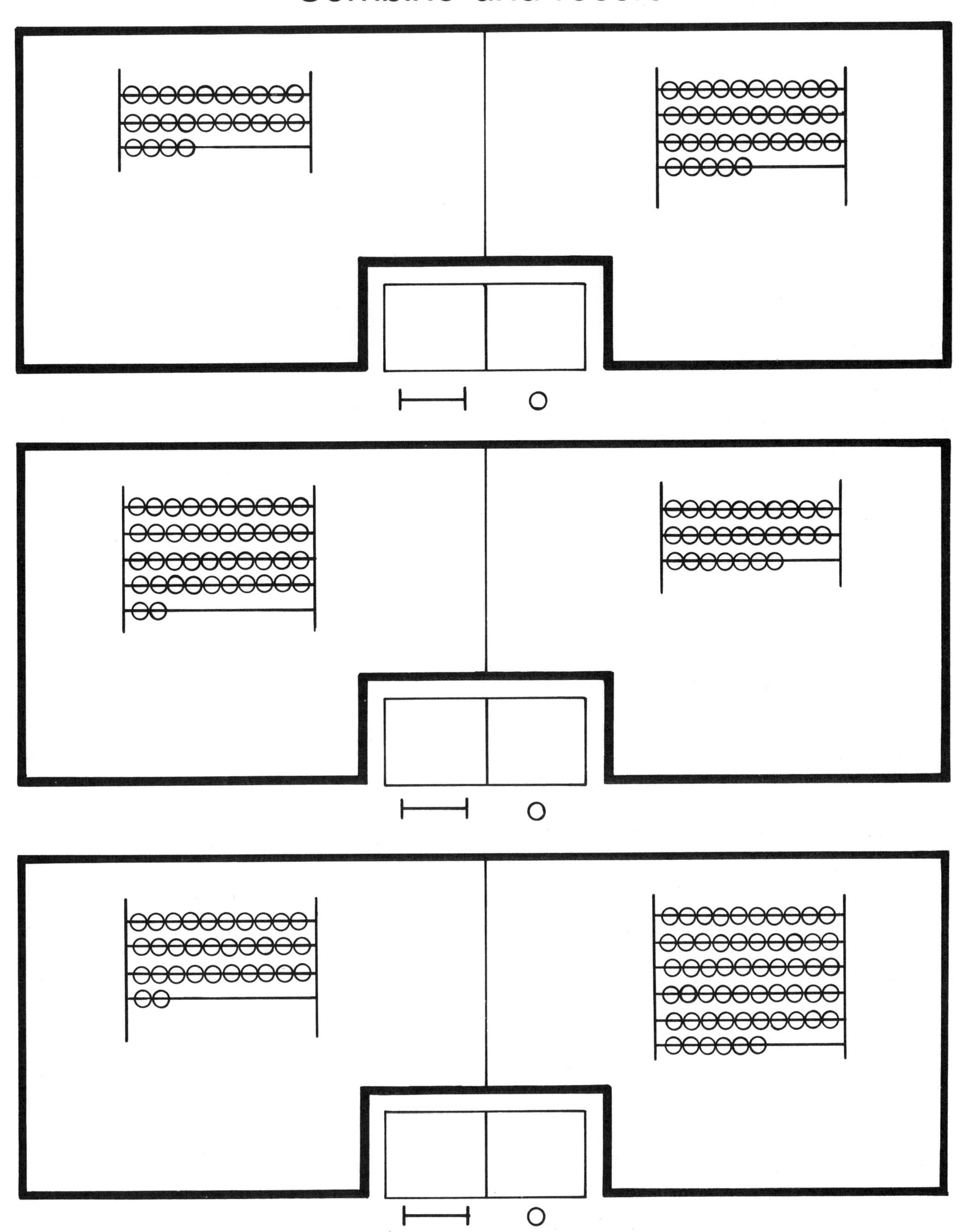

Combine and record.

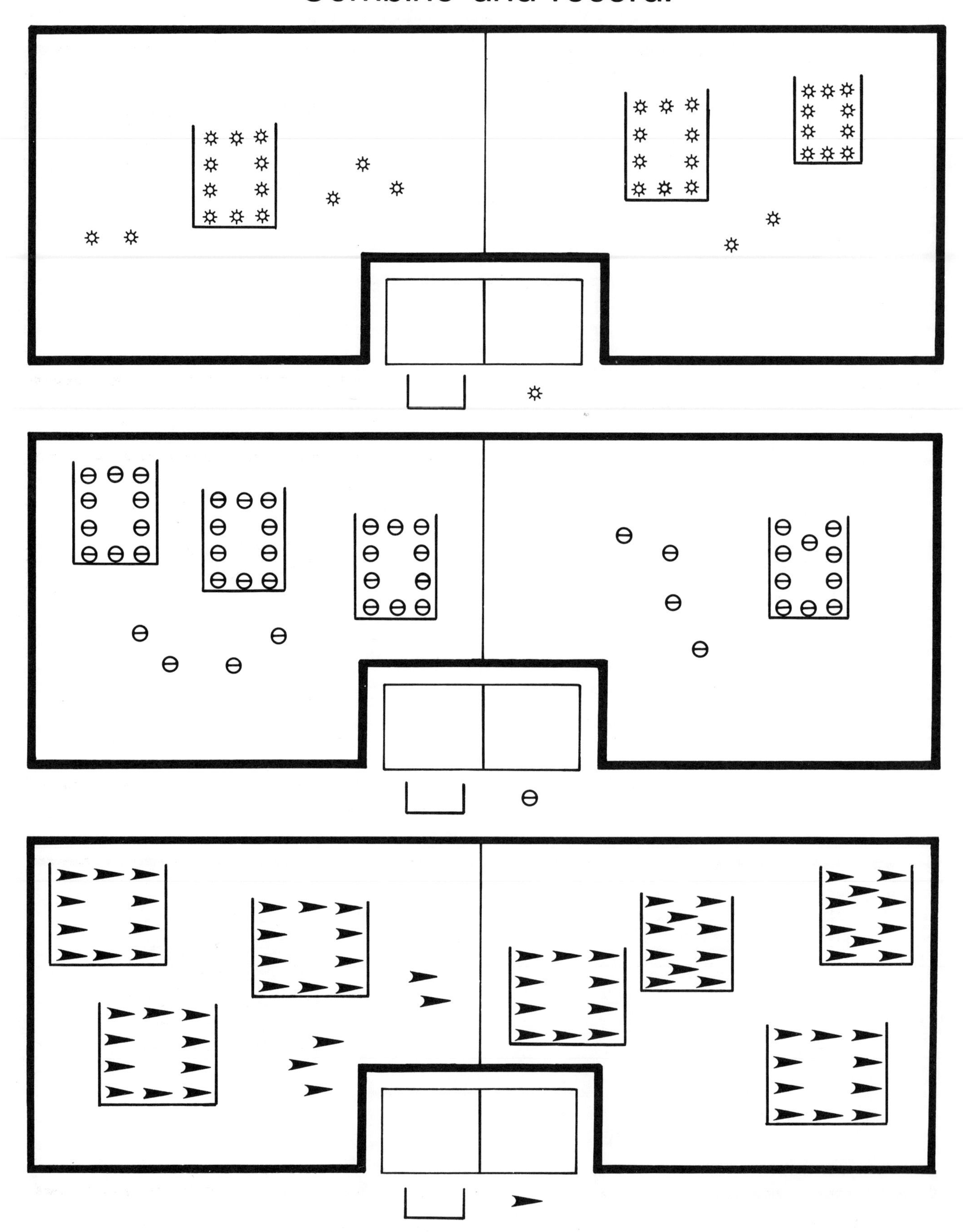

Combine and record.

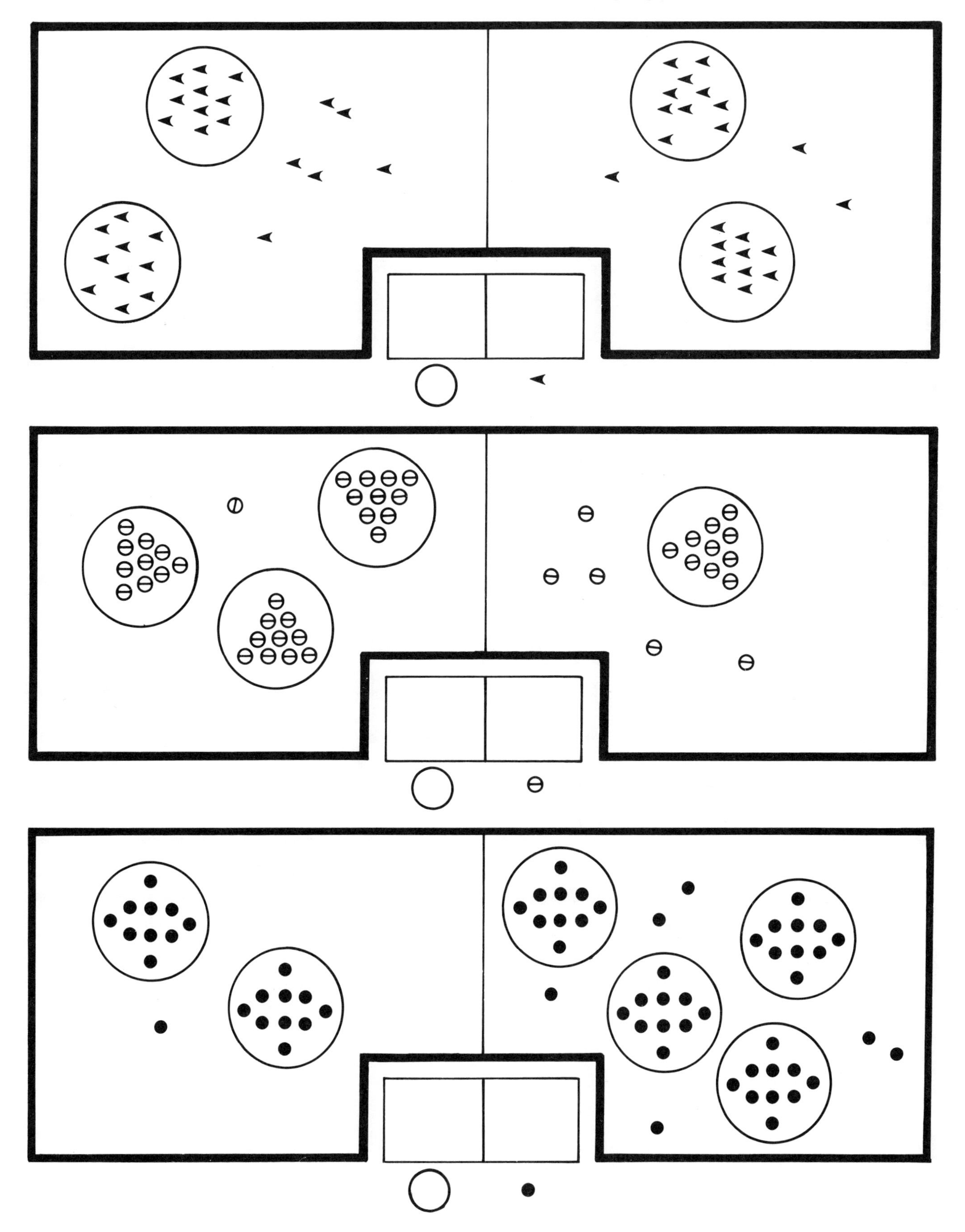

Combine and record.

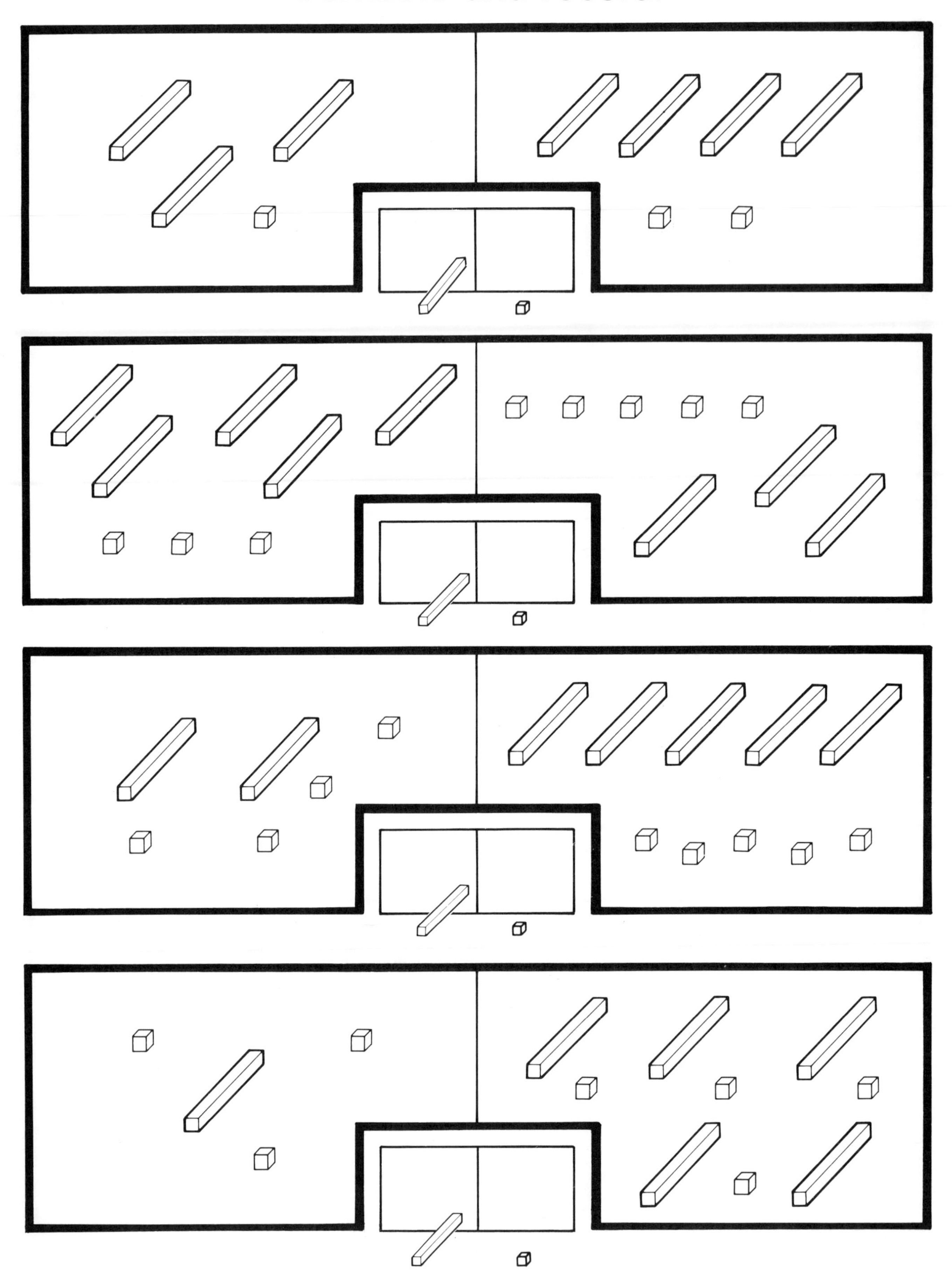

Combine and record.

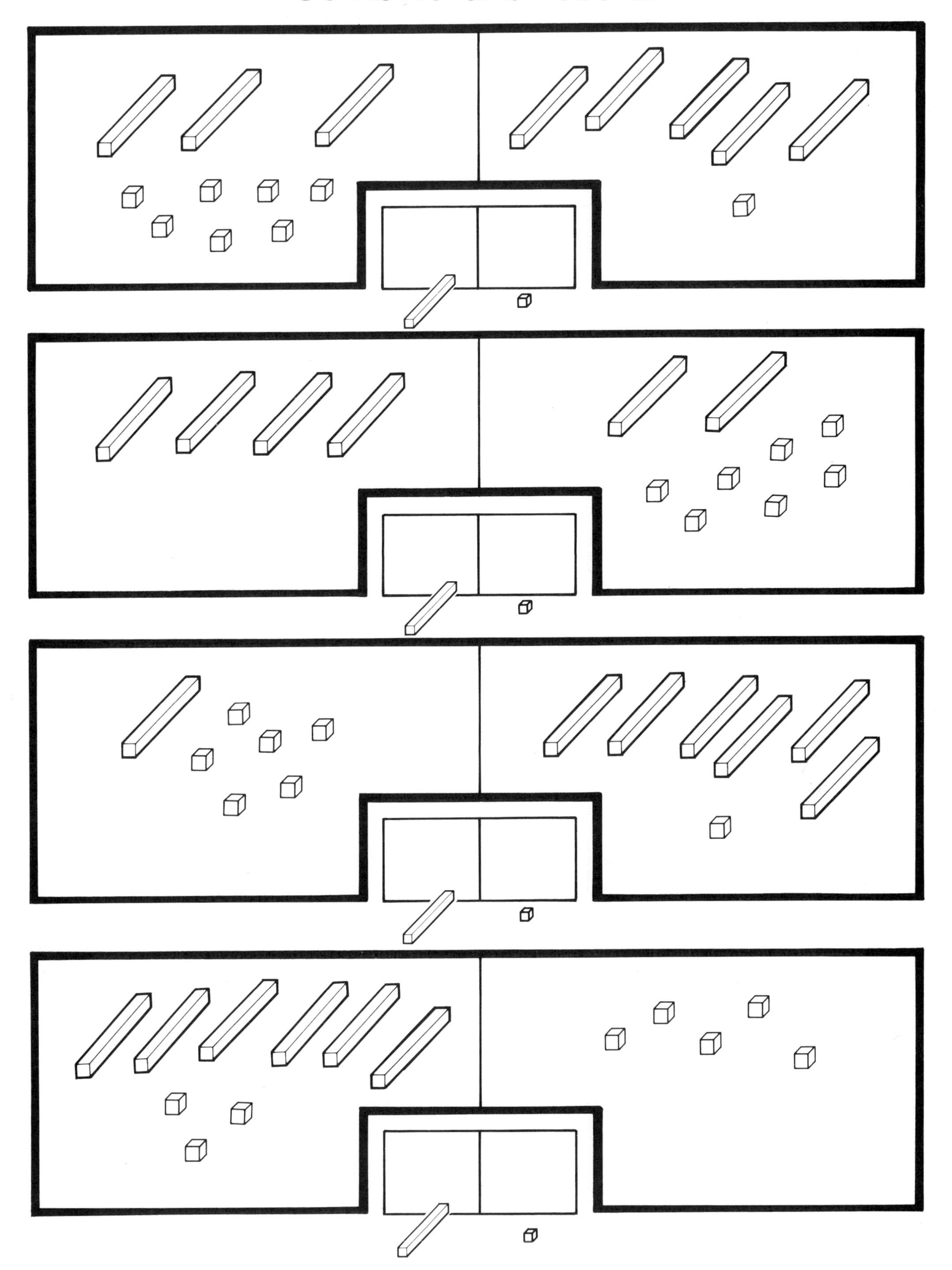

Combine and record.

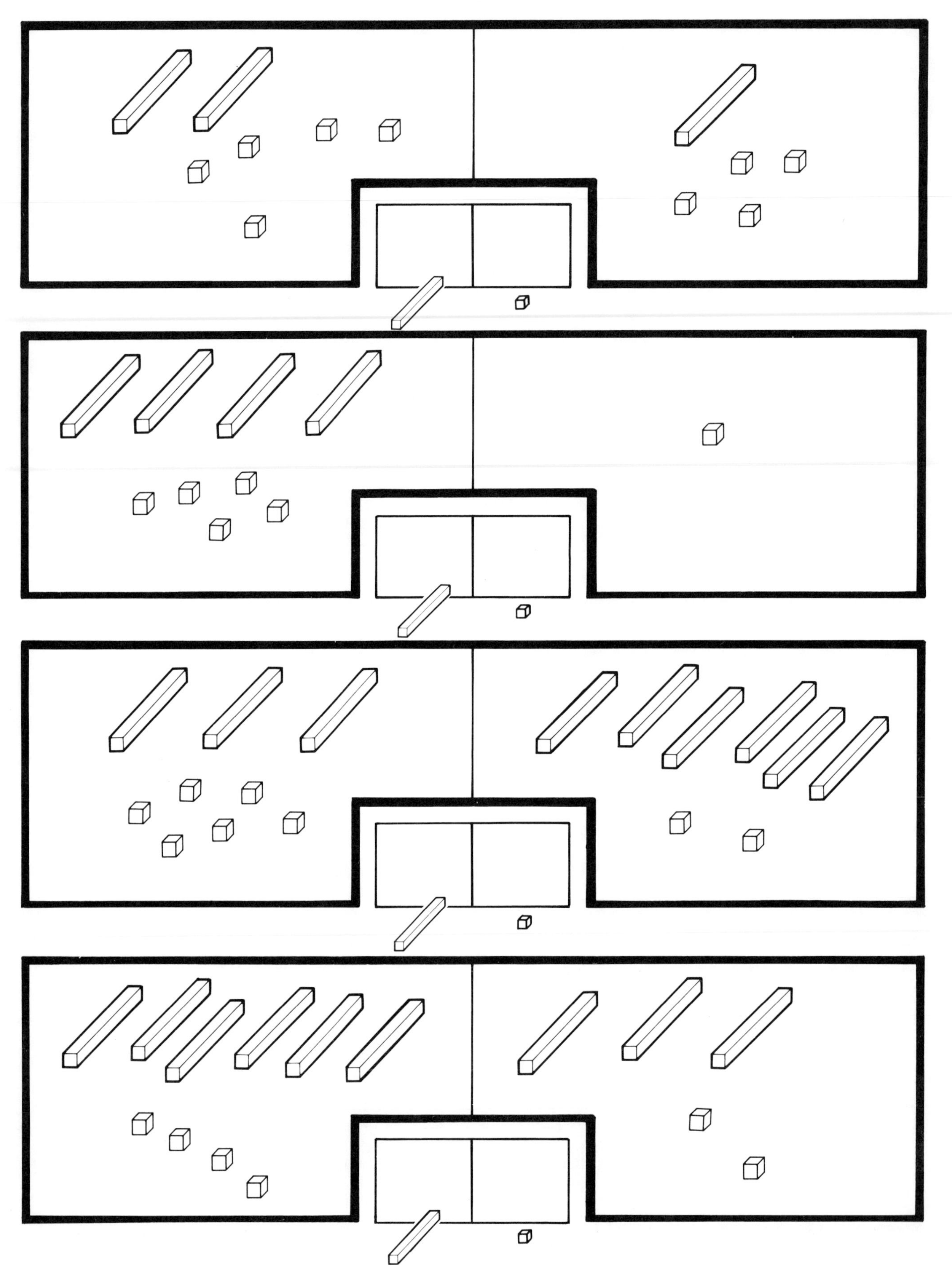

Combine and record.

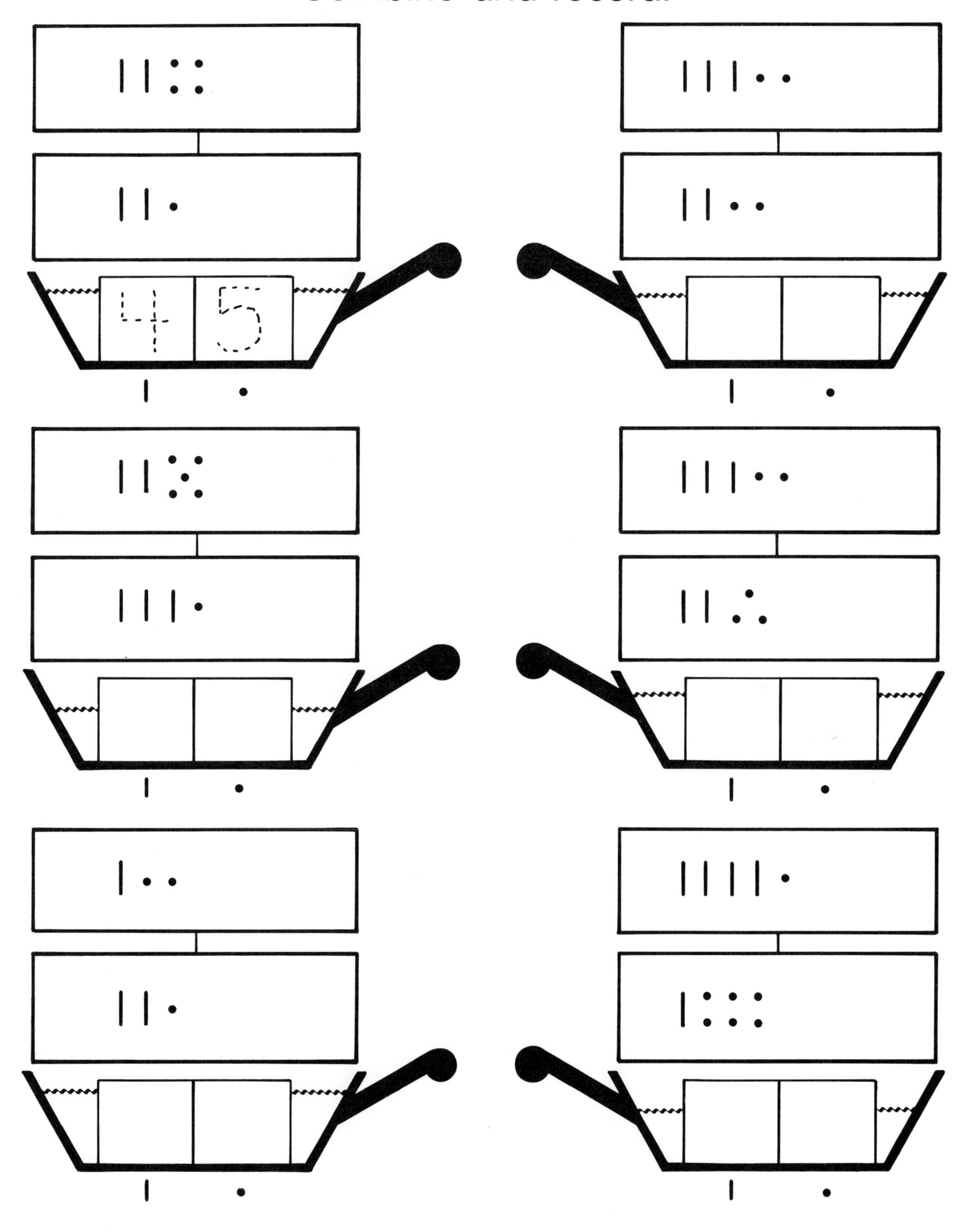

Combine and record.

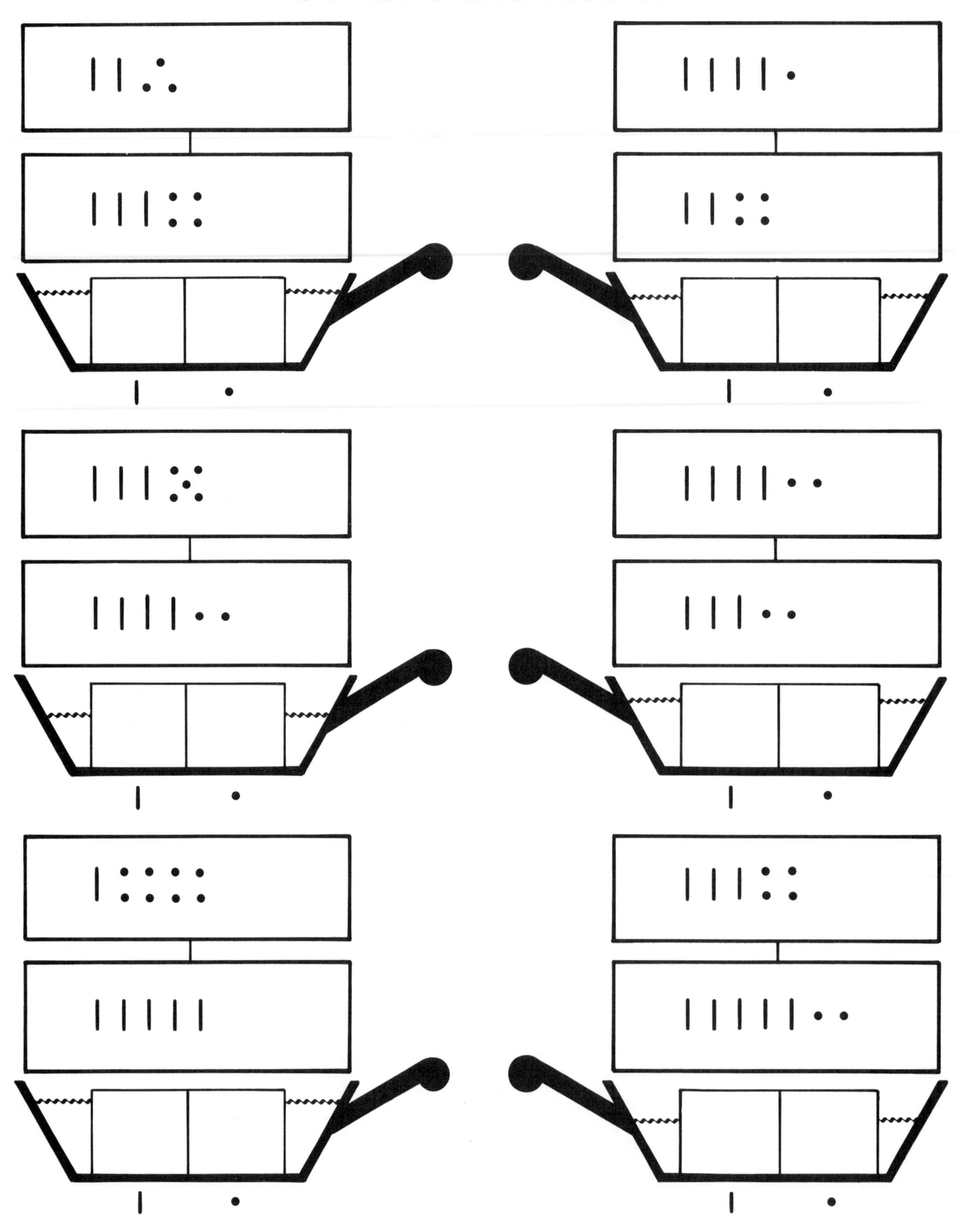

Combine and record.

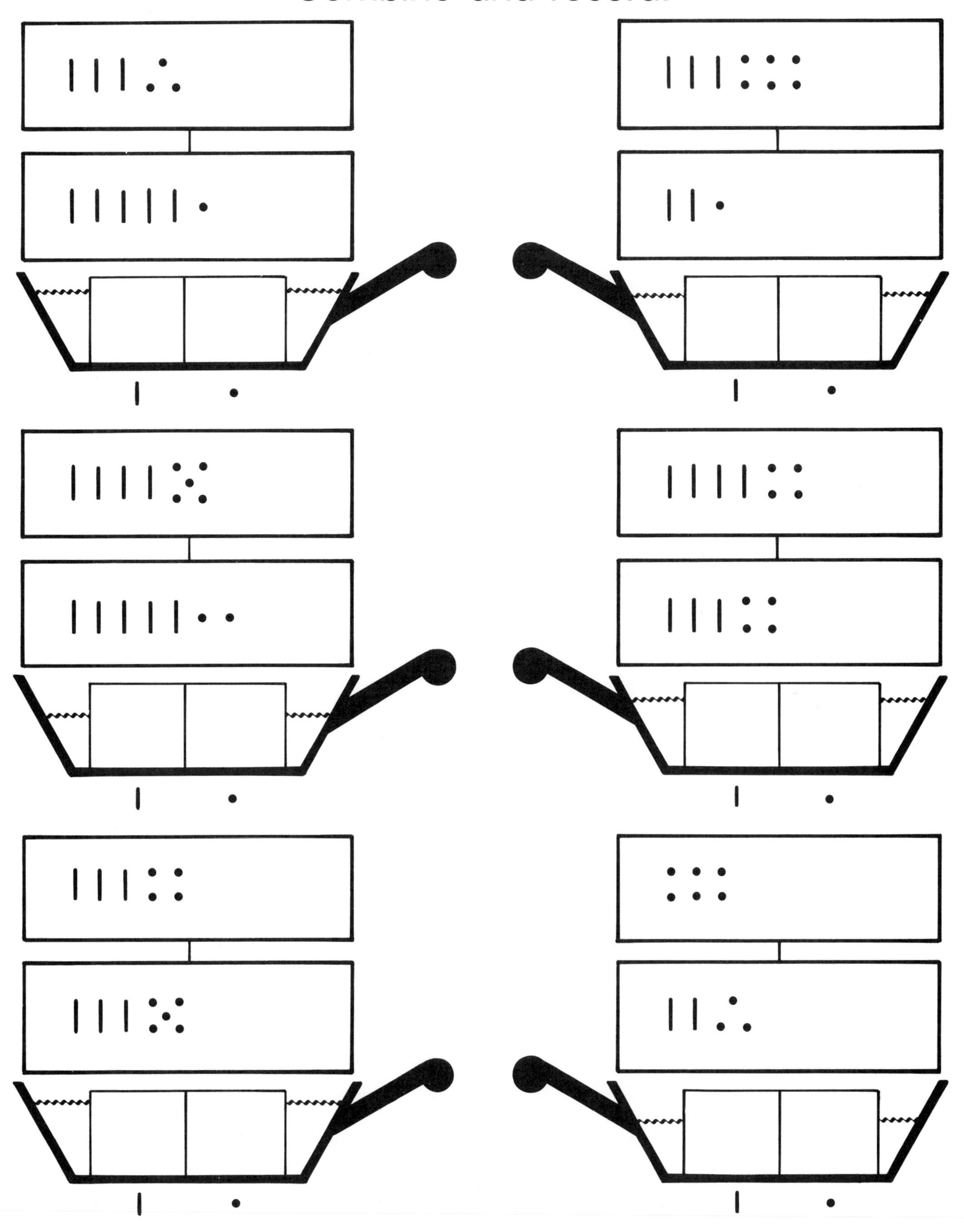

Add.

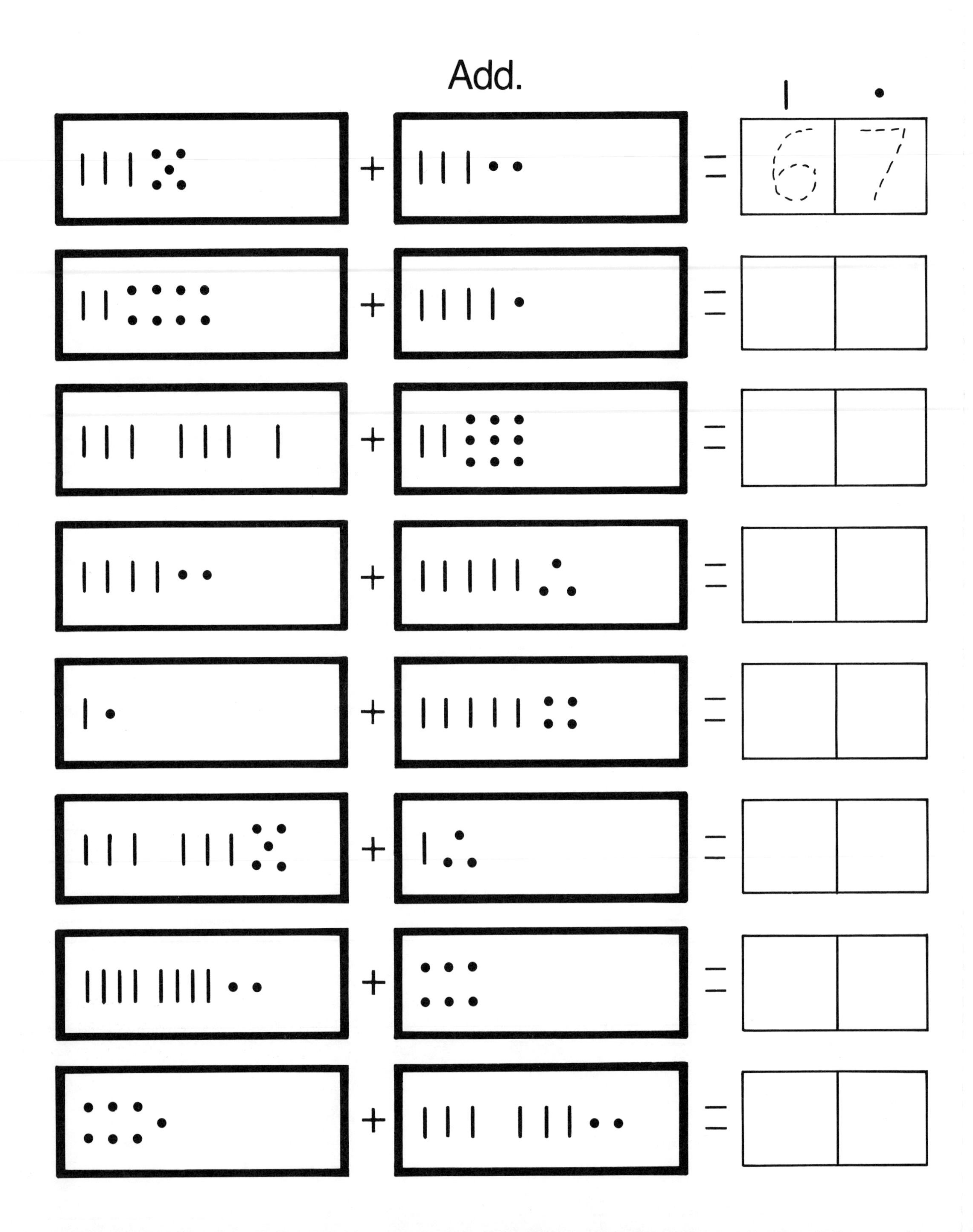

Add.

Add.

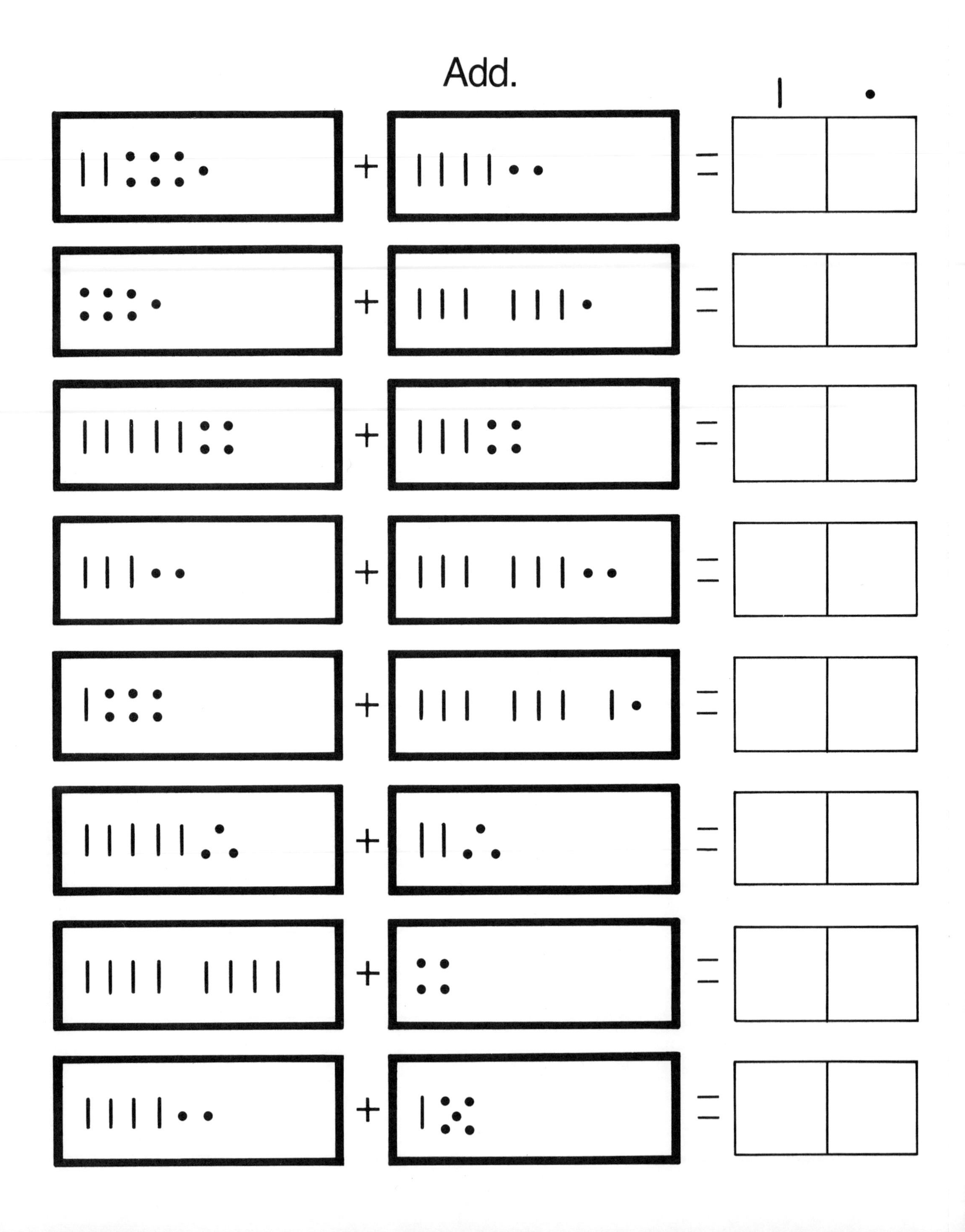

Combine and record.

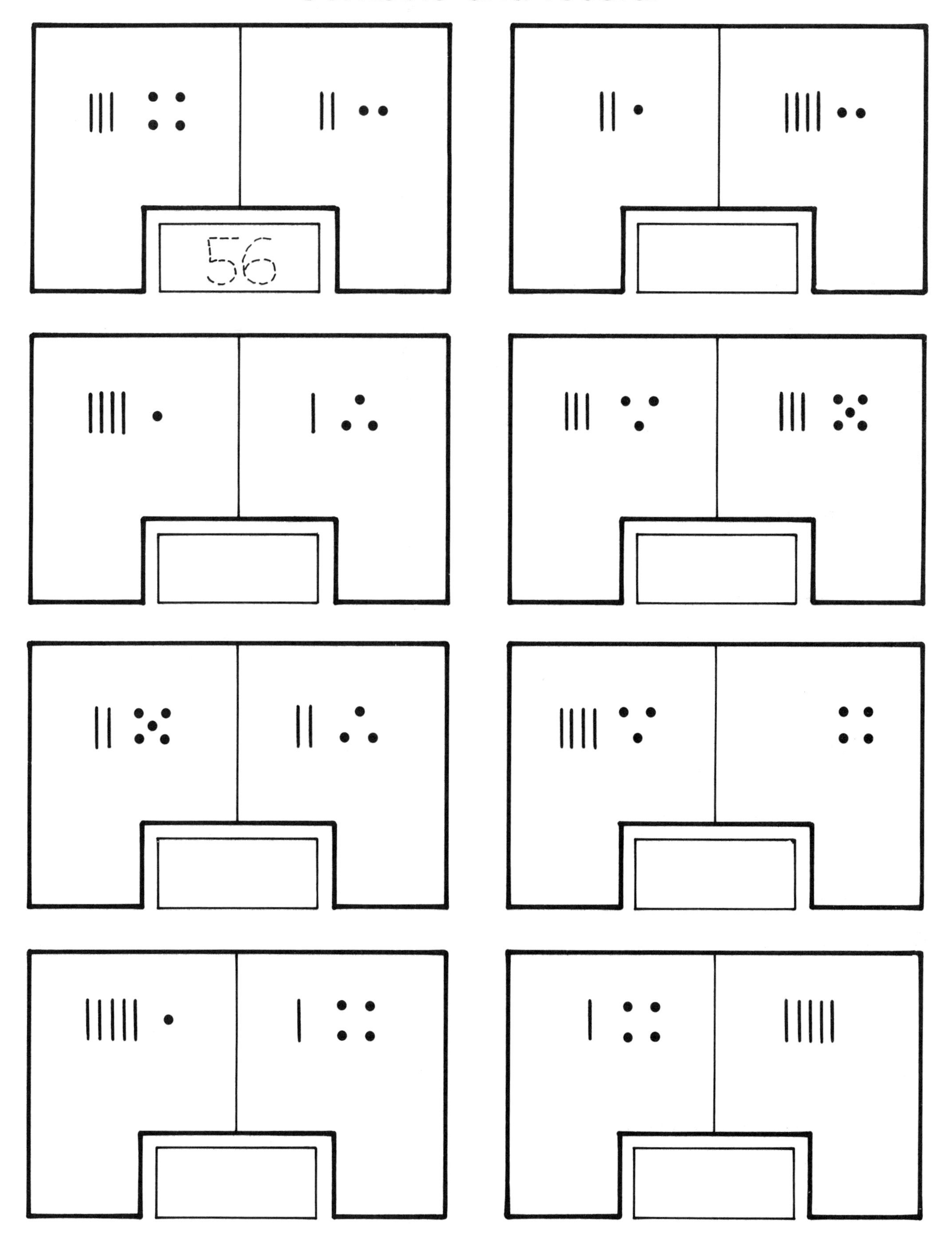

Combine and record.

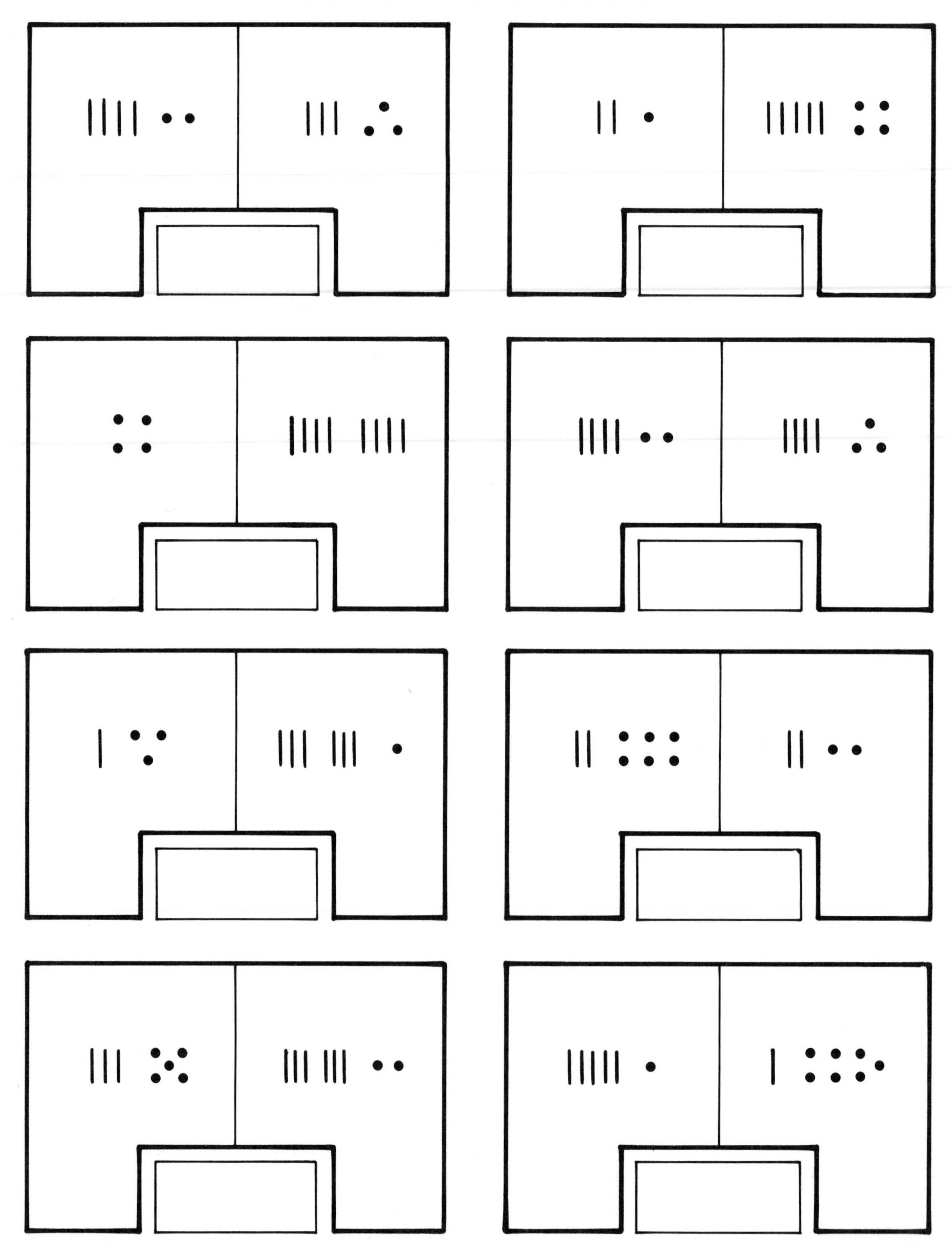

Combine and record.

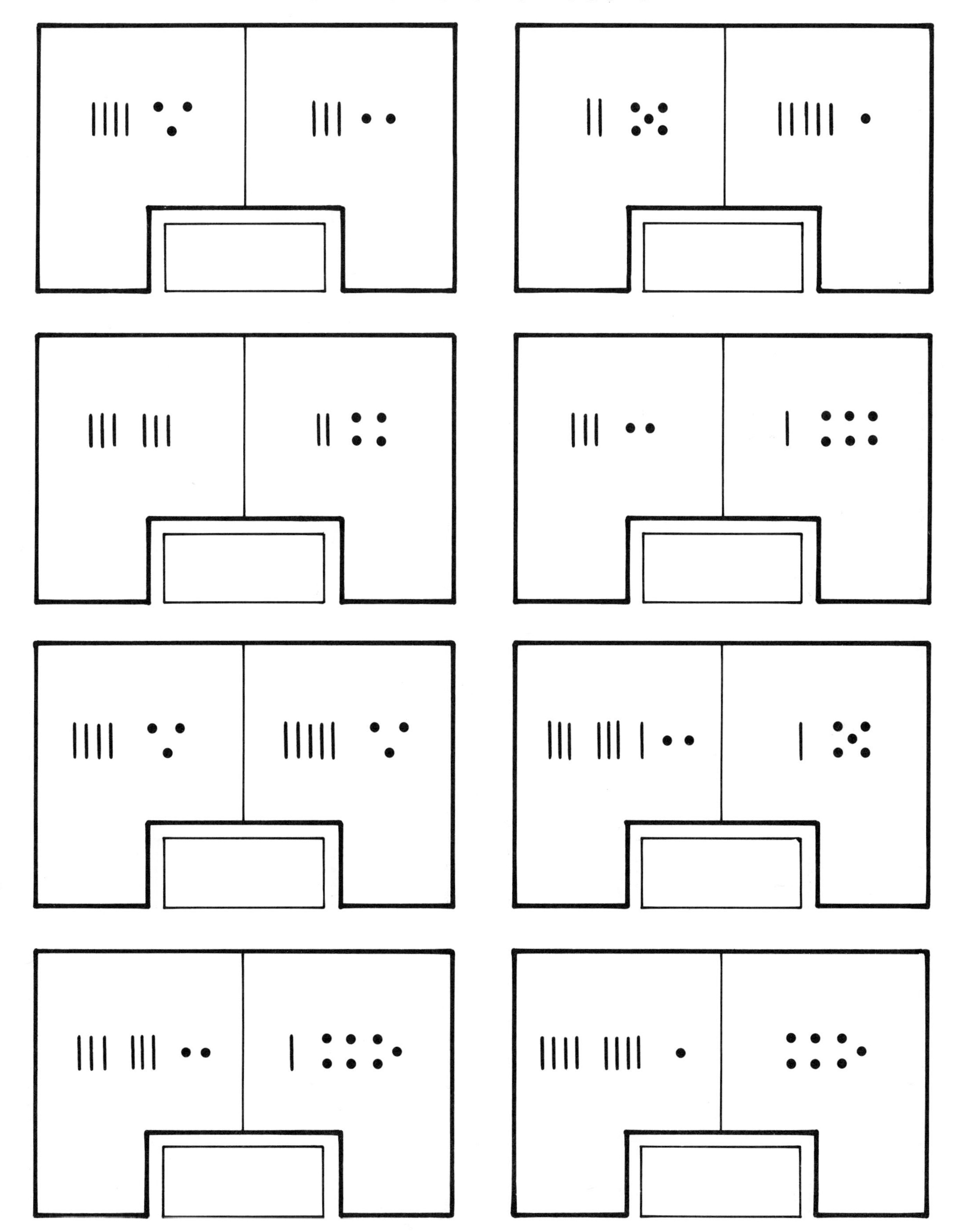

Combine and record.

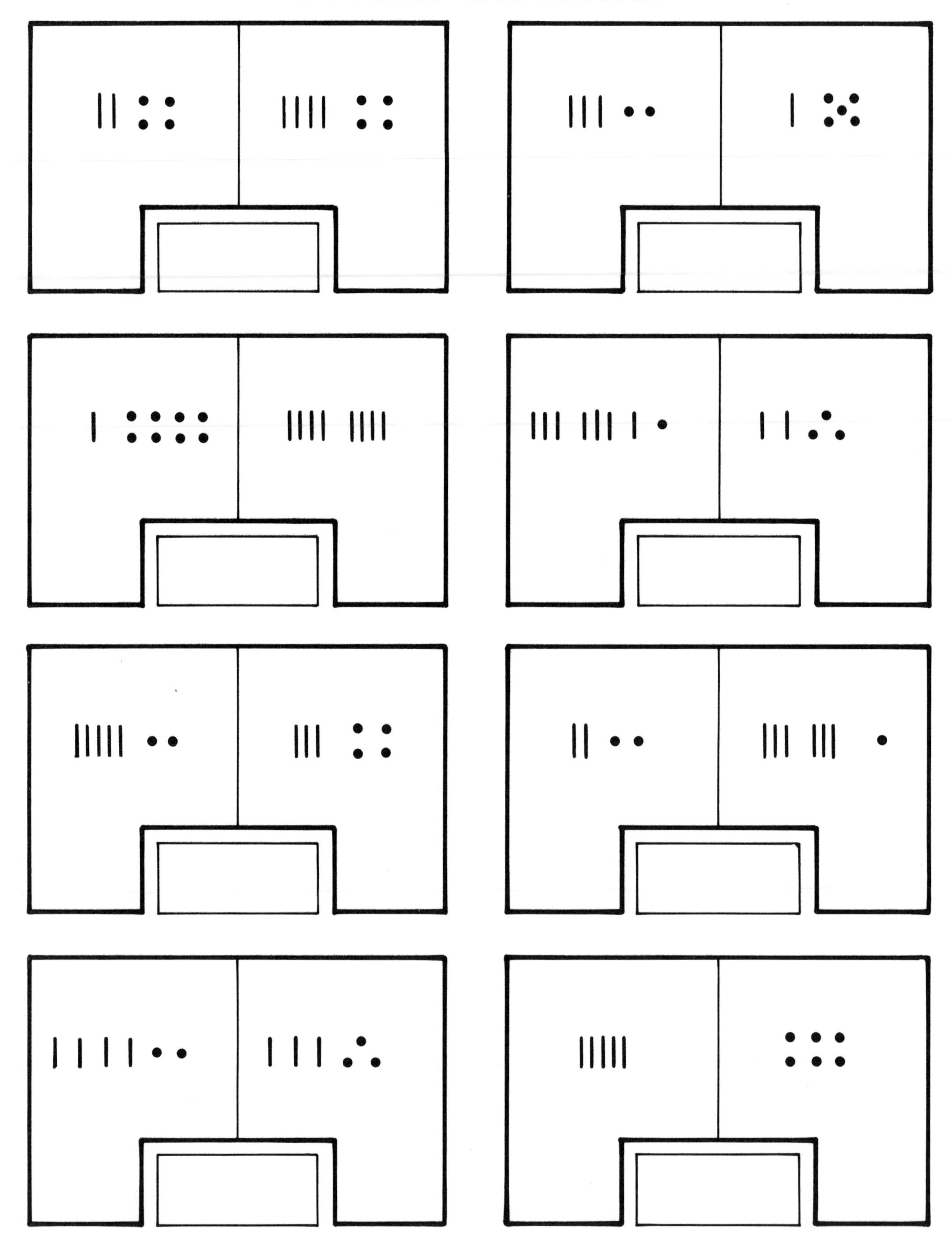

Combine and record.

		24
		22
40	6	46

Combine and record.

Combine and record.

24

61

Combine and record.

I I	• • • • •	
I I I I I	•	

I I I	• • • • • •	
I	• •	

		42
		21

		35
		23

I I I I I I	• • • • • • •	
I I	•	

		34
		33

I I	•	
I I I I	• • • • • • •	

I I I I I	• • • • • • • •	
I I	•	

Color the tens and ones. Add.

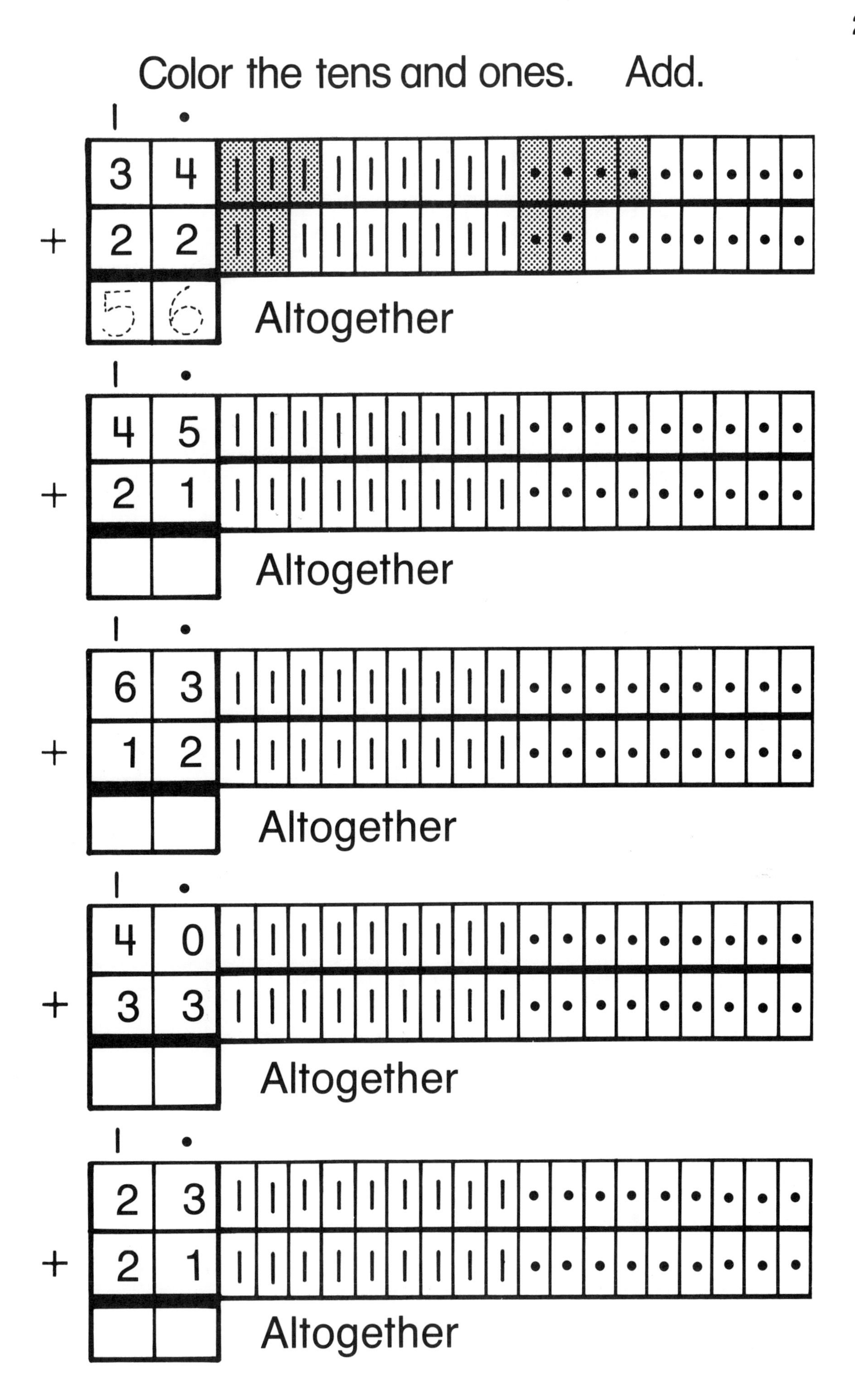

Color the tens and ones. Add.

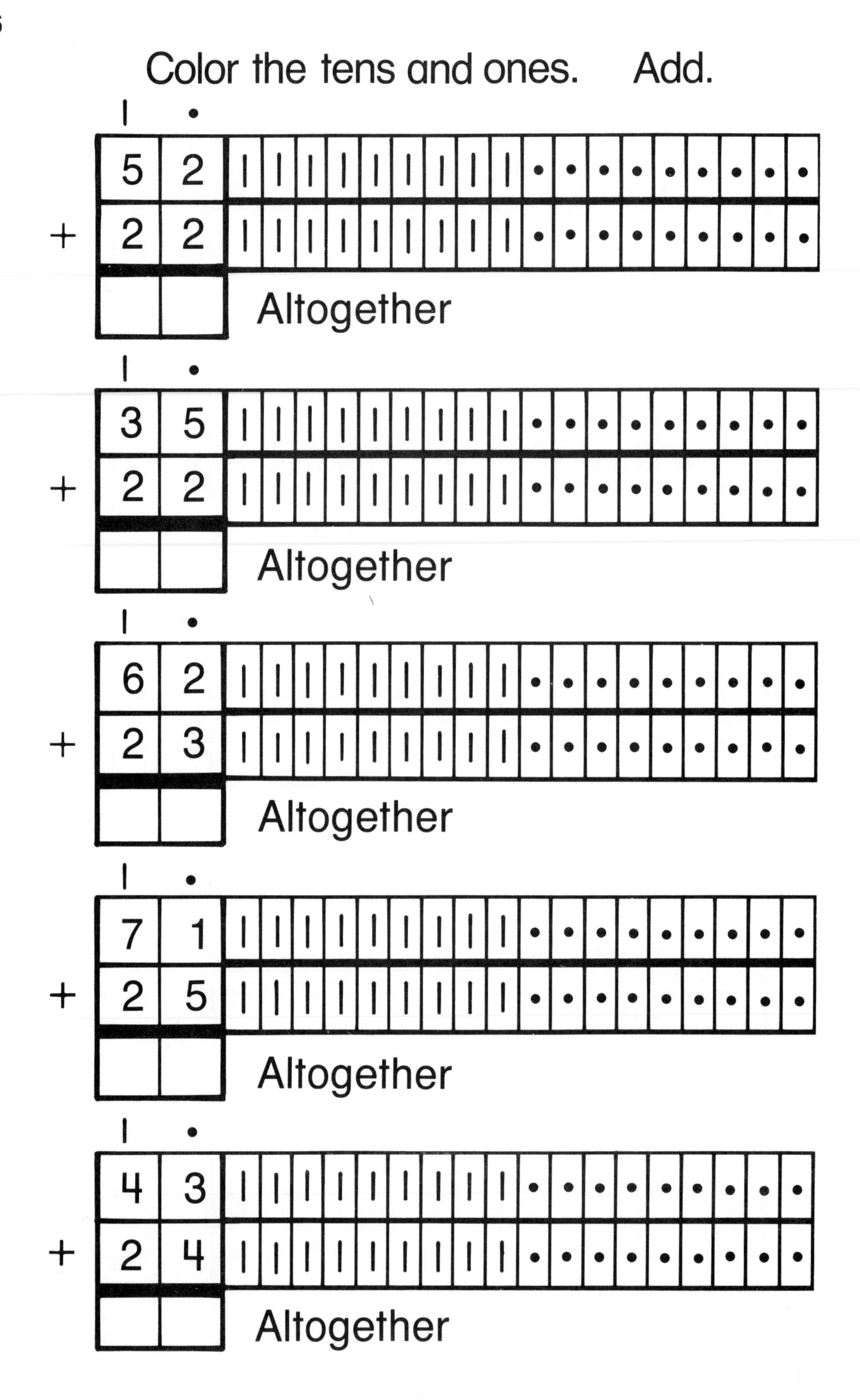

Color the tens and ones. Add.

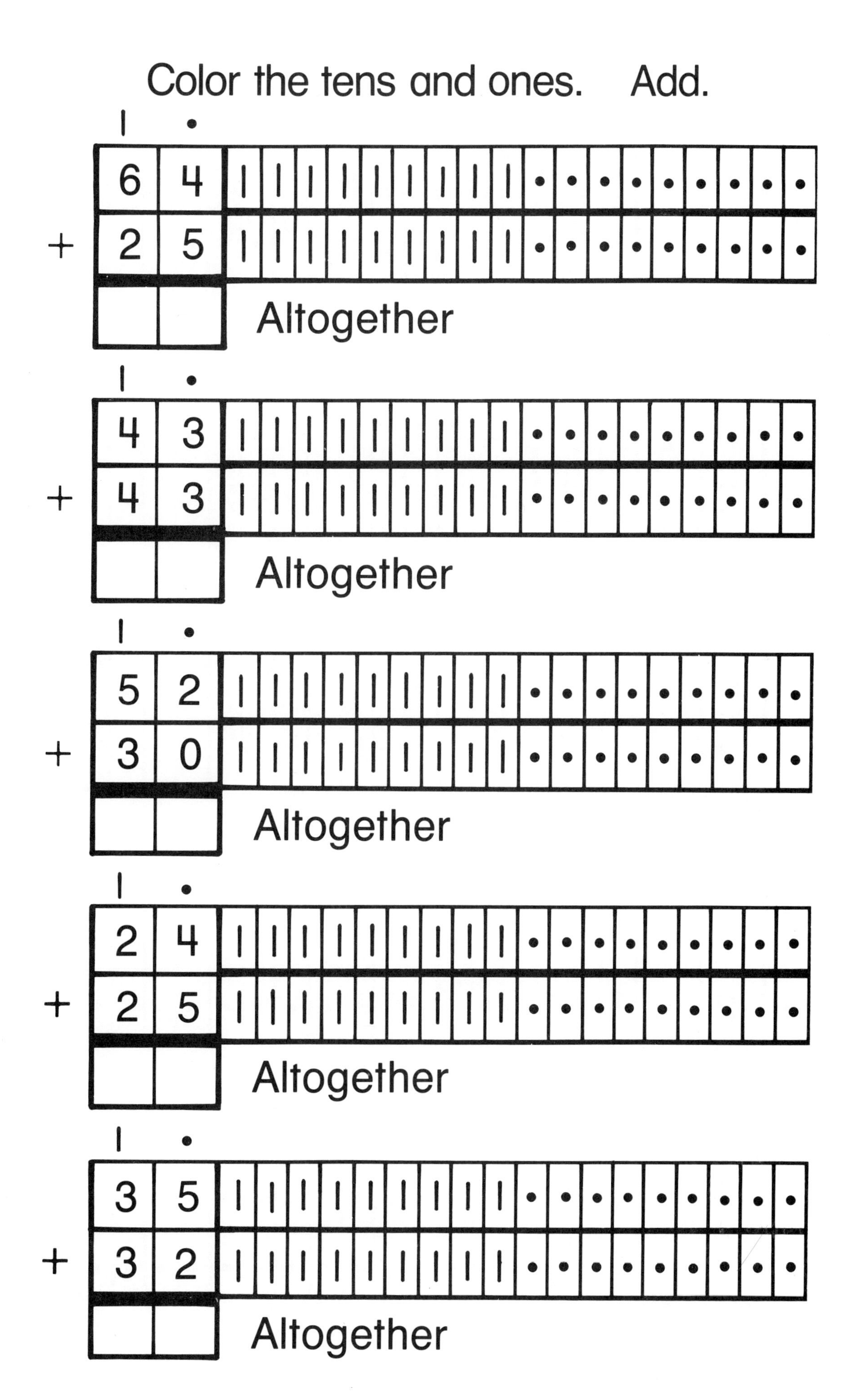

Color the tens and ones. Add.

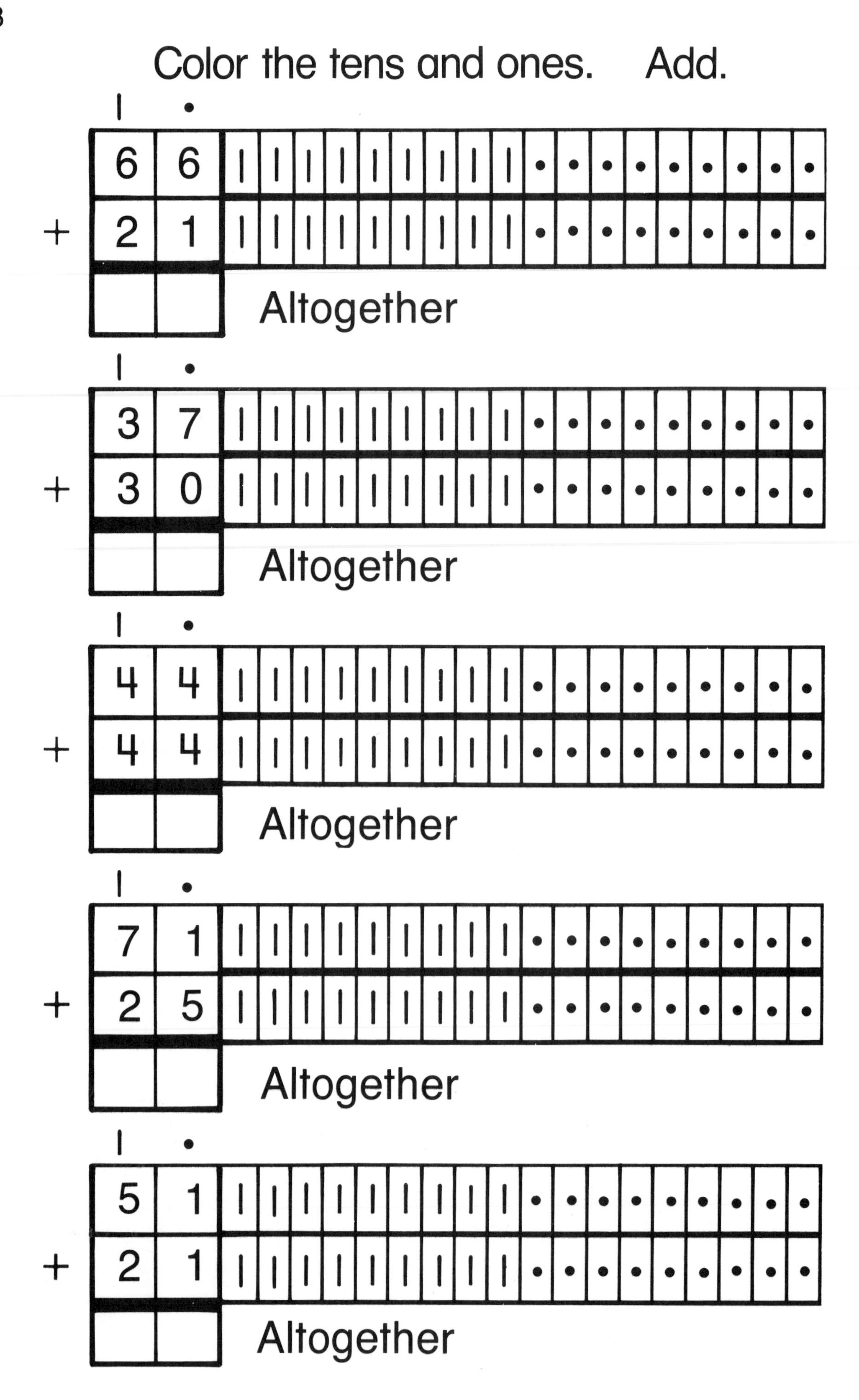

Color the tens and ones. Add.

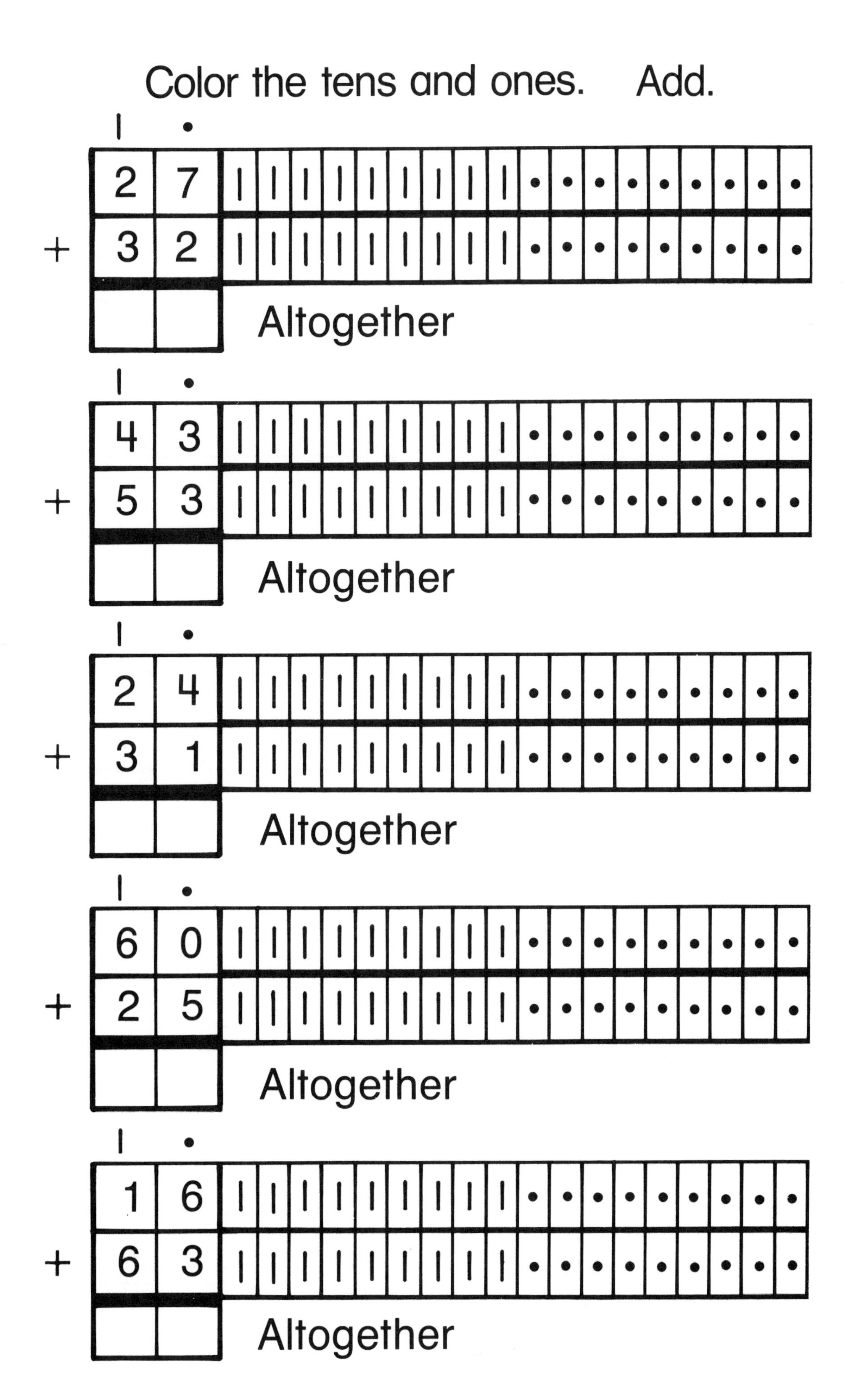

27
+ 32
Altogether
43
+ 53
Altogether
24
+ 31
Altogether
60
+ 25
Altogether
16
+ 63
Altogether

Combine and record.

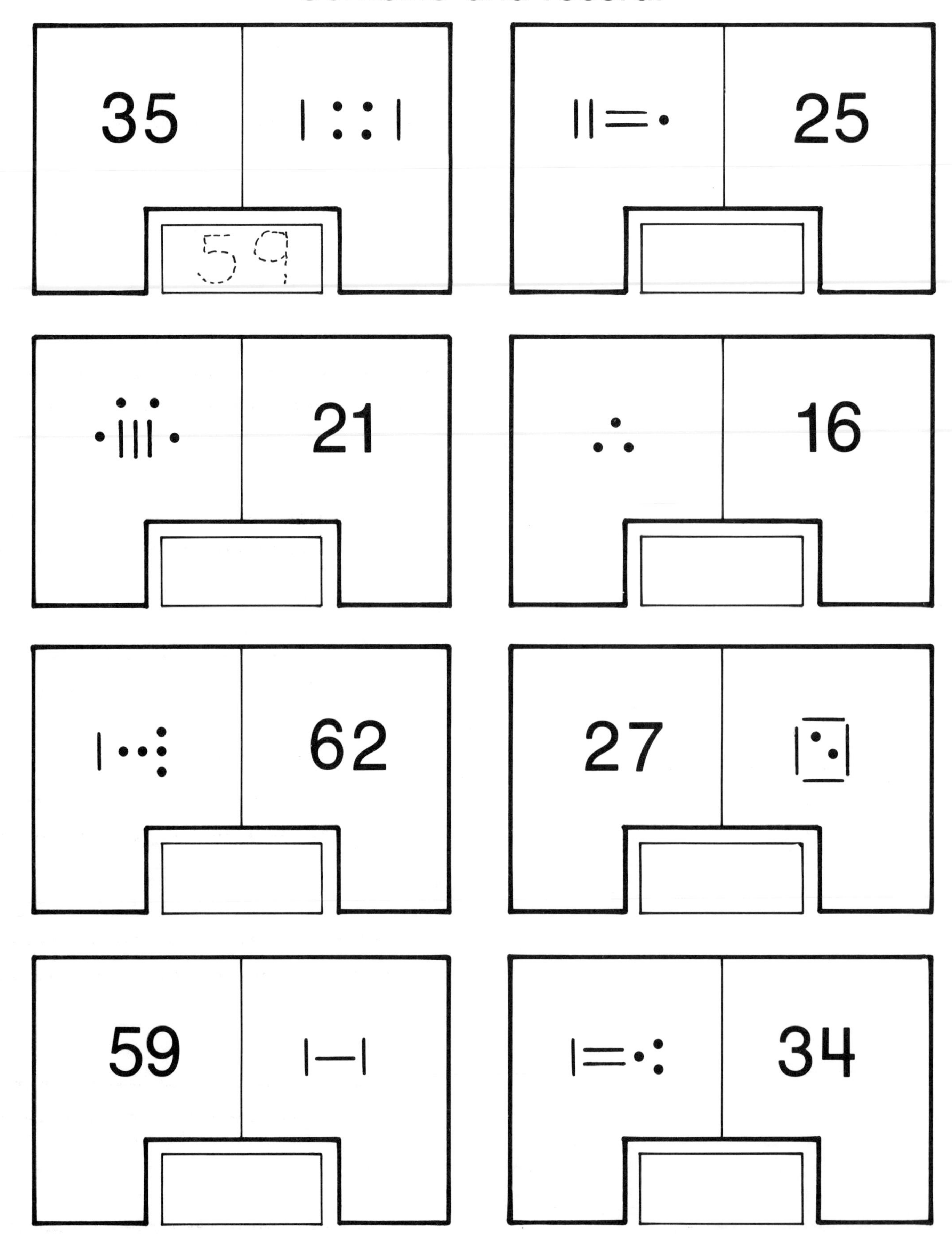

Combine and record.

23	45	16
52	61	33
73	35	71
51	67	54
82	17	42

Complete each problem.

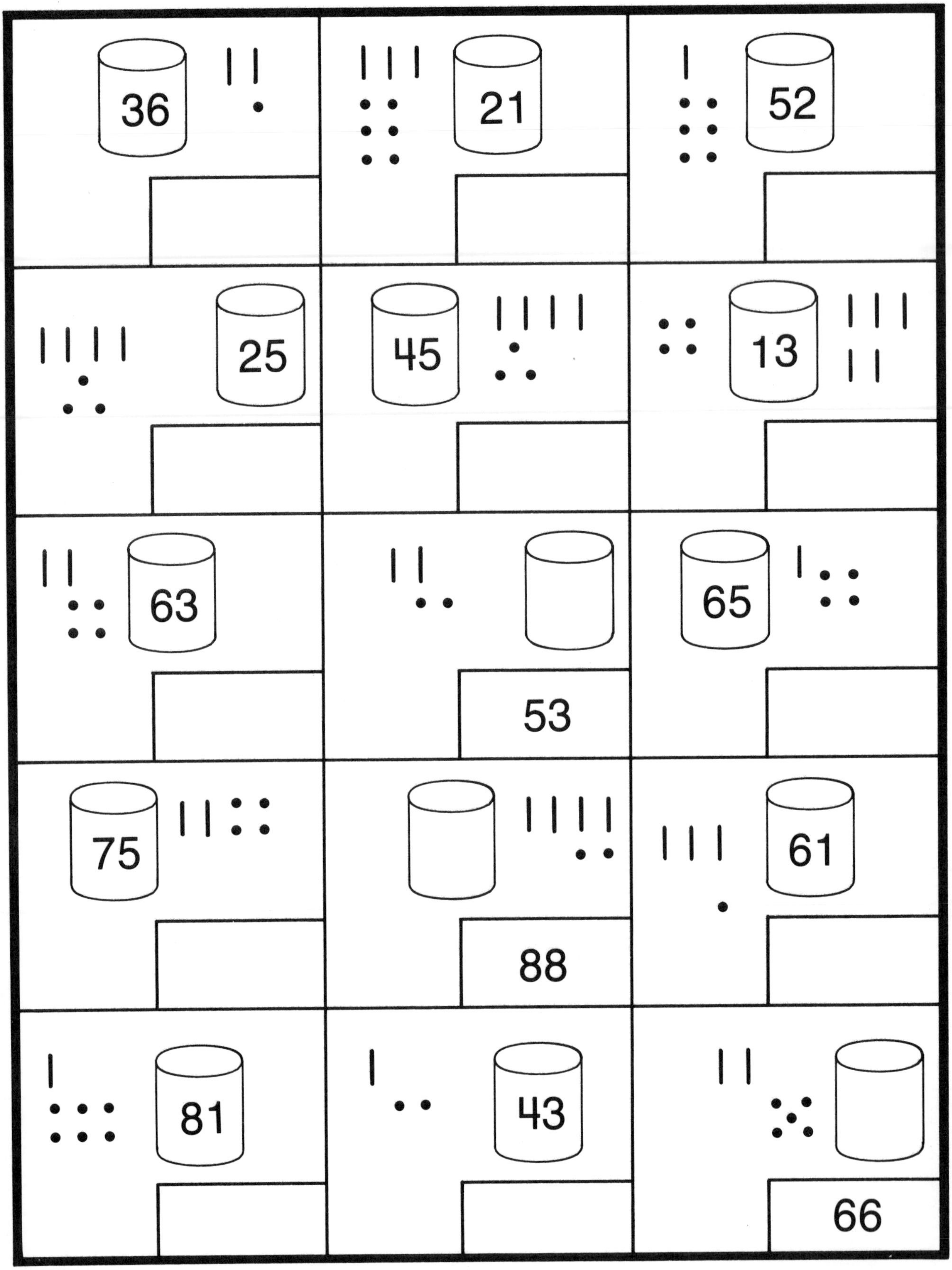

36

21

52

25

45

13

63

65

53

75

61

88

81

43

66

Combine and record.

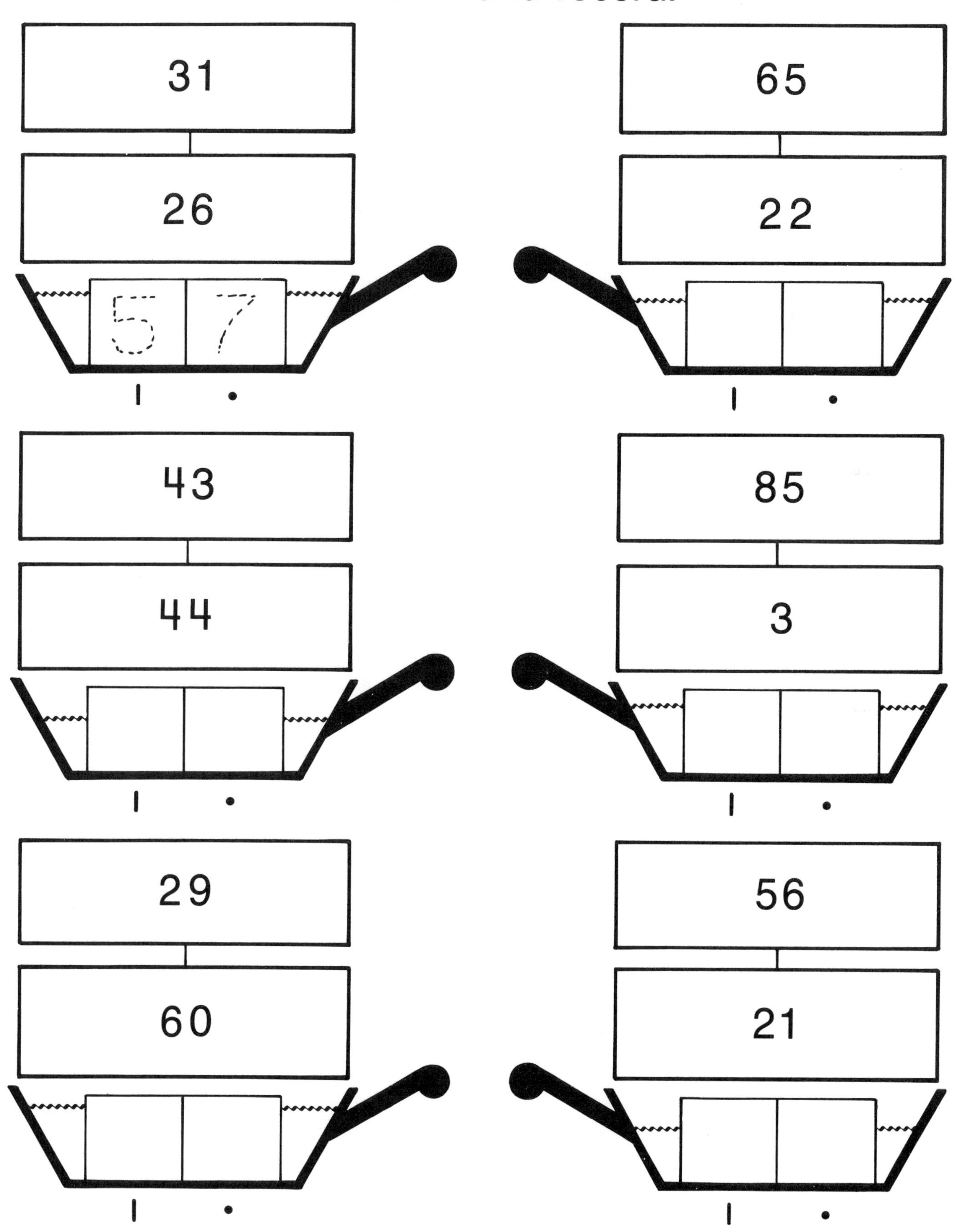

Combine and record. Trade if necessary.

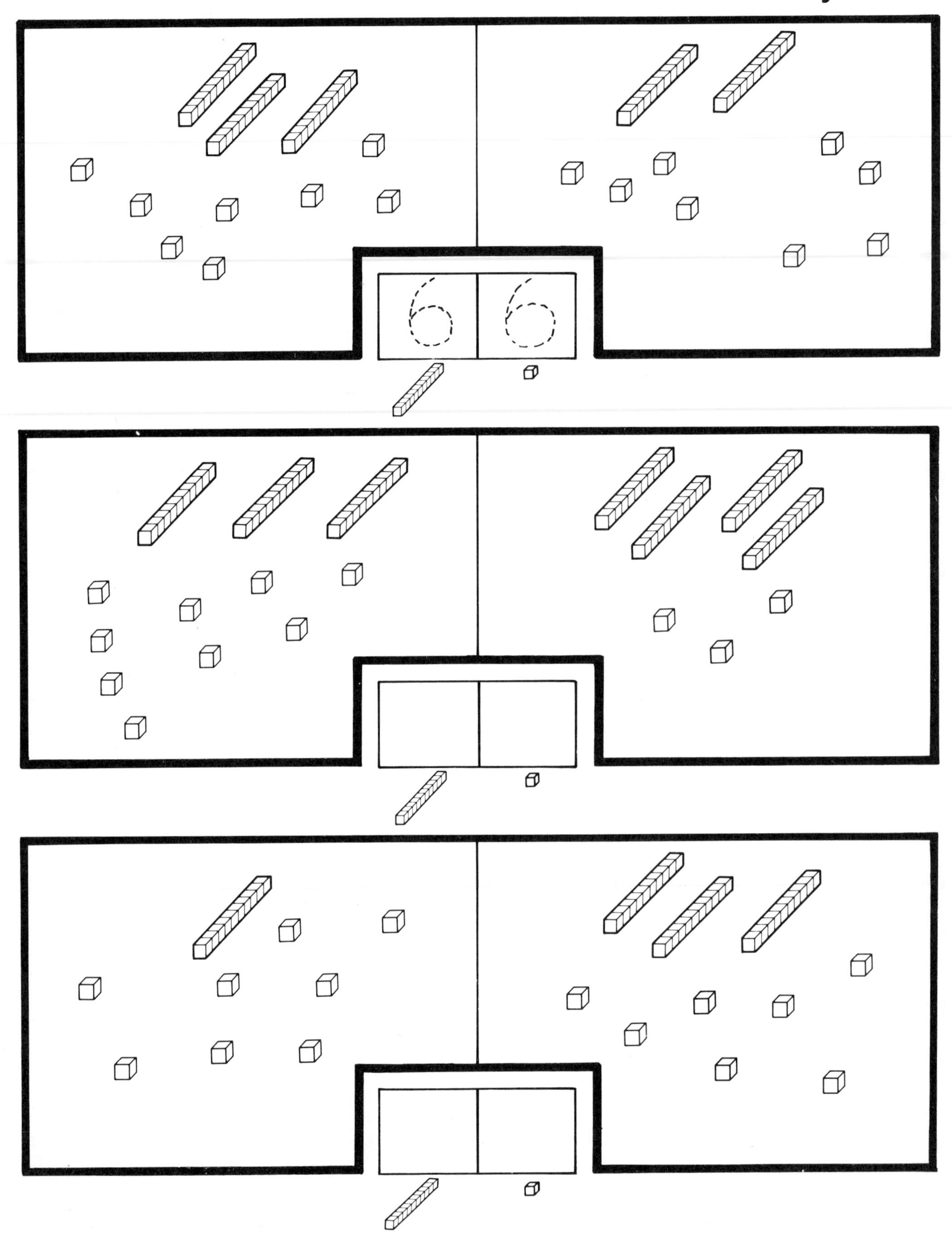

Combine and record. Trade if necessary.

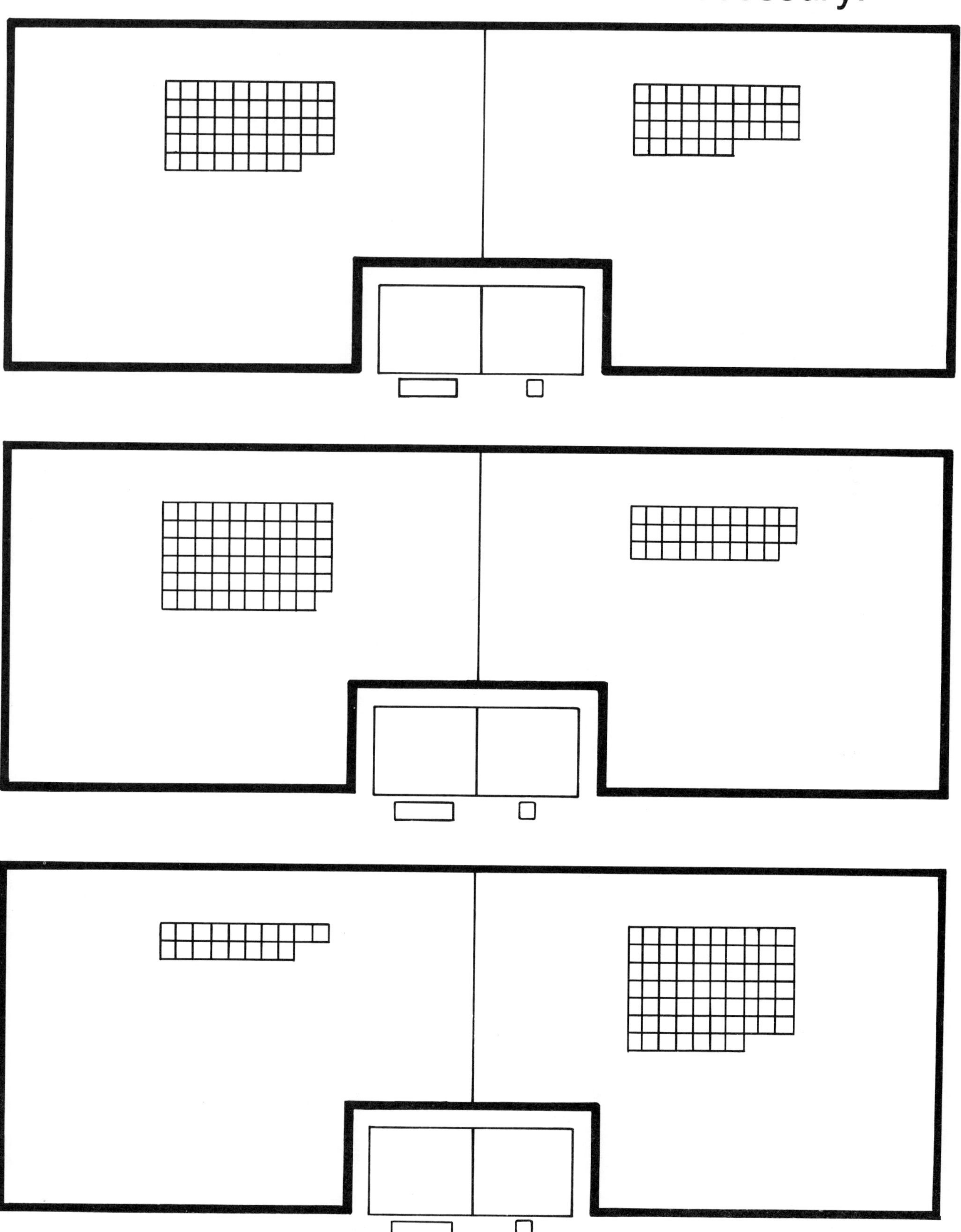

Combine and record. Trade if necessary.

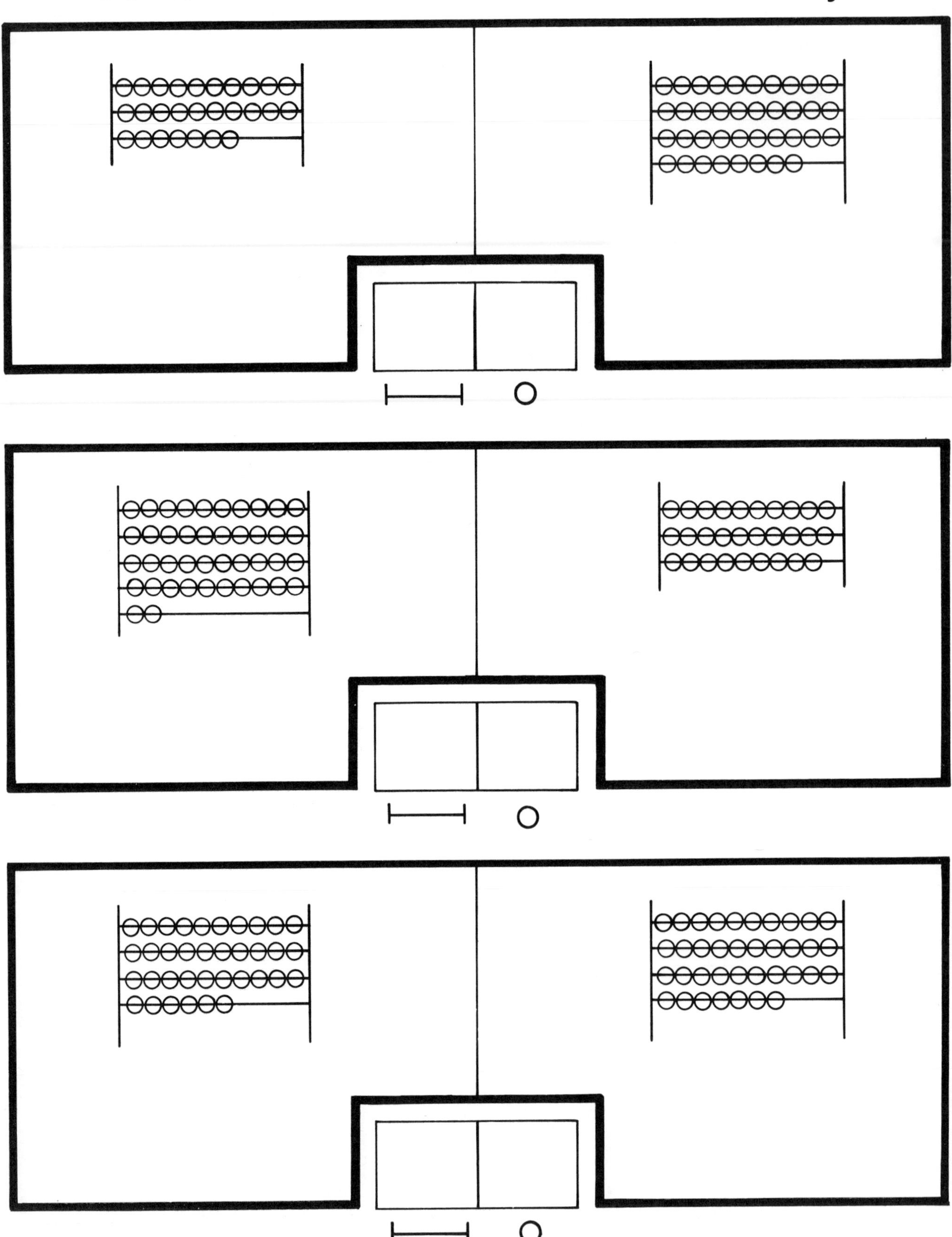

Combine and record. Trade if necessary.

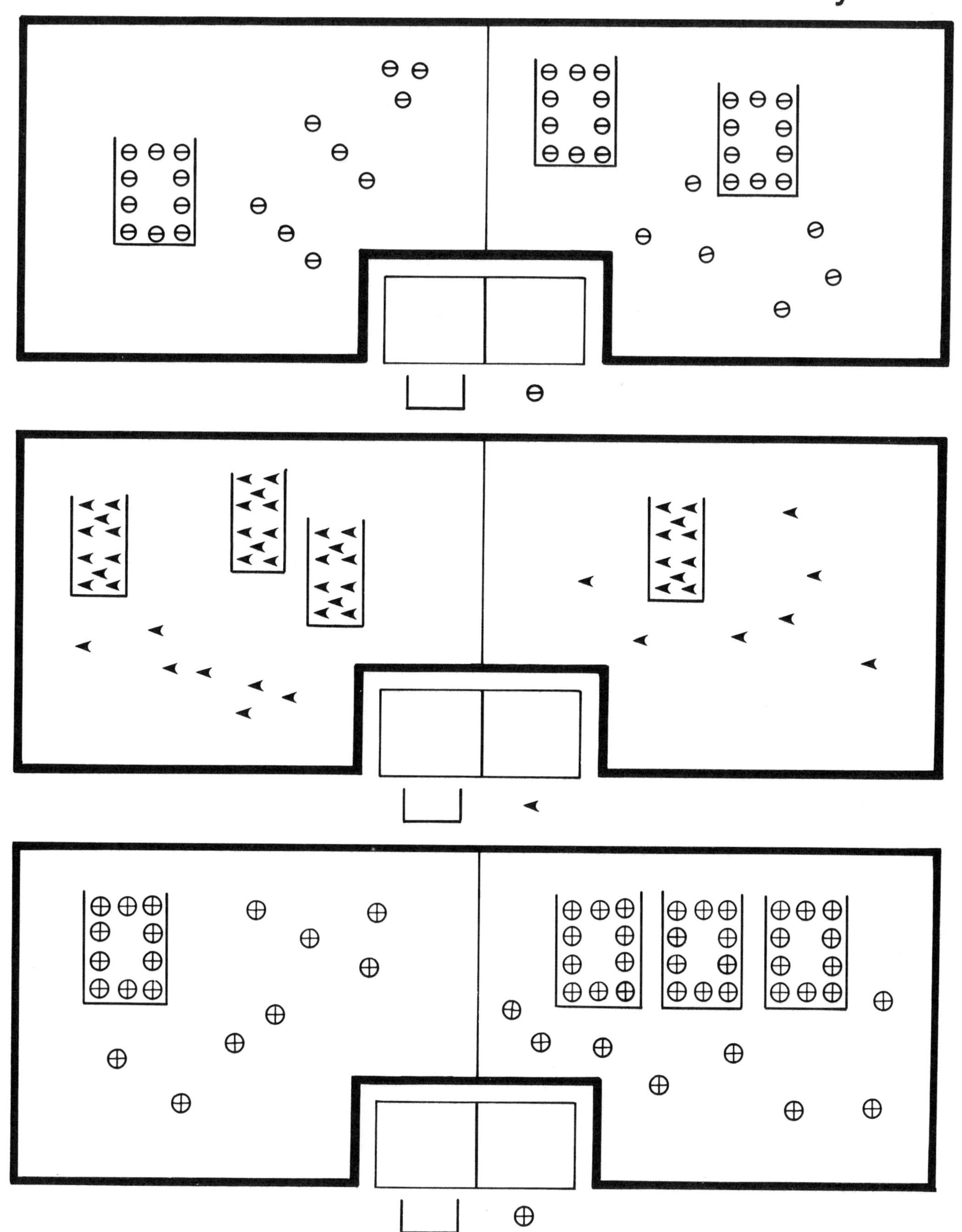

Combine and record. Trade if necessary.

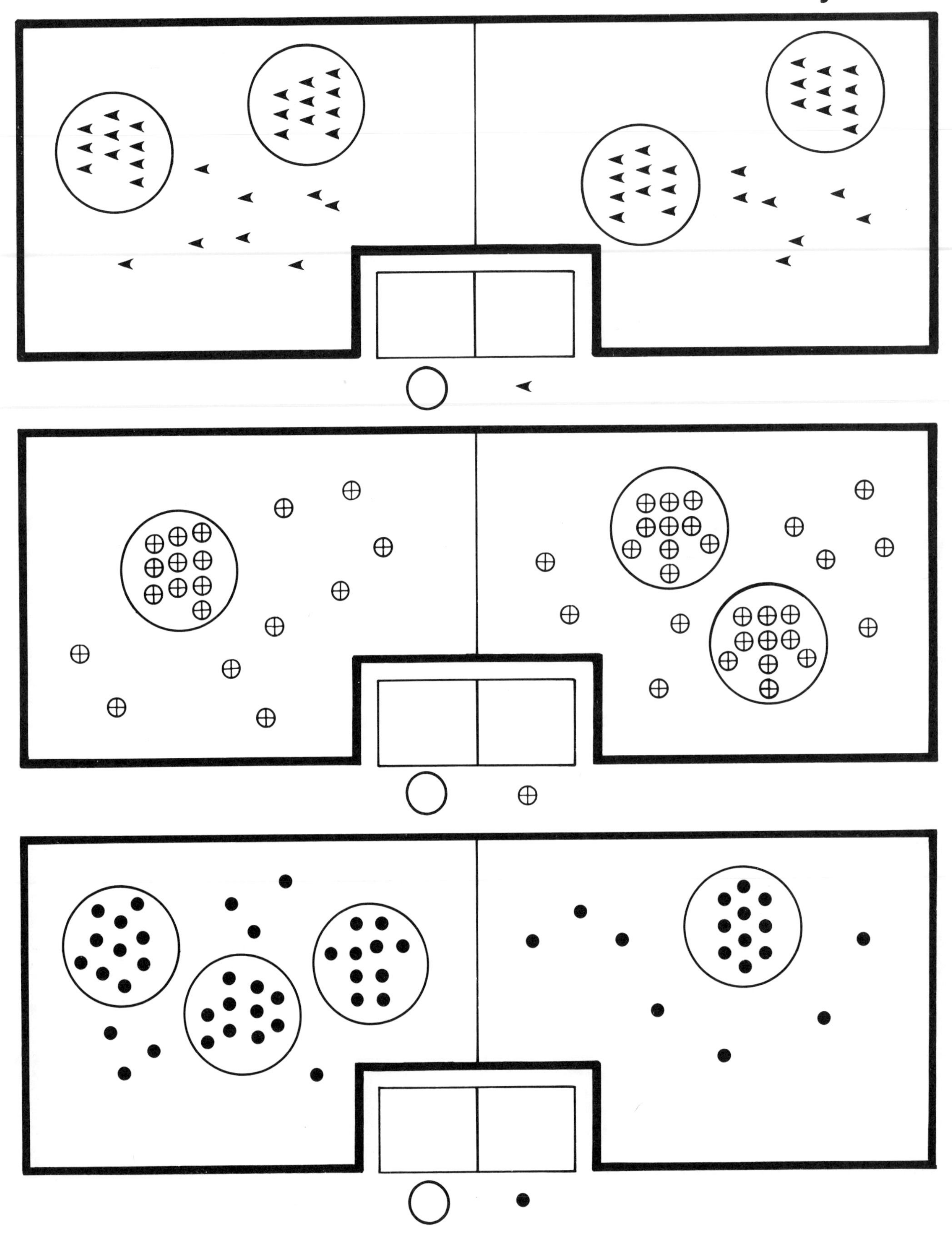

Combine and record. Trade if necessary.

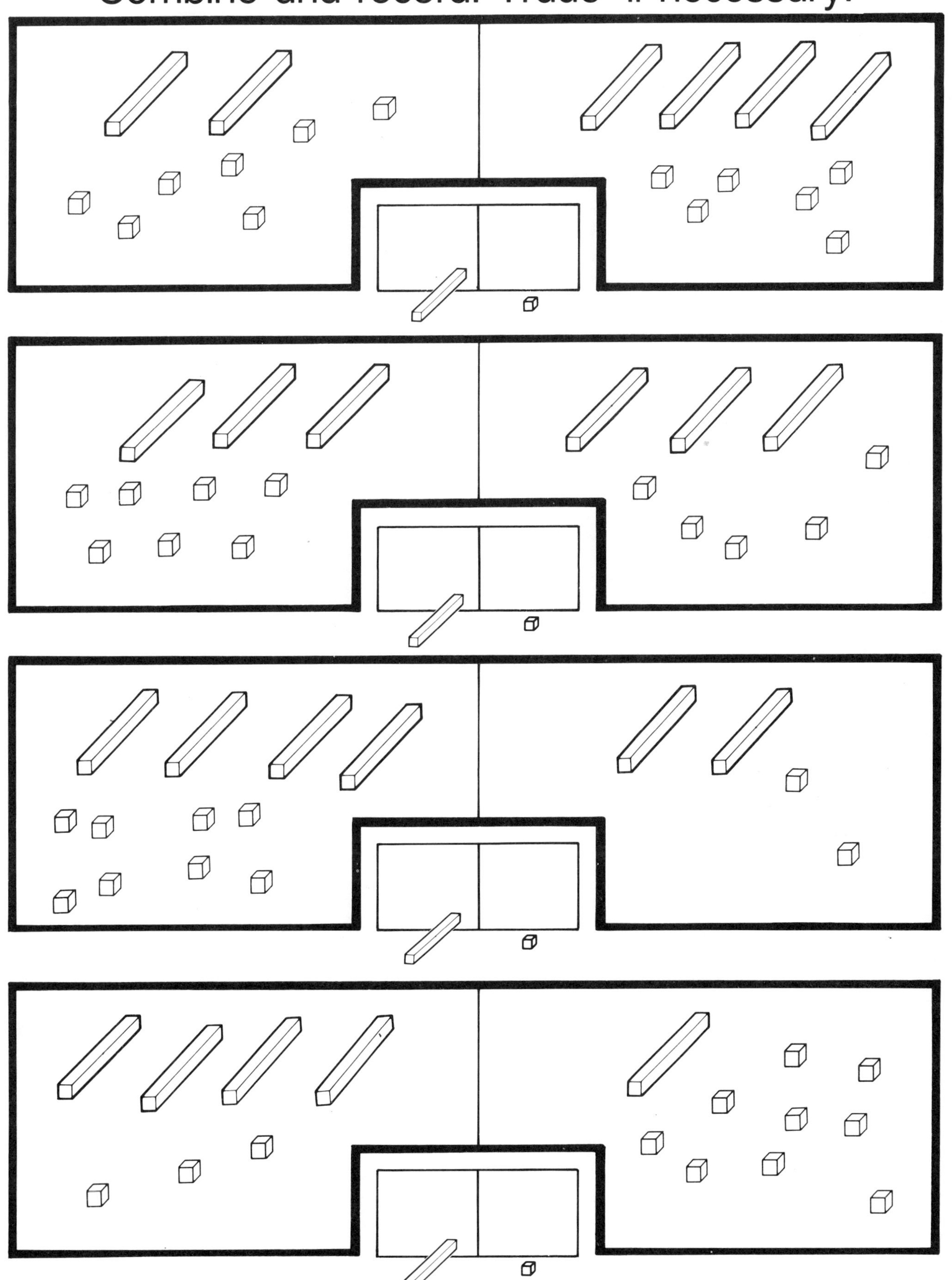

Combine and record. Trade if necessary.

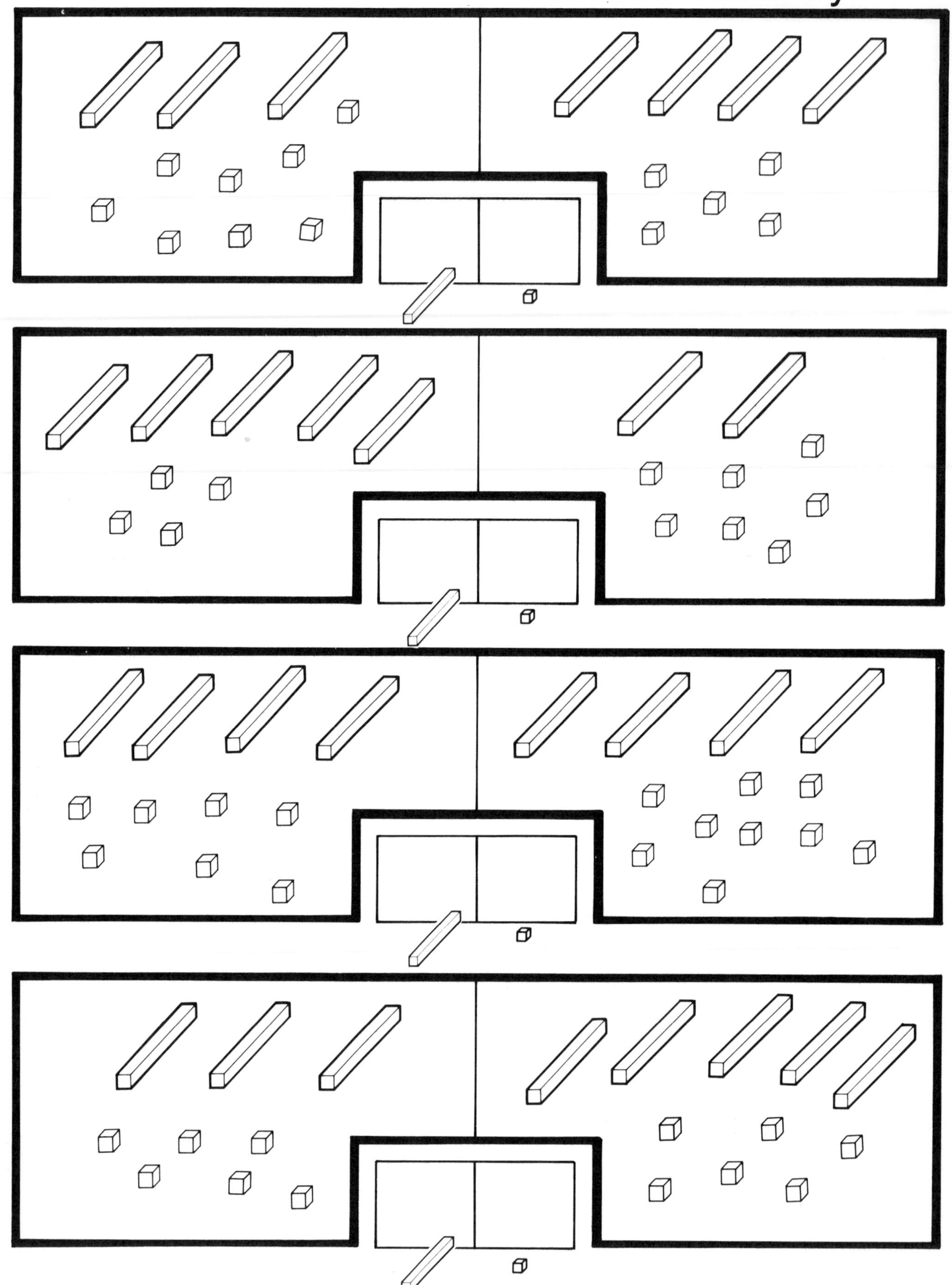

Combine and record. Trade if necessary.

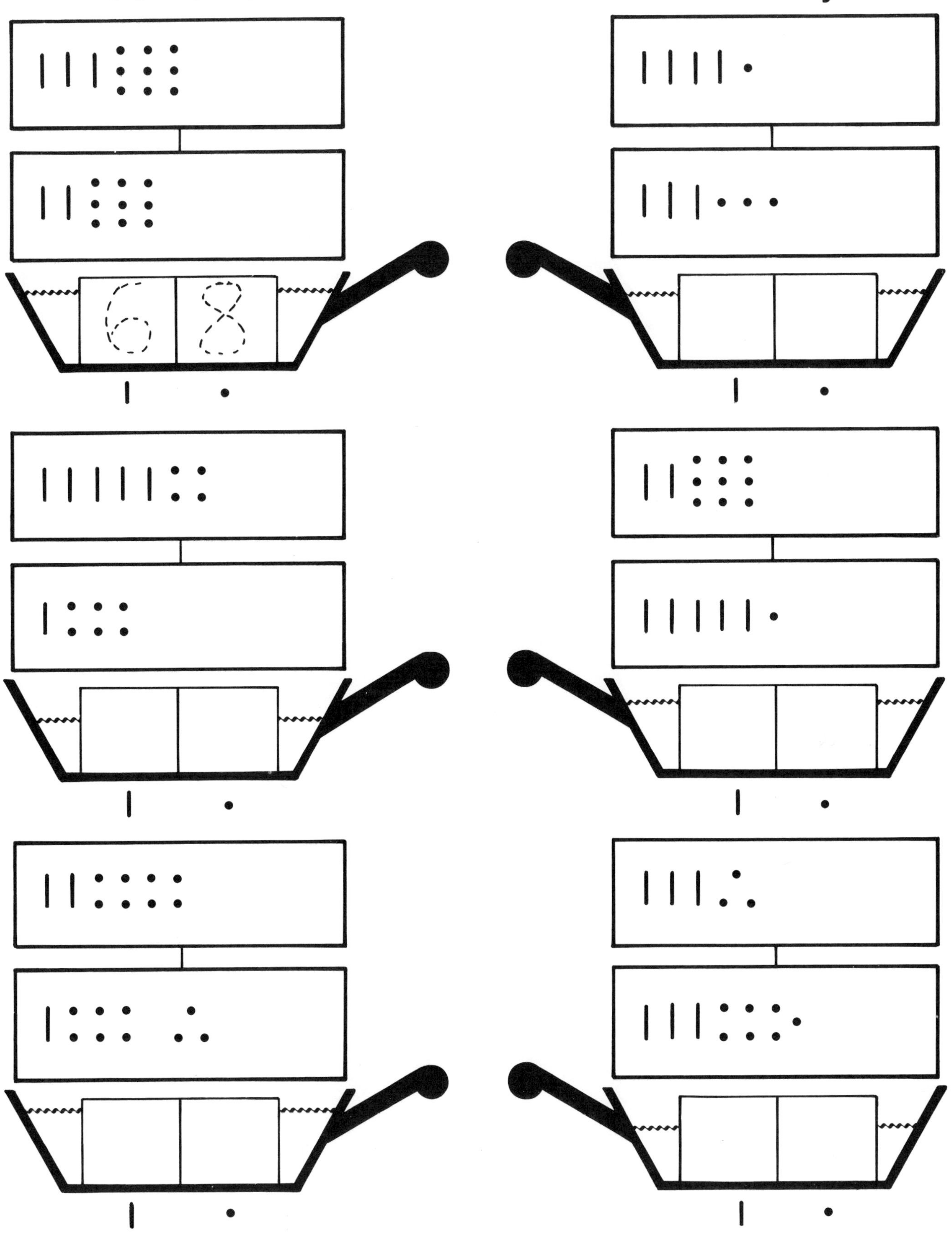

Combine and record. Trade if necessary.

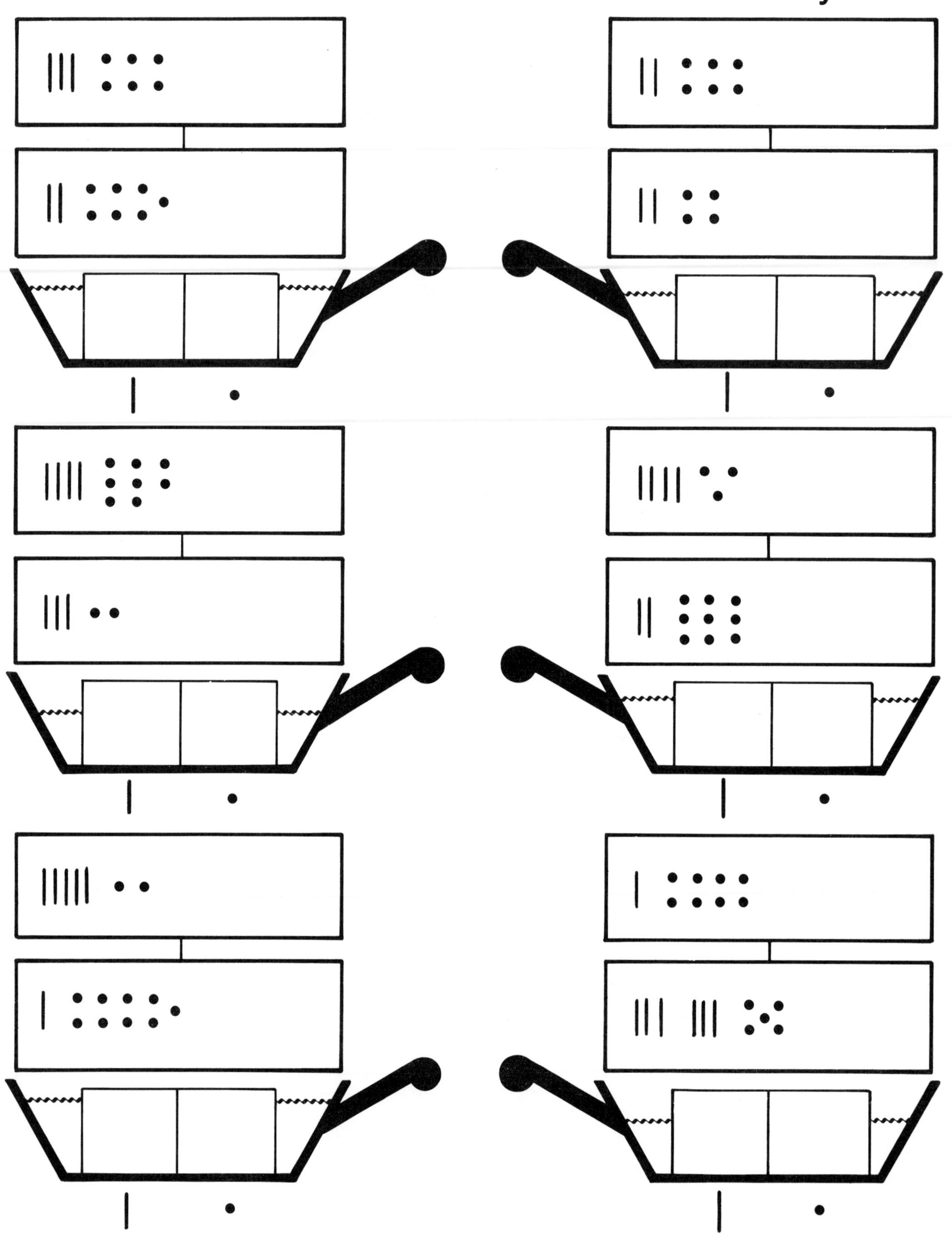

Combine and record. Trade if necessary.

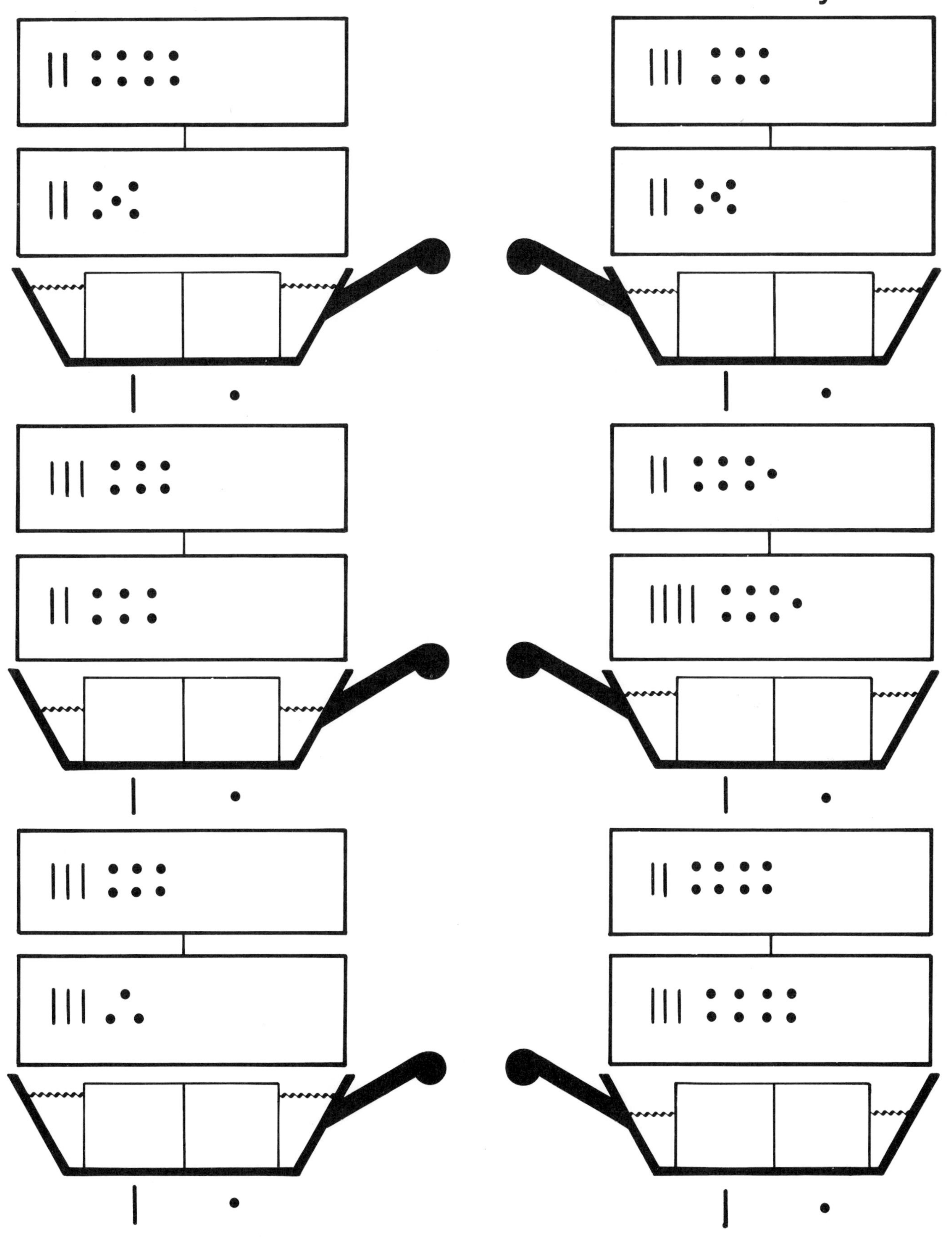

Combine and record. Trade if necessary.

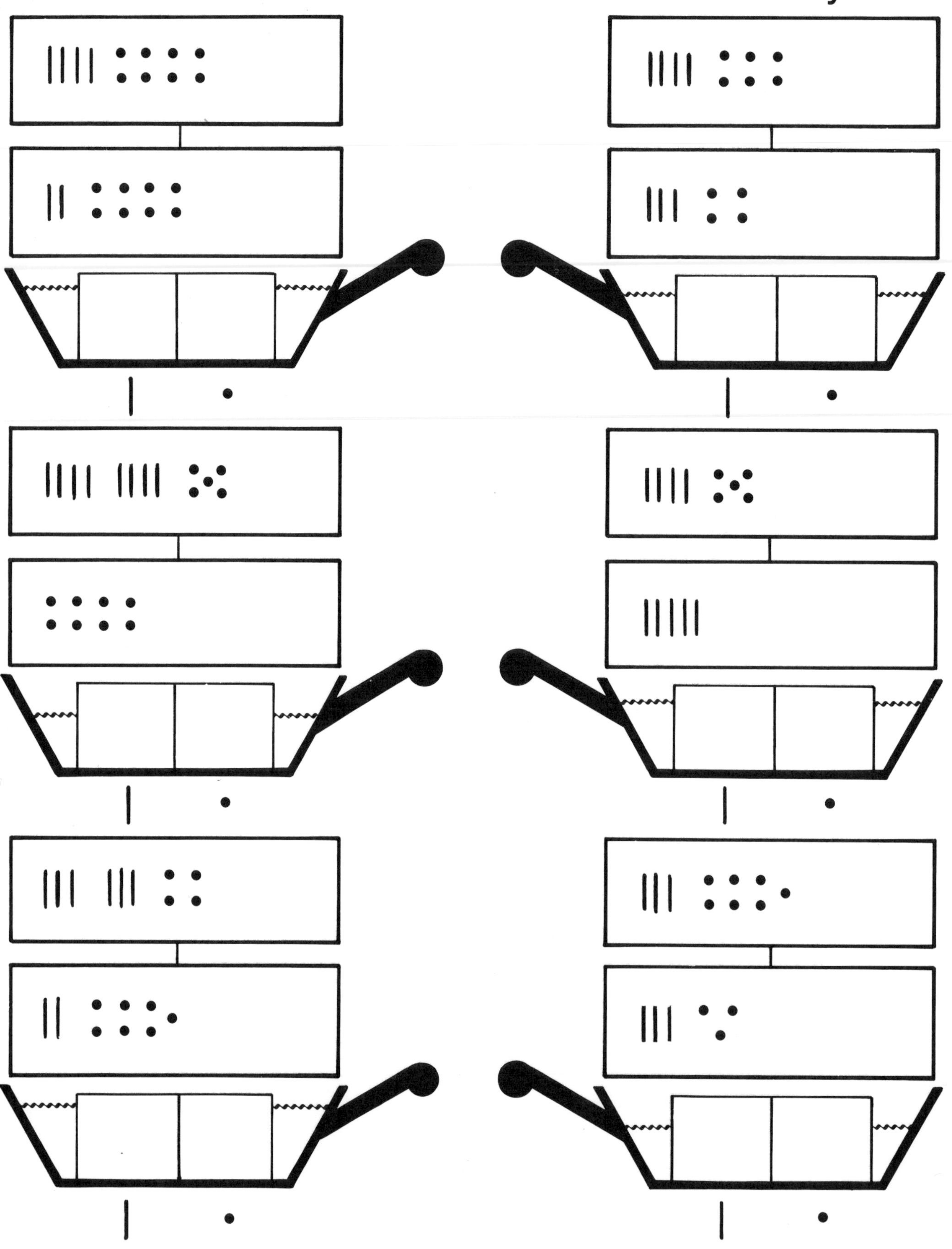

Add. Trade if necessary.

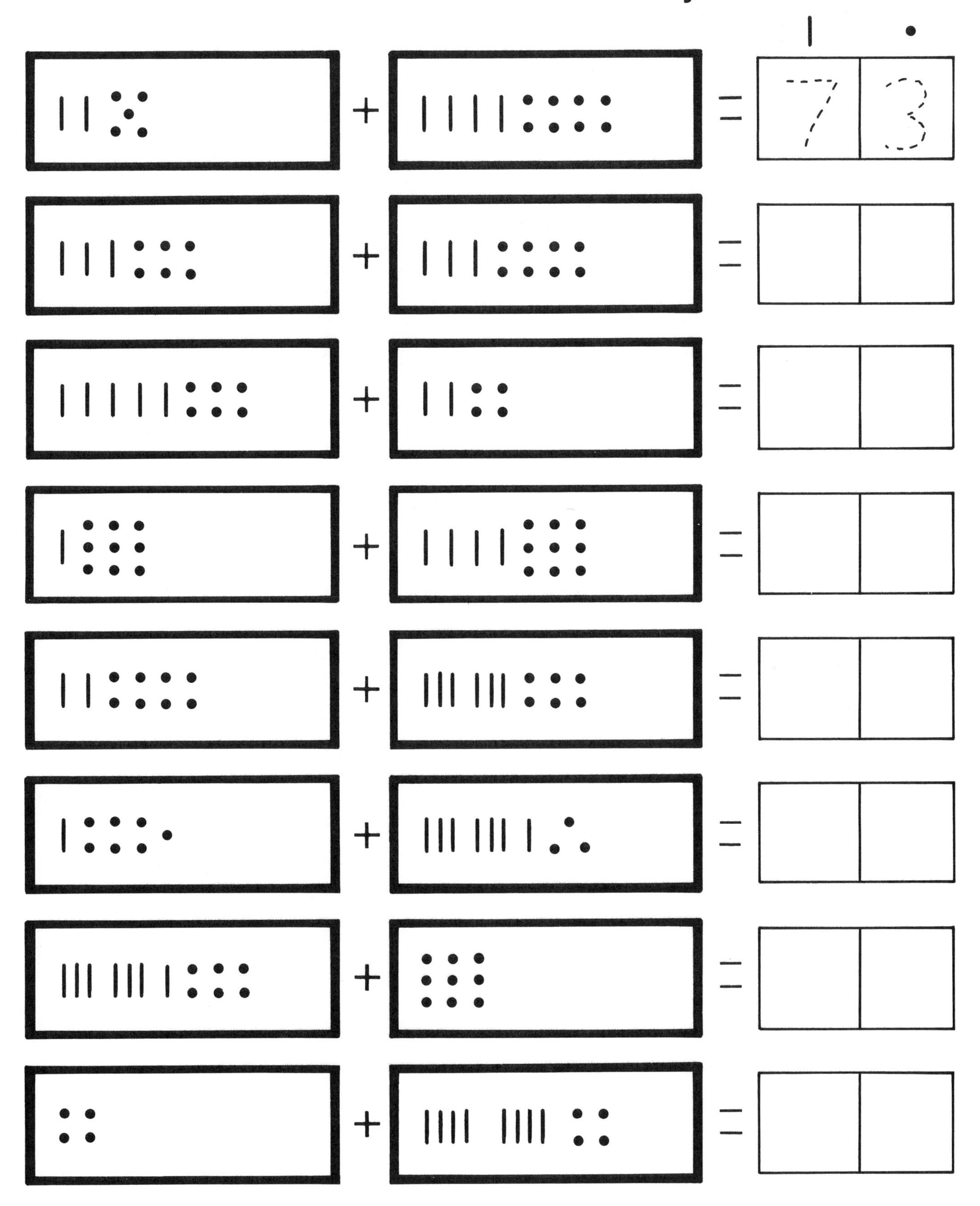

O

Add. Trade if necessary.

Add. Trade if necessary.

O

Add. Trade if necessary.

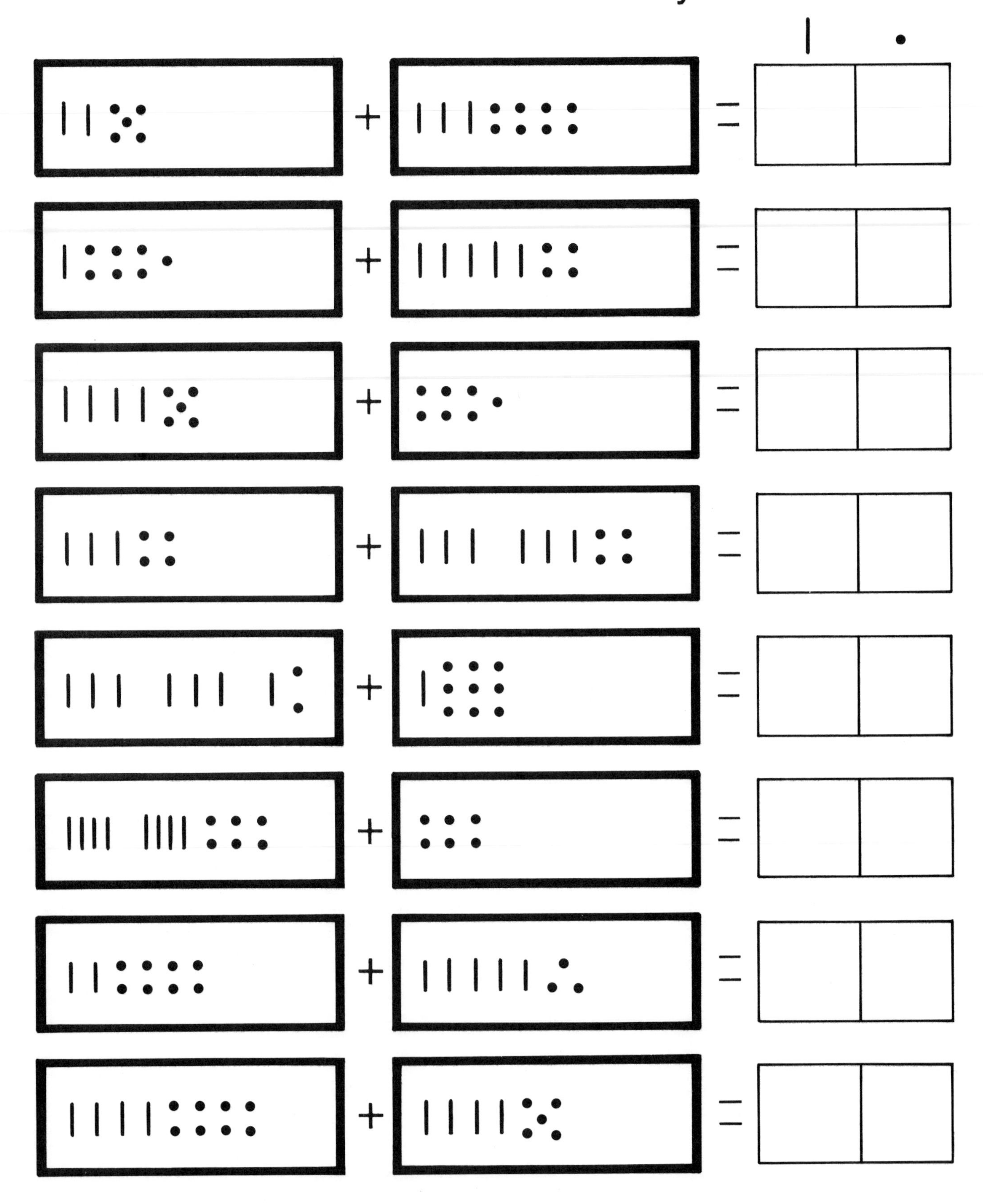

Combine and record.

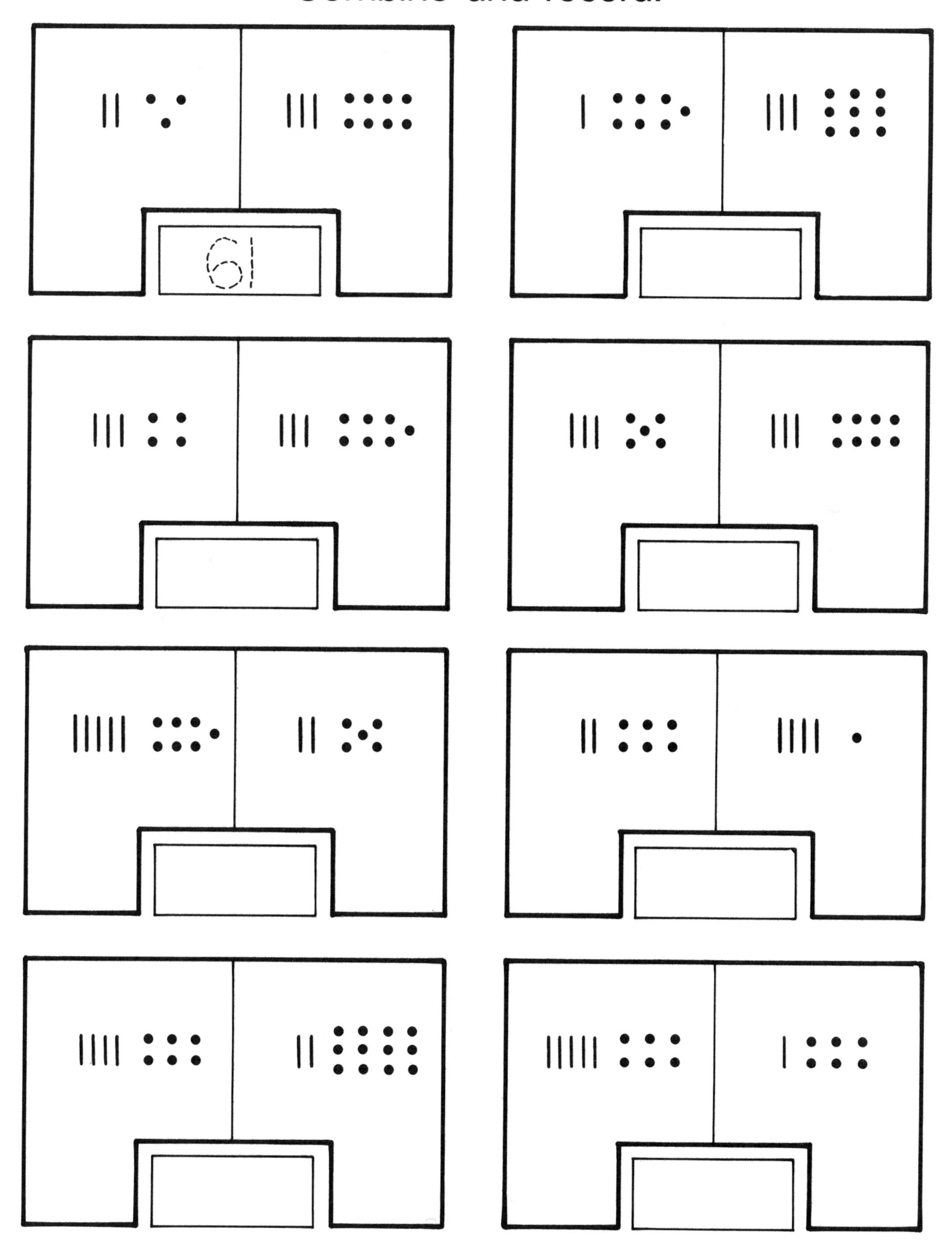

Combine and record.

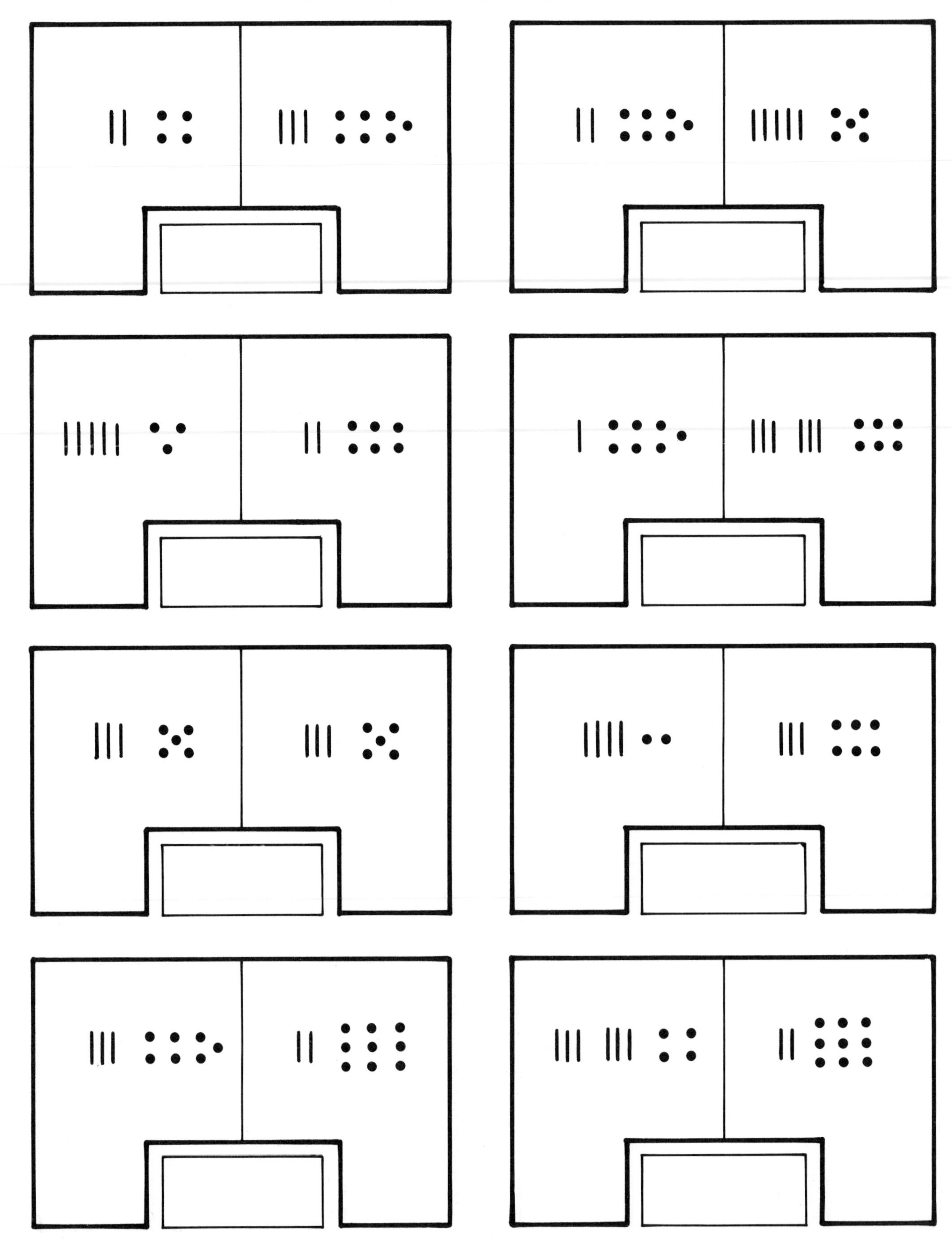

Combine and record.

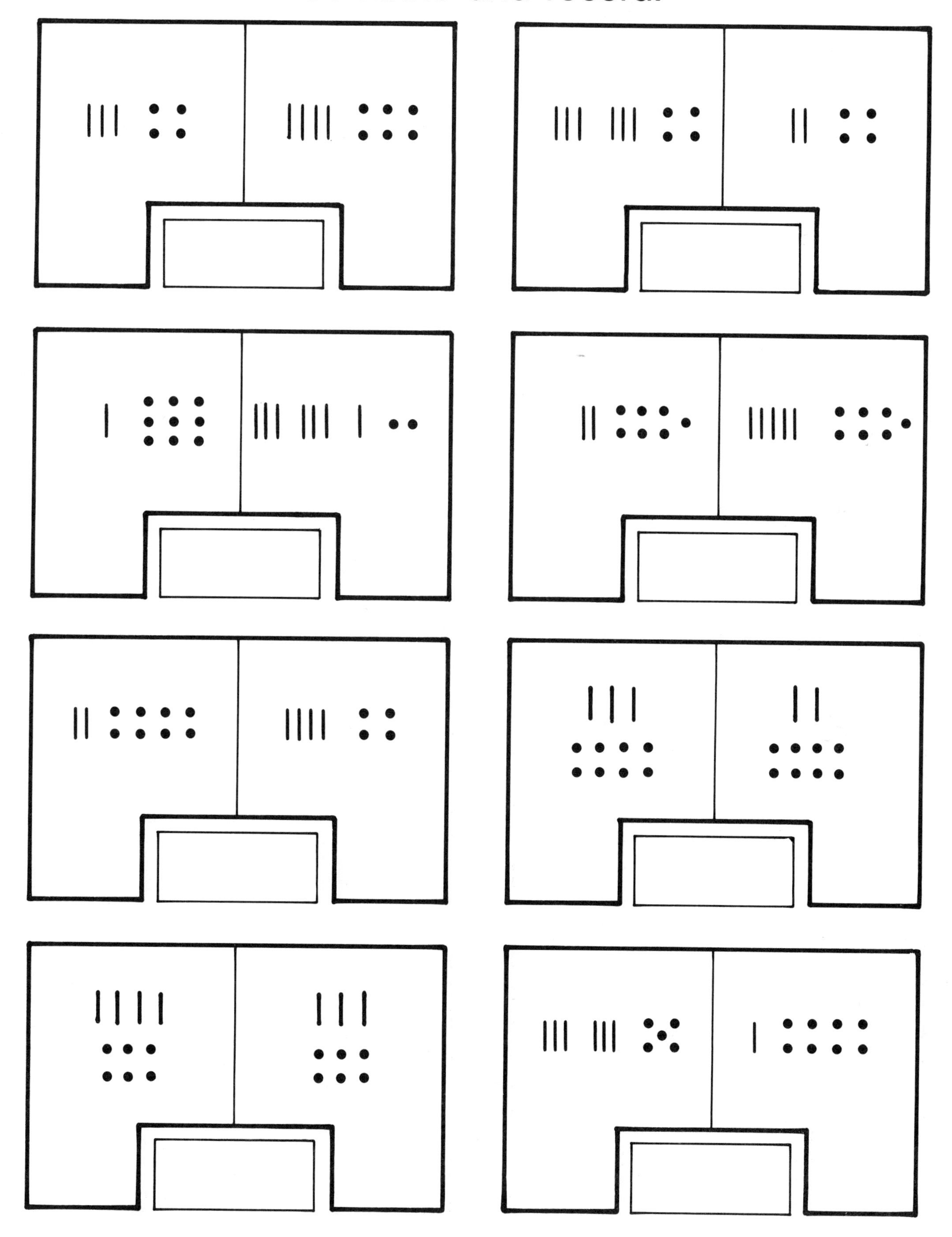

Combine and record.

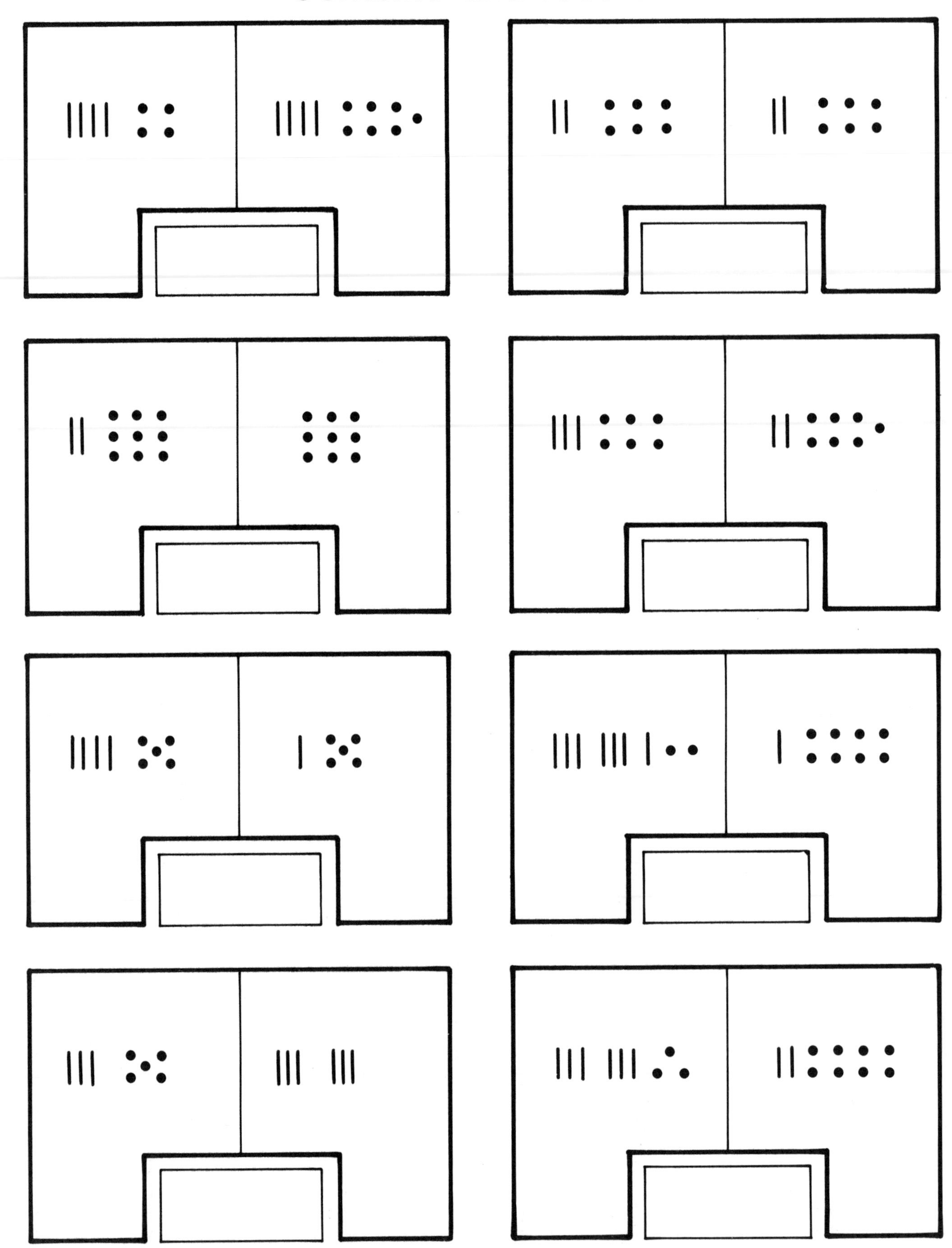

Combine and record.

		34
		36
60	10	70

Combine and record.

		27
		48

		45
		36

Combine and record.

I I	• • • • •	
I I I I	• • • • • • •	

I I I I I I	• • •	
I I I	• • • • • • •	

		39
		29

I I I I I I	• • • • • • • • •	
I	• •	

		17
		67

		46
		47

		35
		39

I I I I I I I	• • •	
I	• • • • • • • •	

Combine and record.

		38
		48

		75
		15

		63
		19

		57
		27

Color the tens and ones. Add.

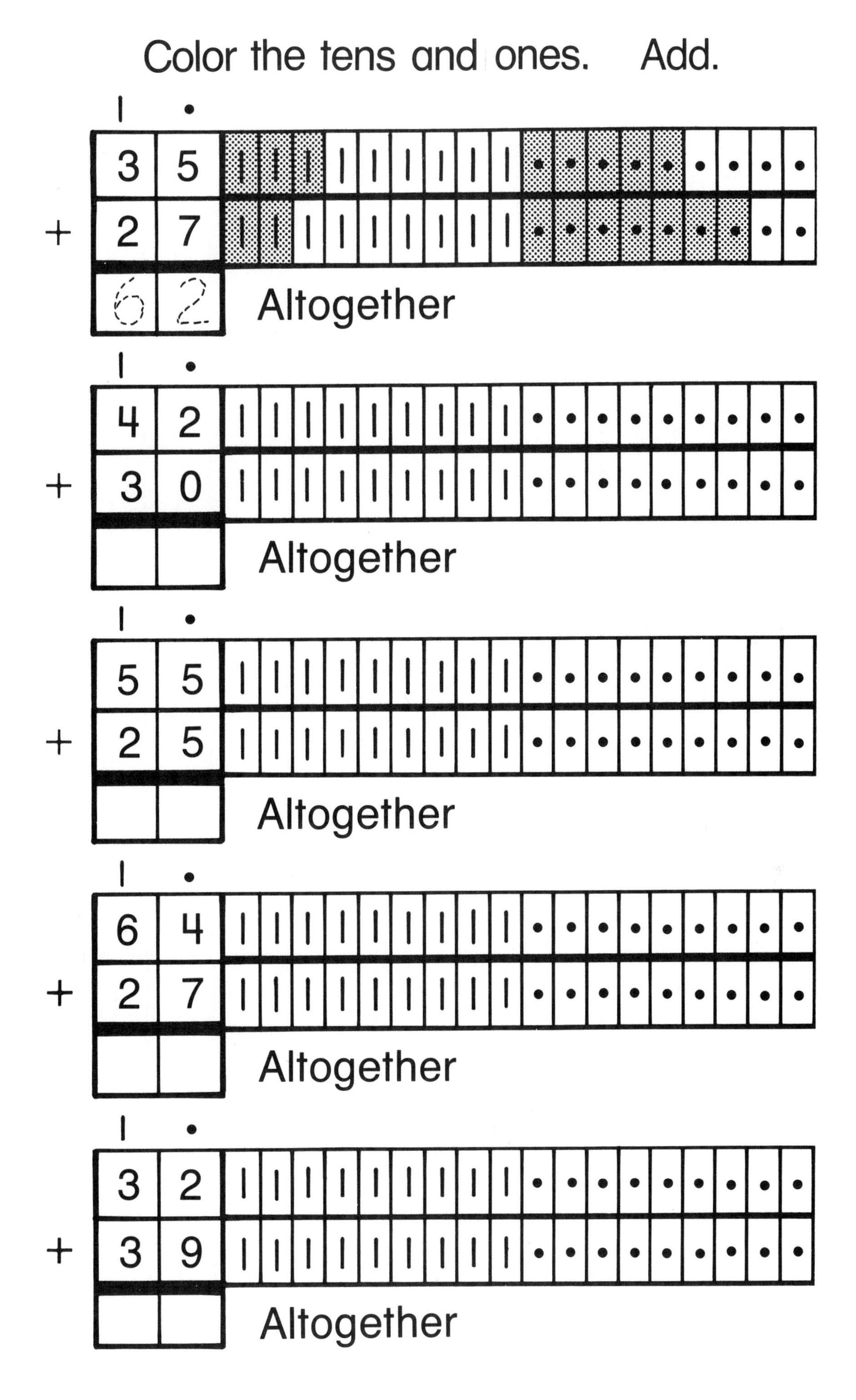

I	•
3	5
2	7
6	2

Altogether

I	•
4	2
3	0

Altogether

I	•
5	5
2	5

Altogether

I	•
6	4
2	7

Altogether

I	•
3	2
3	9

Altogether

Color the tens and ones. Add.

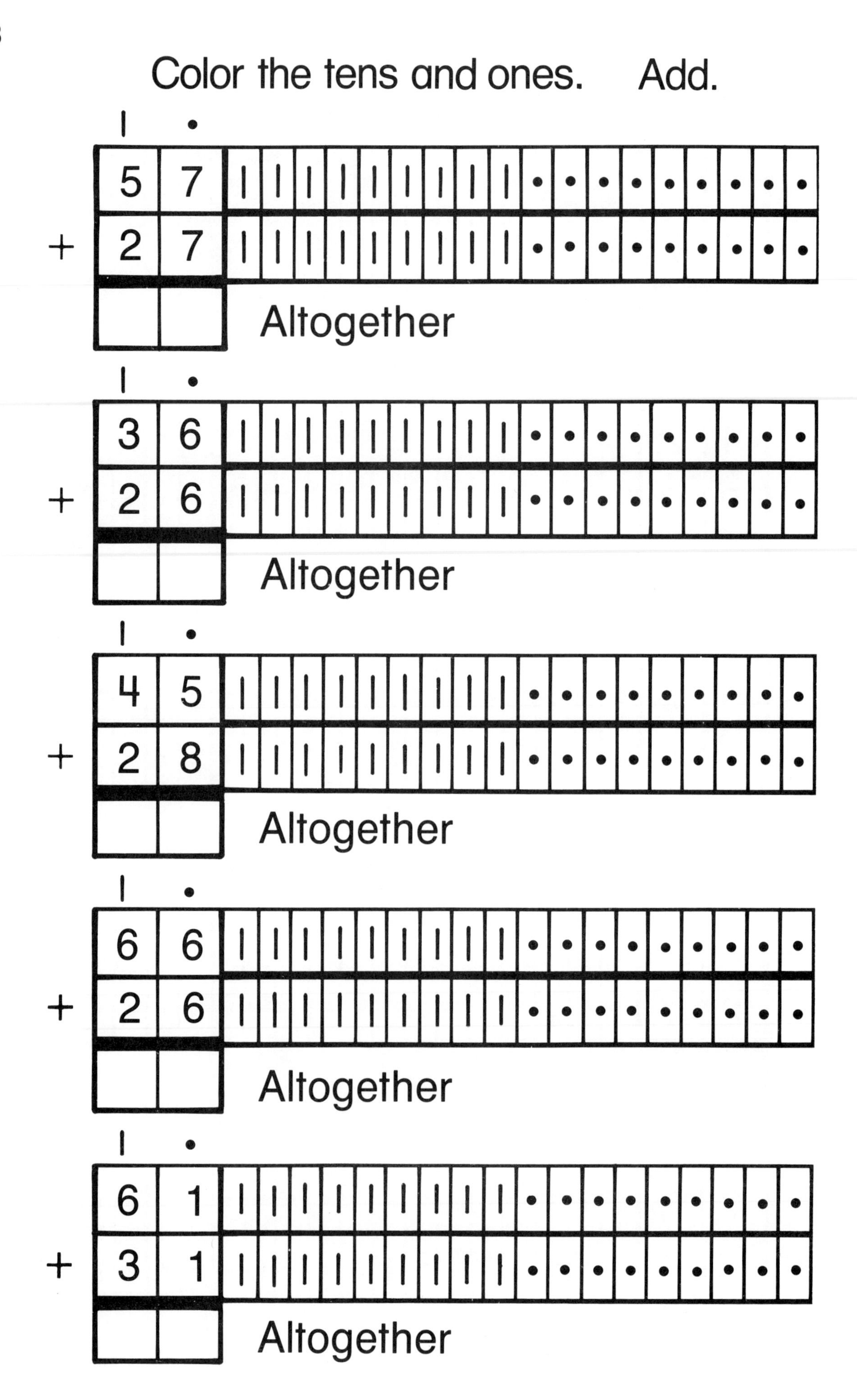

Color the tens and ones. Add.

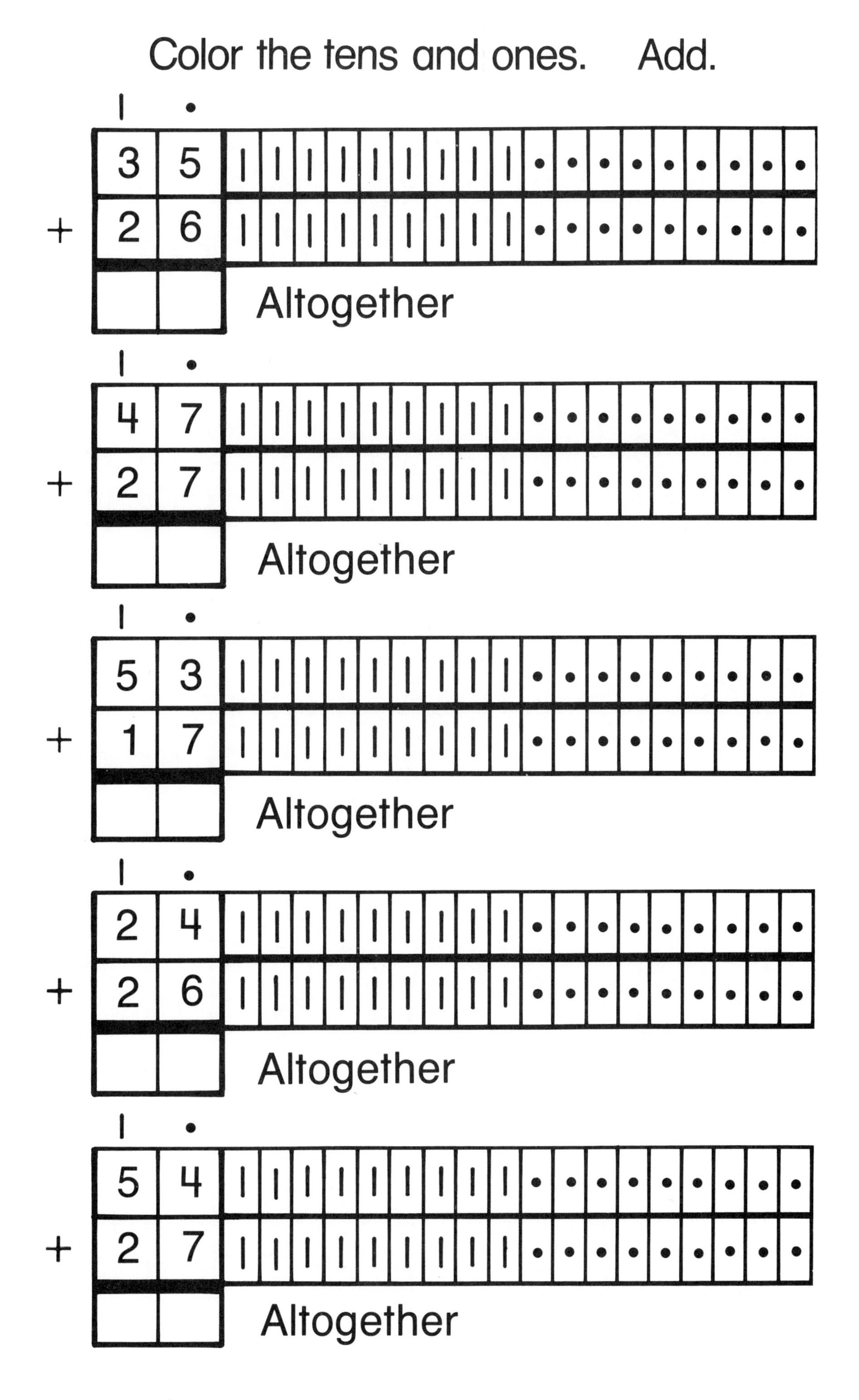

Color the tens and ones. Add.

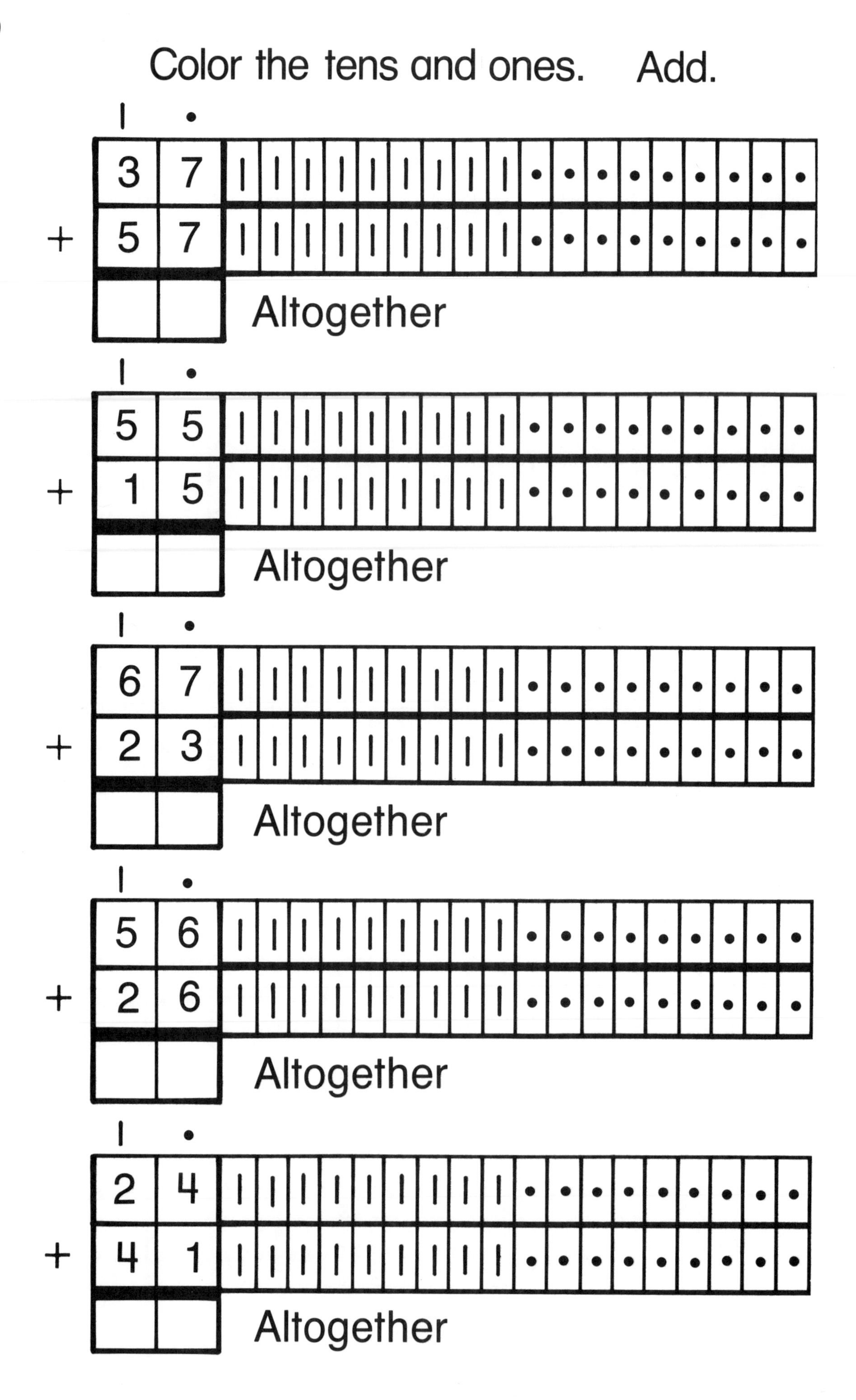

Color the tens and ones. Add.

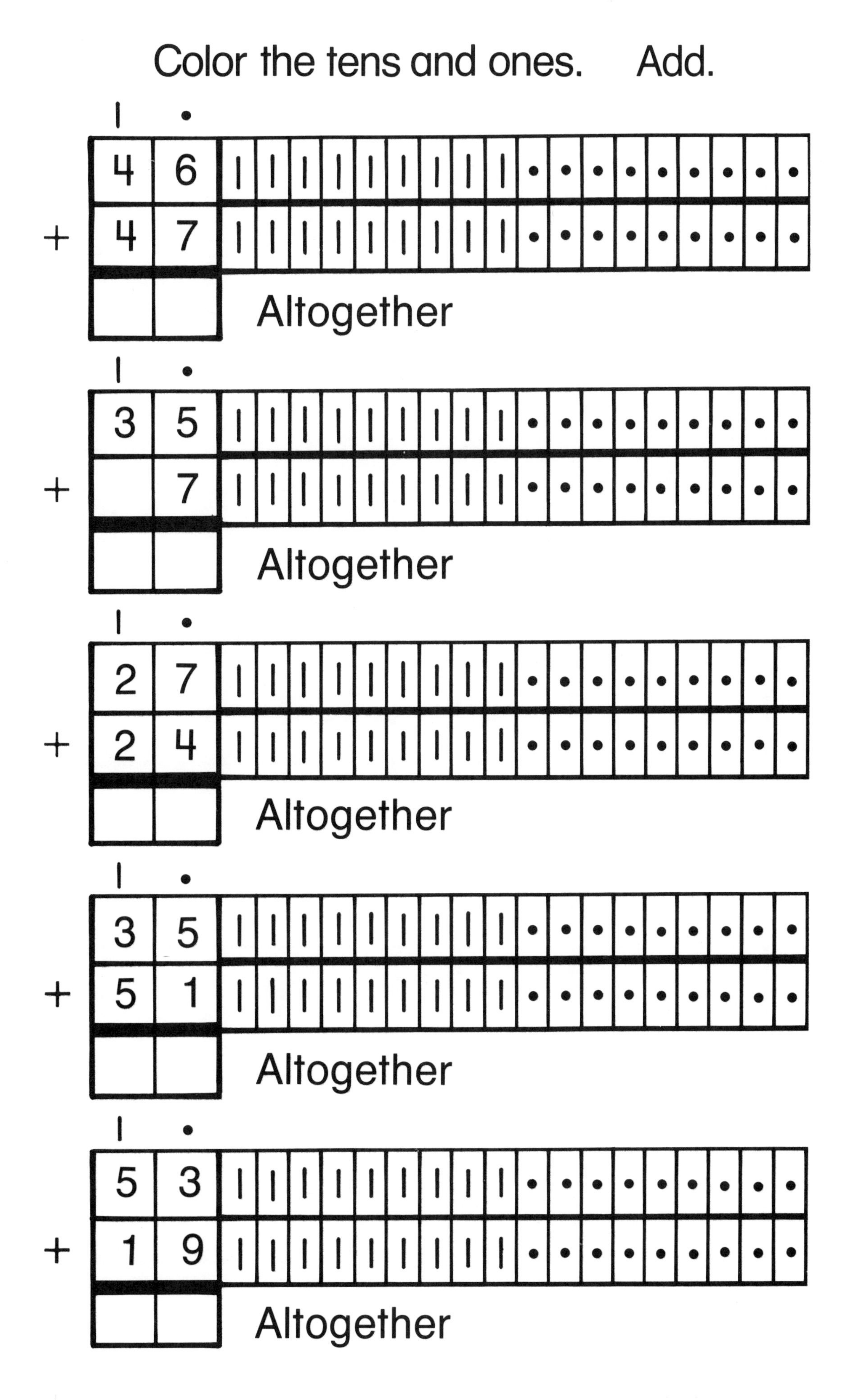
46
+ 47
Altogether
35
+ 7
Altogether
27
+ 24
Altogether
35
+ 51
Altogether
53
+ 19
Altogether

Combine and record.

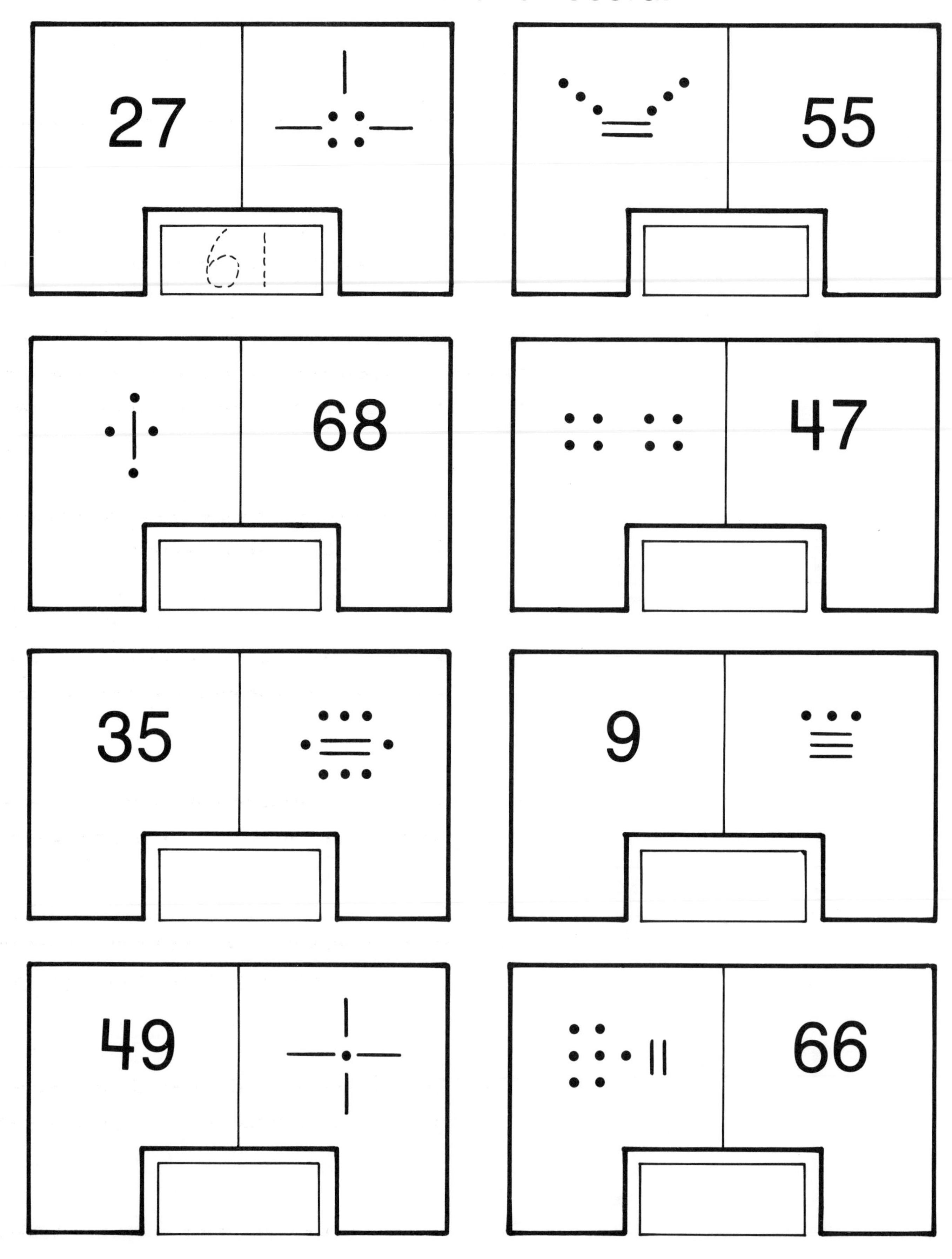

Combine and record.

27	44	67
53	38	18
36	15	53
66	52	48
75	46	17

Combine and record. Trade if necessary.

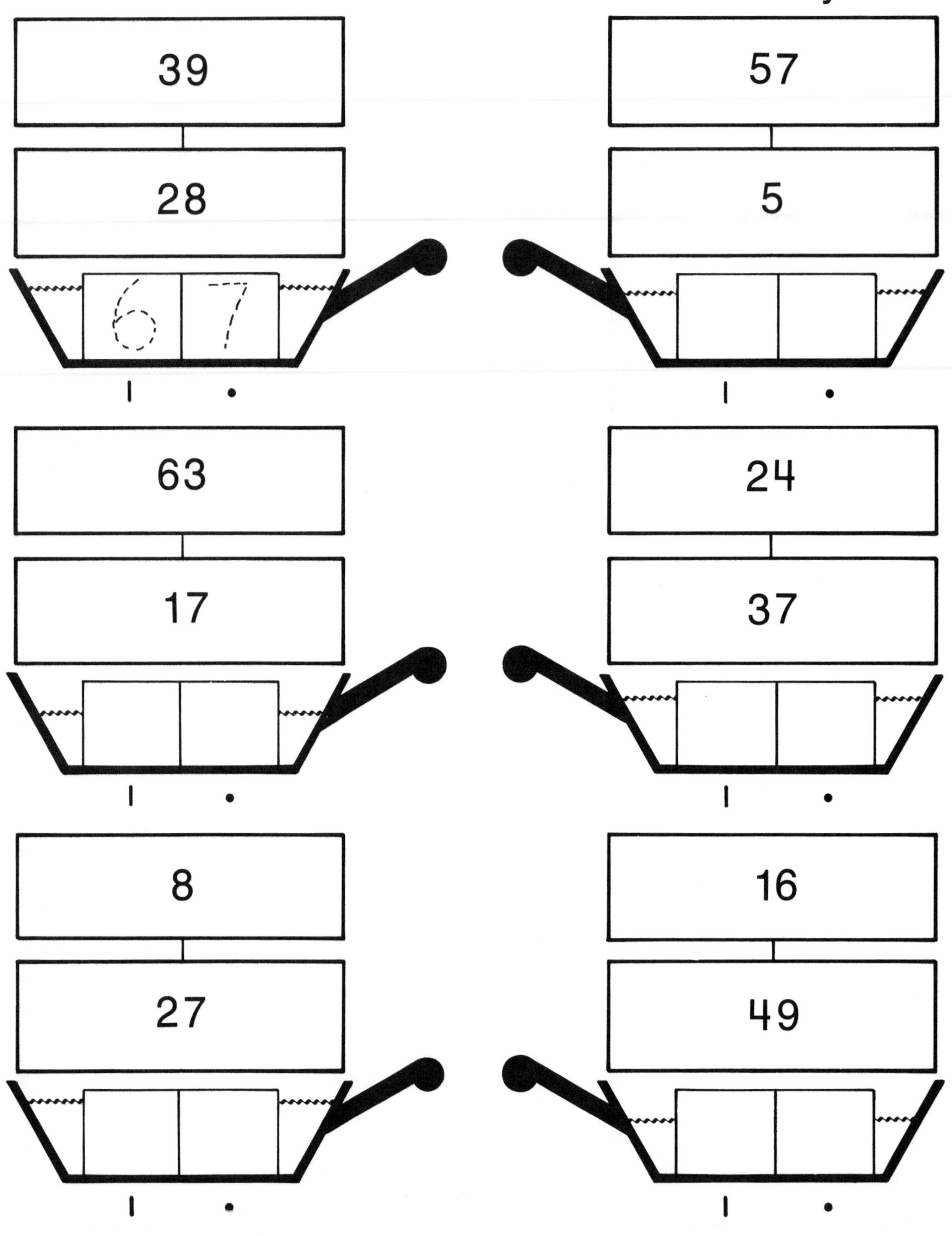

Combine and record.

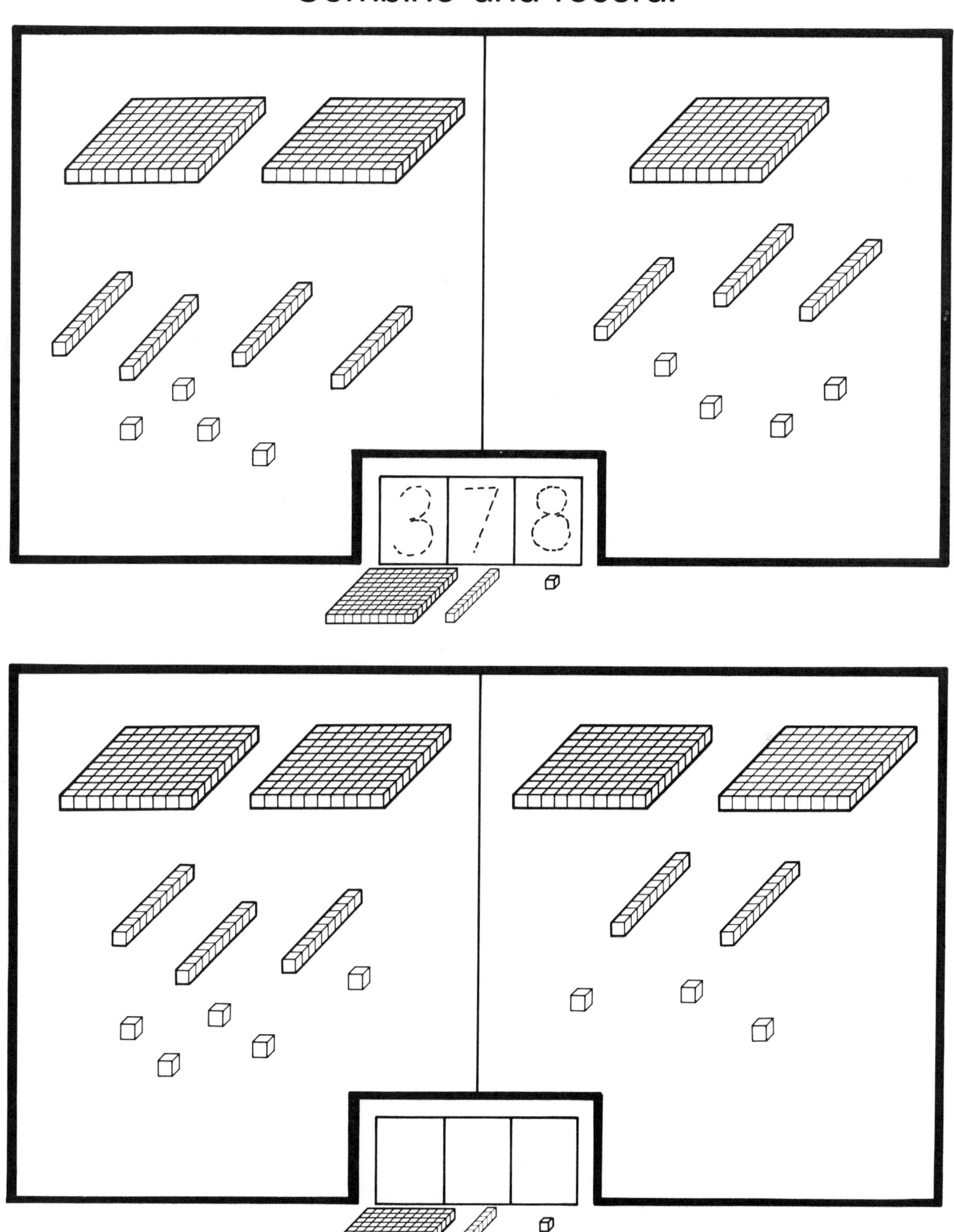

Combine and record.

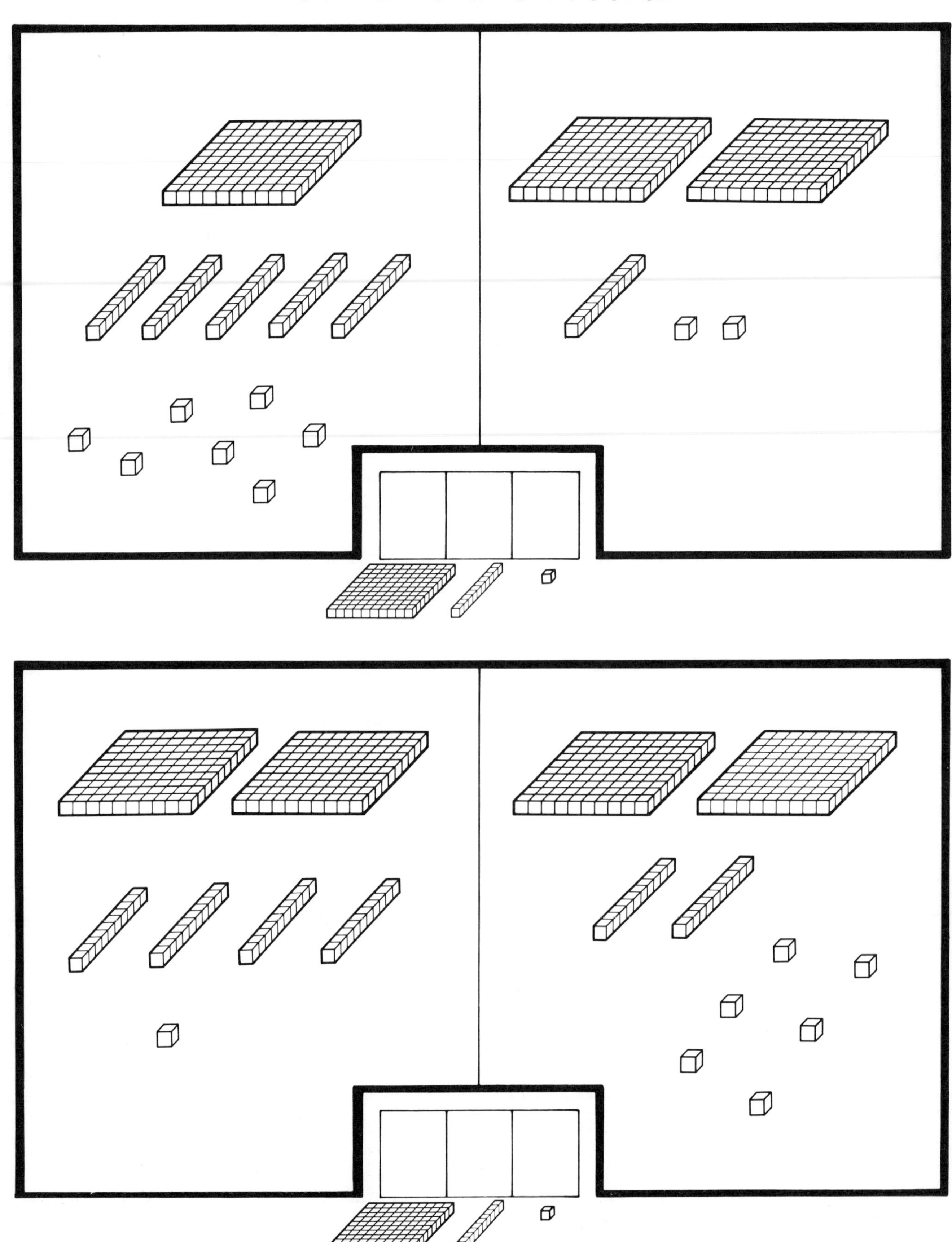

Combine and record.

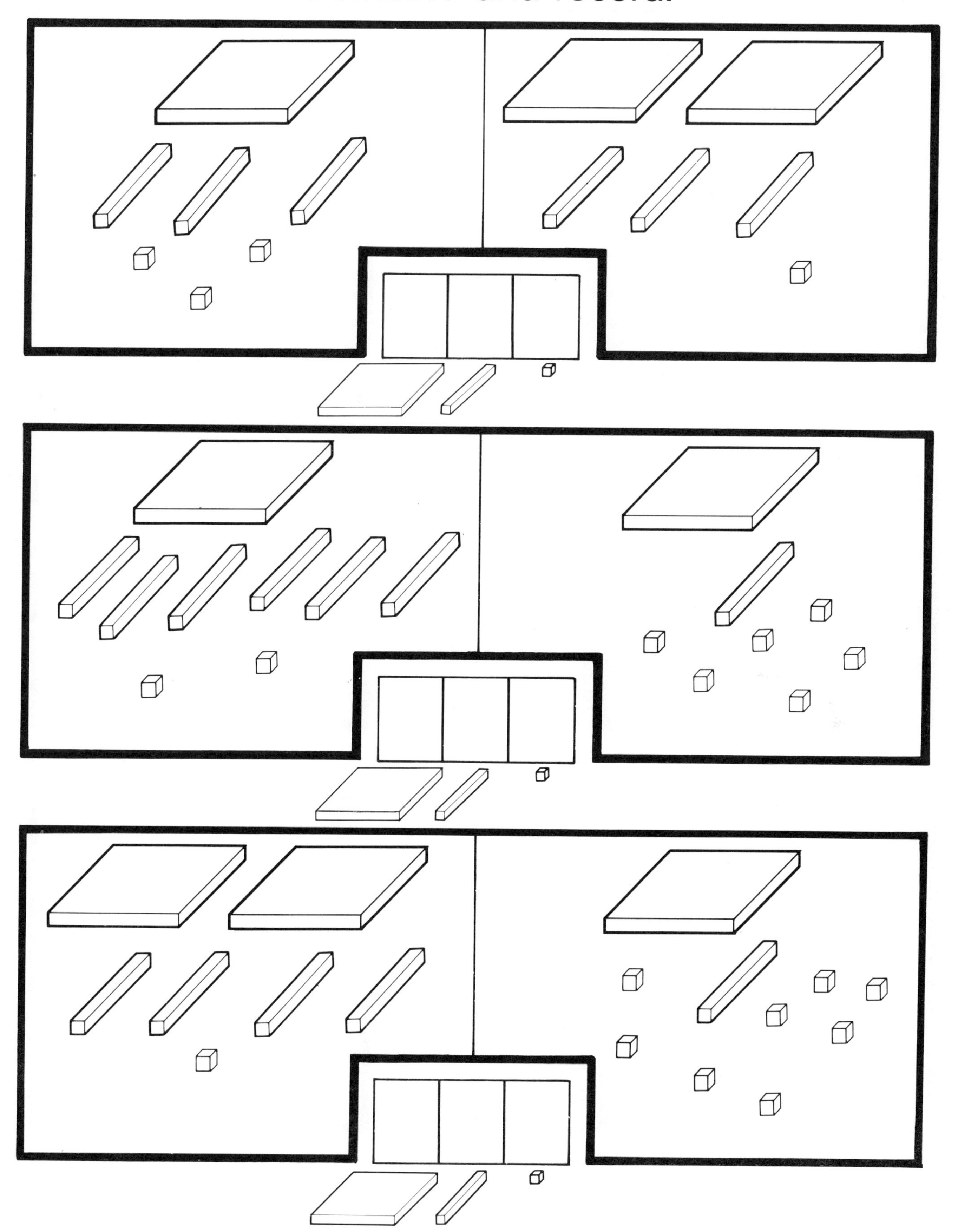

Combine and record.

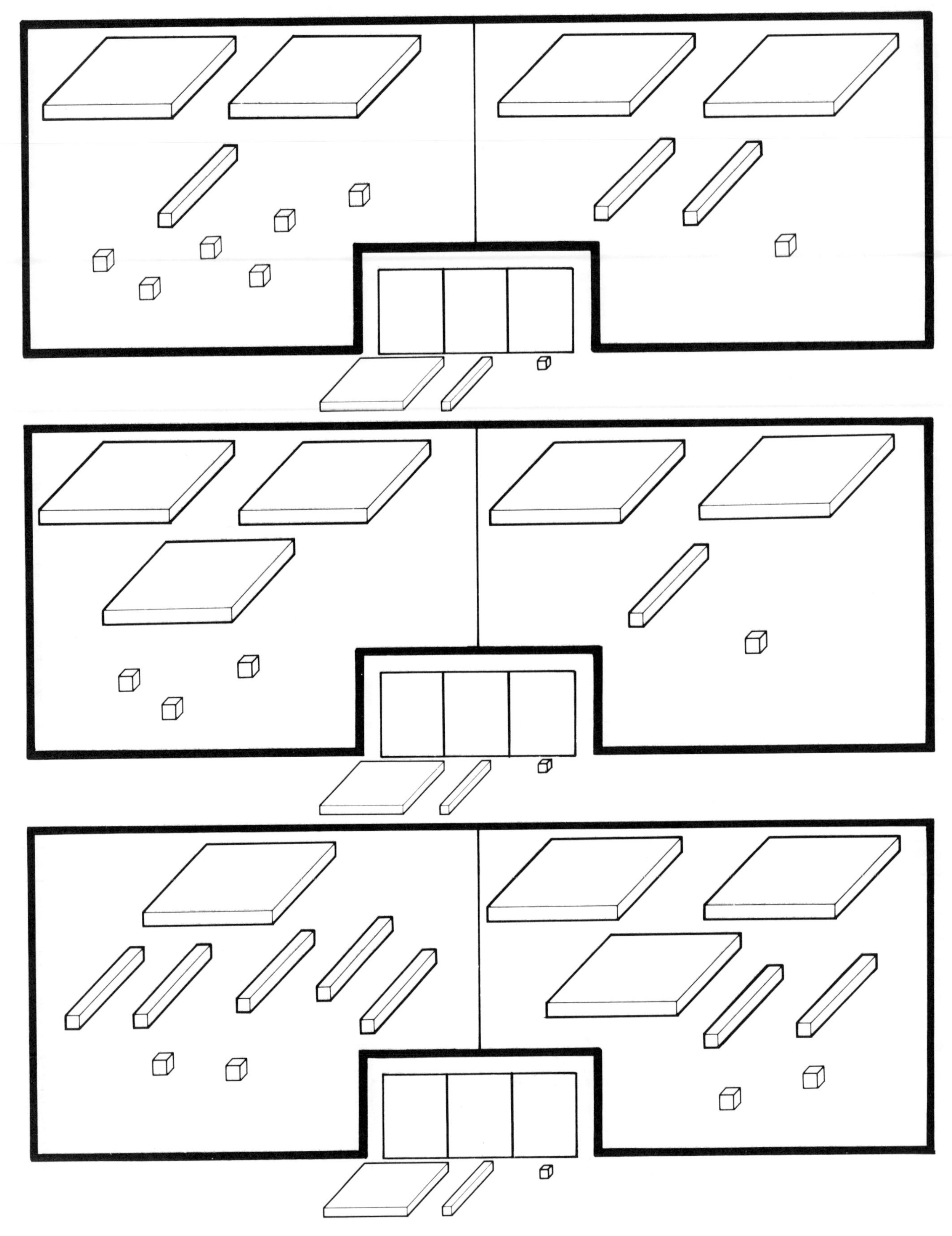

Combine and record.

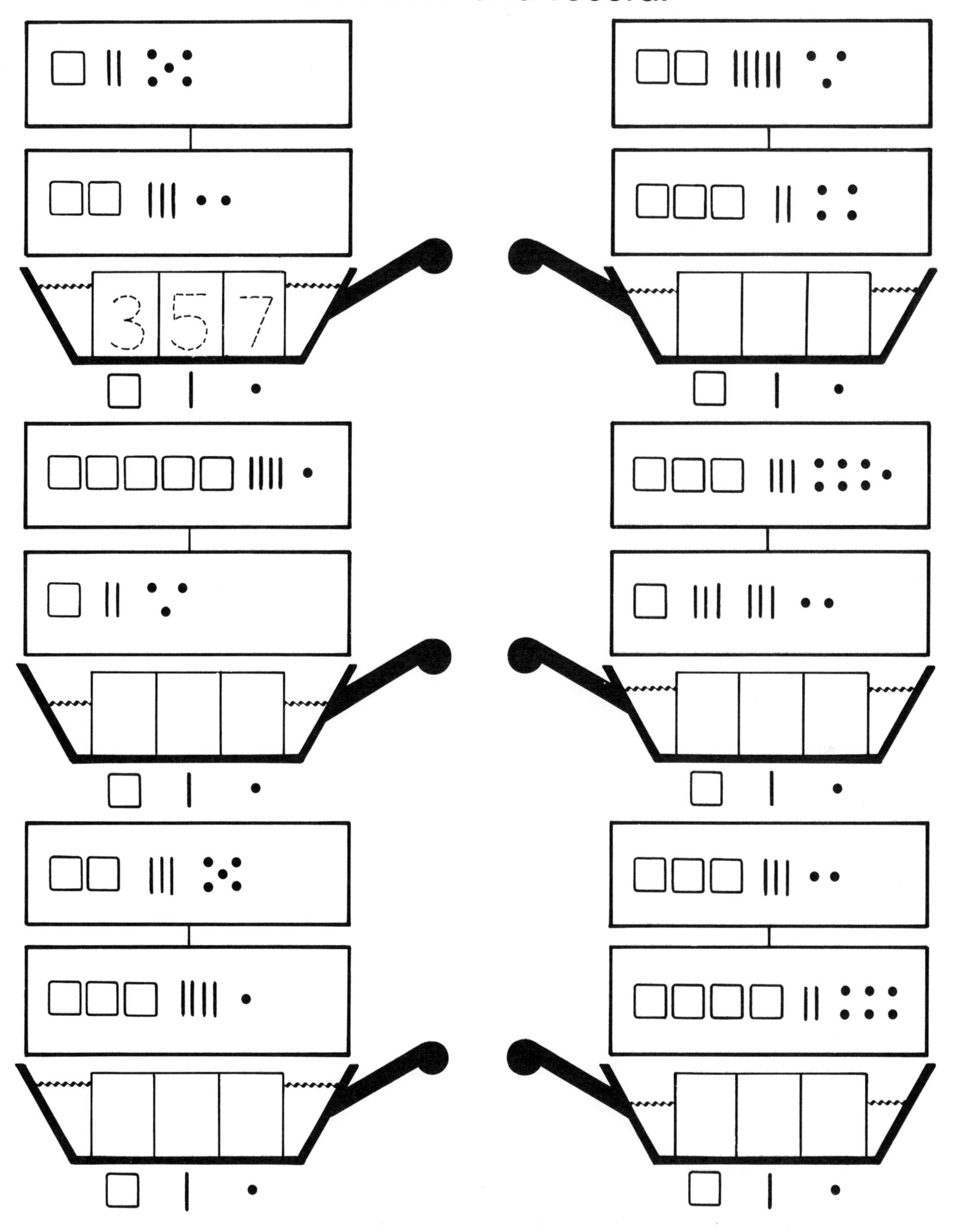

Combine and record.

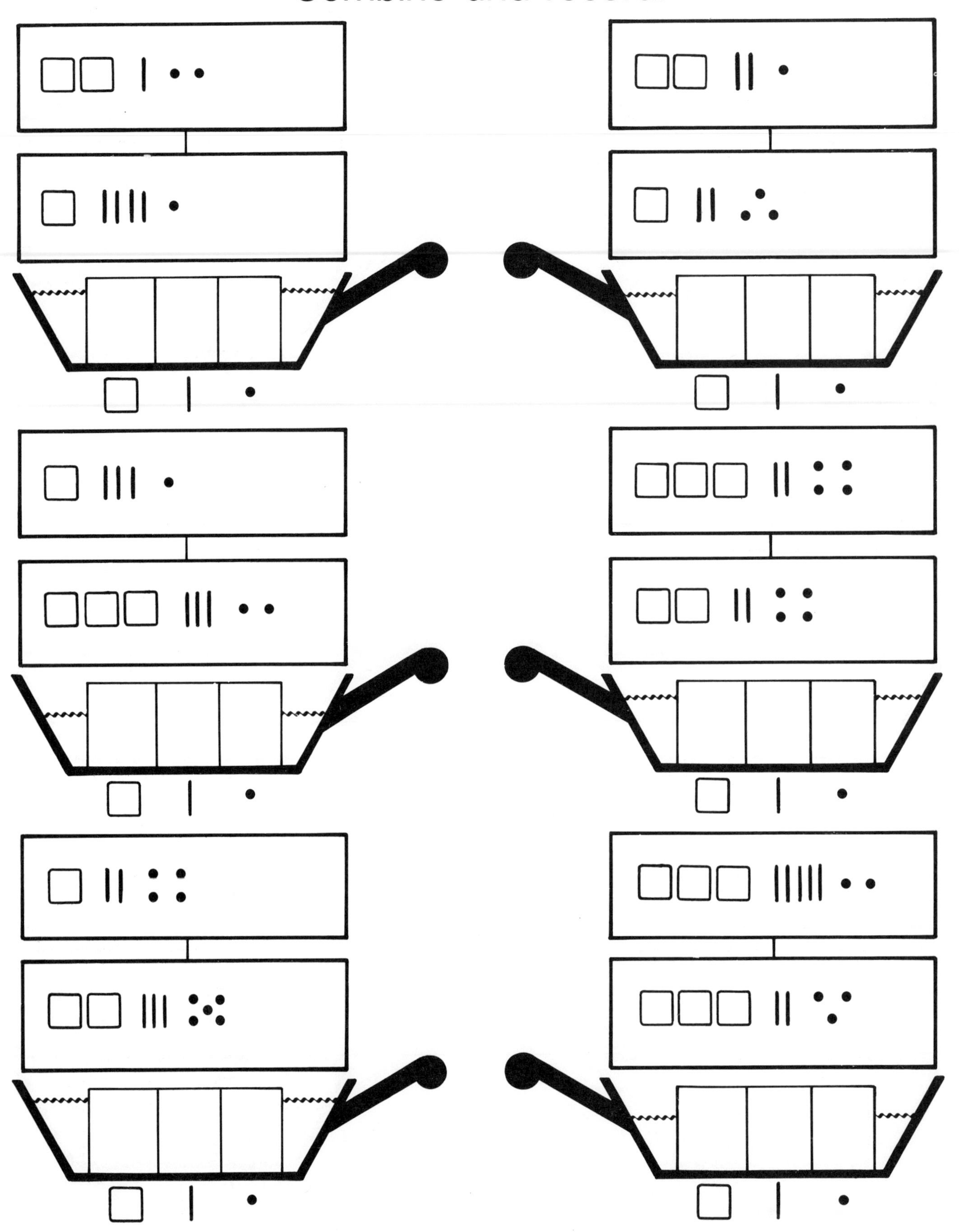

Combine and record.

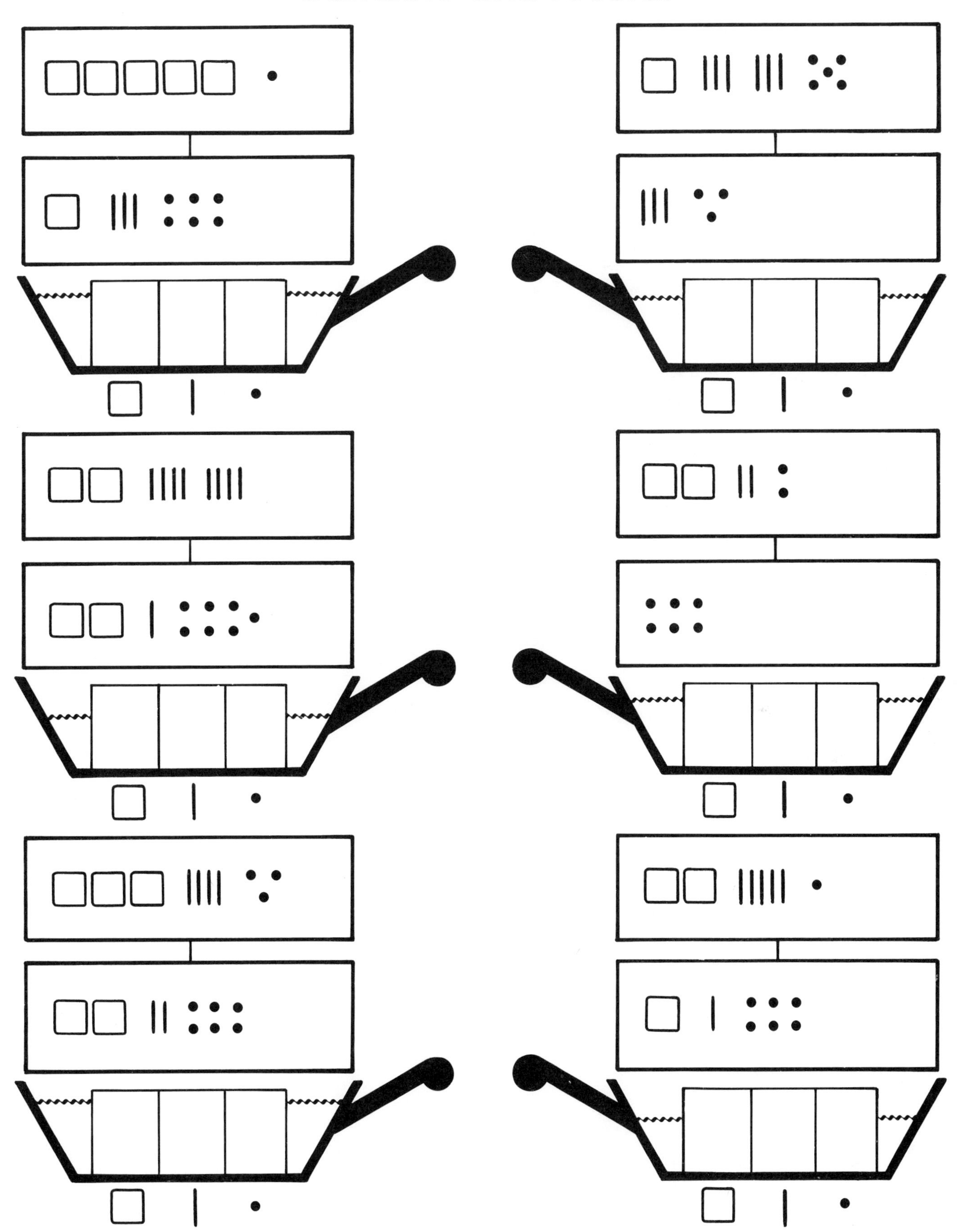

Combine and record.

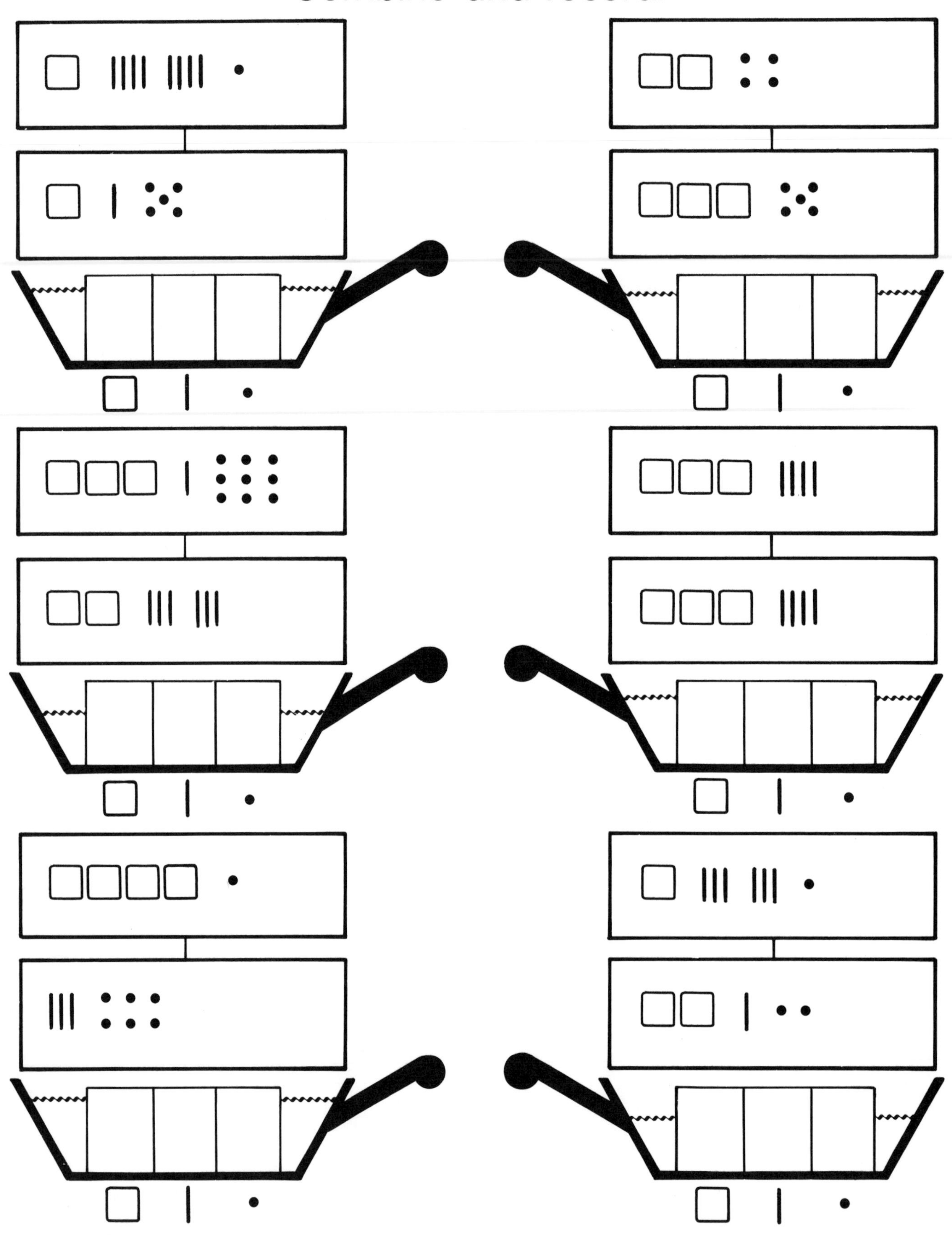

Add.

3 6 4

Add.

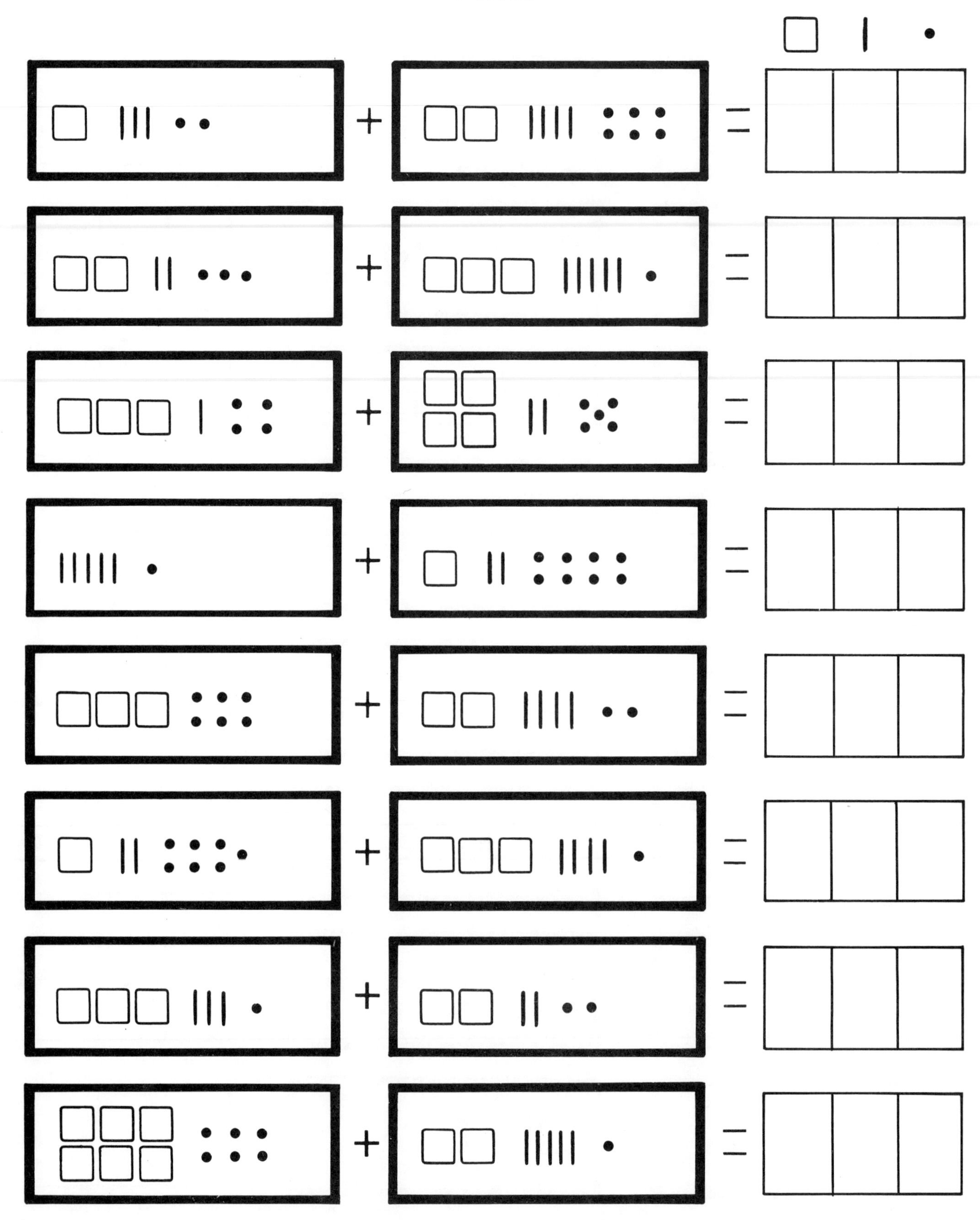

Add.

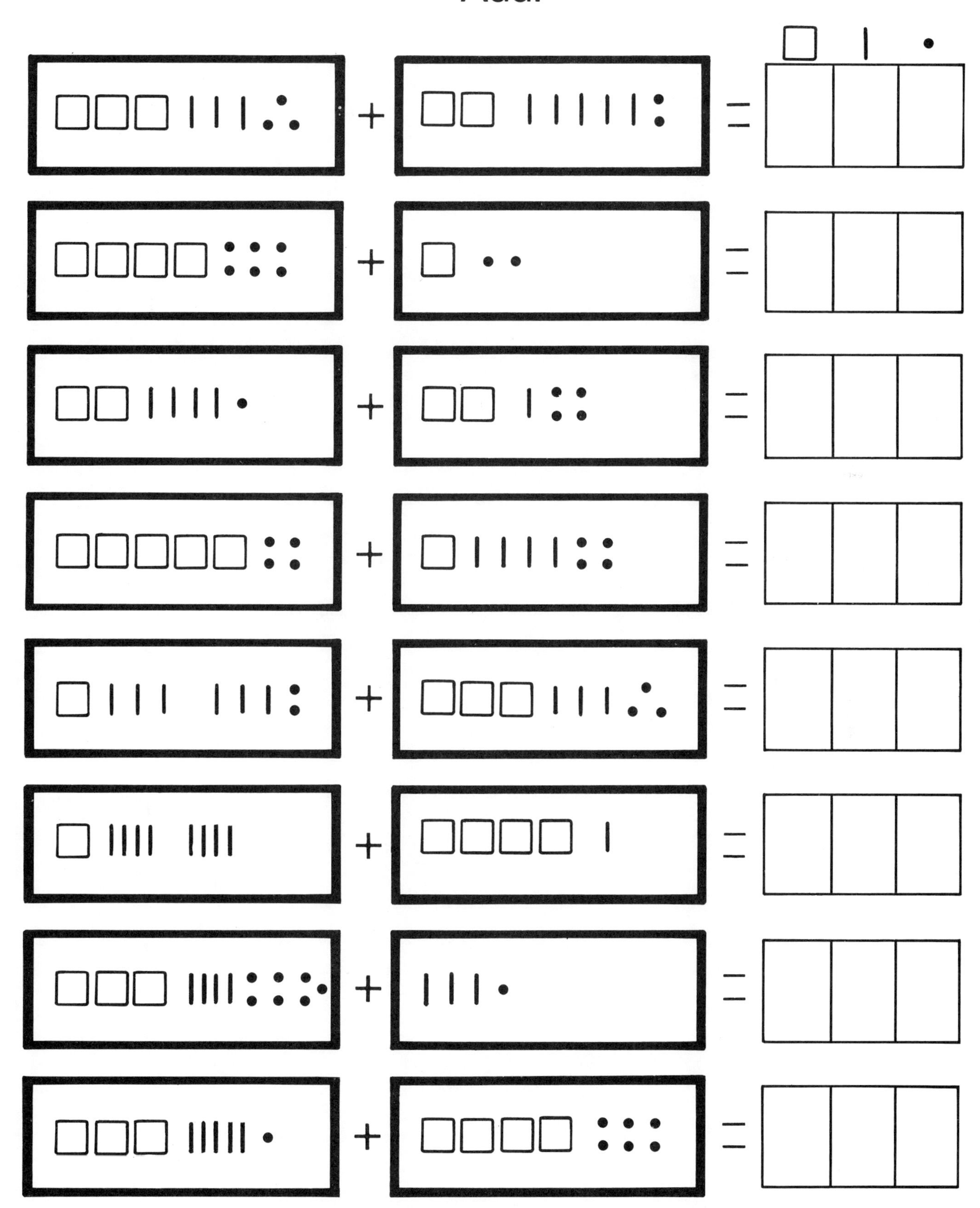

Add.

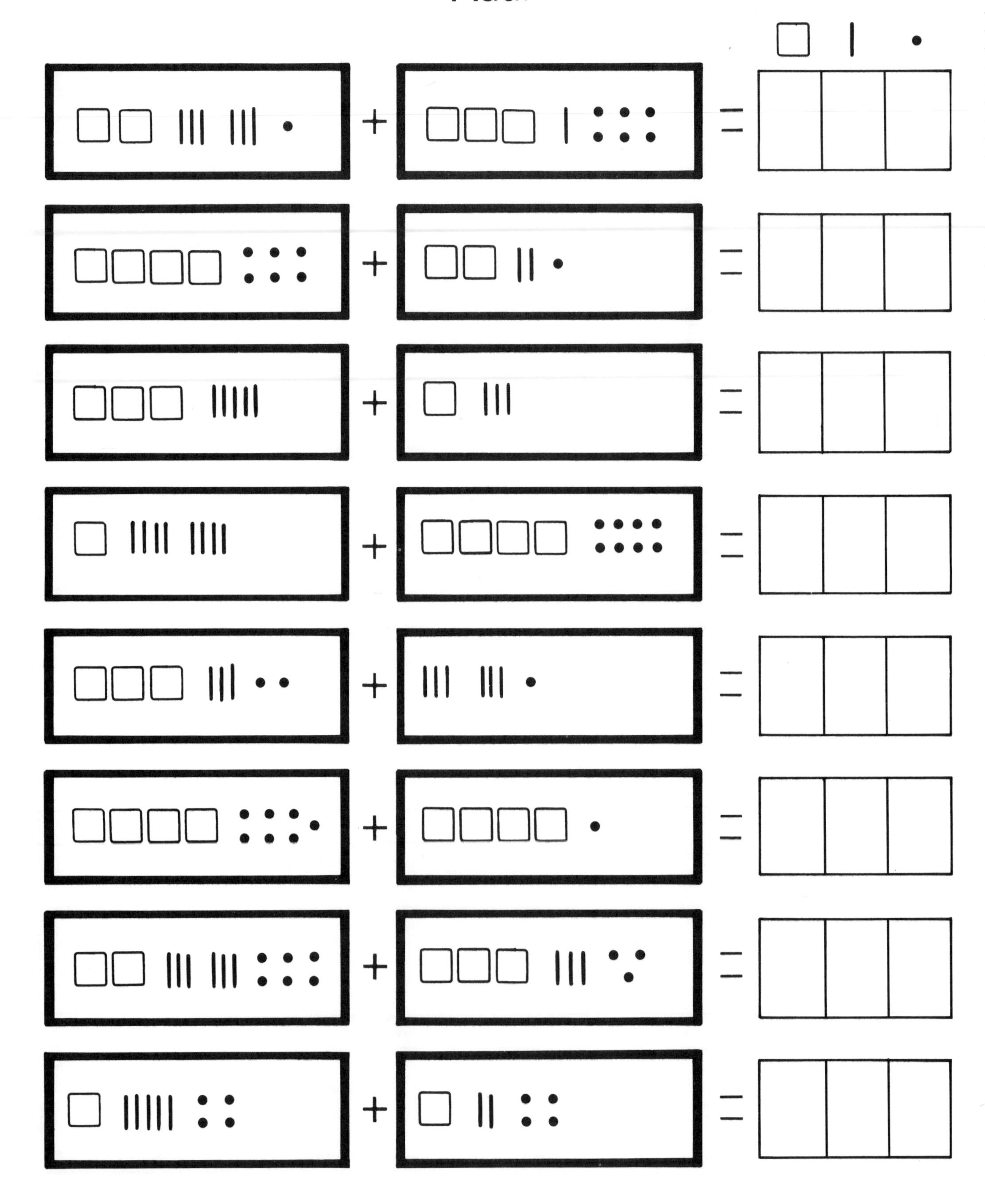

Combine and record.

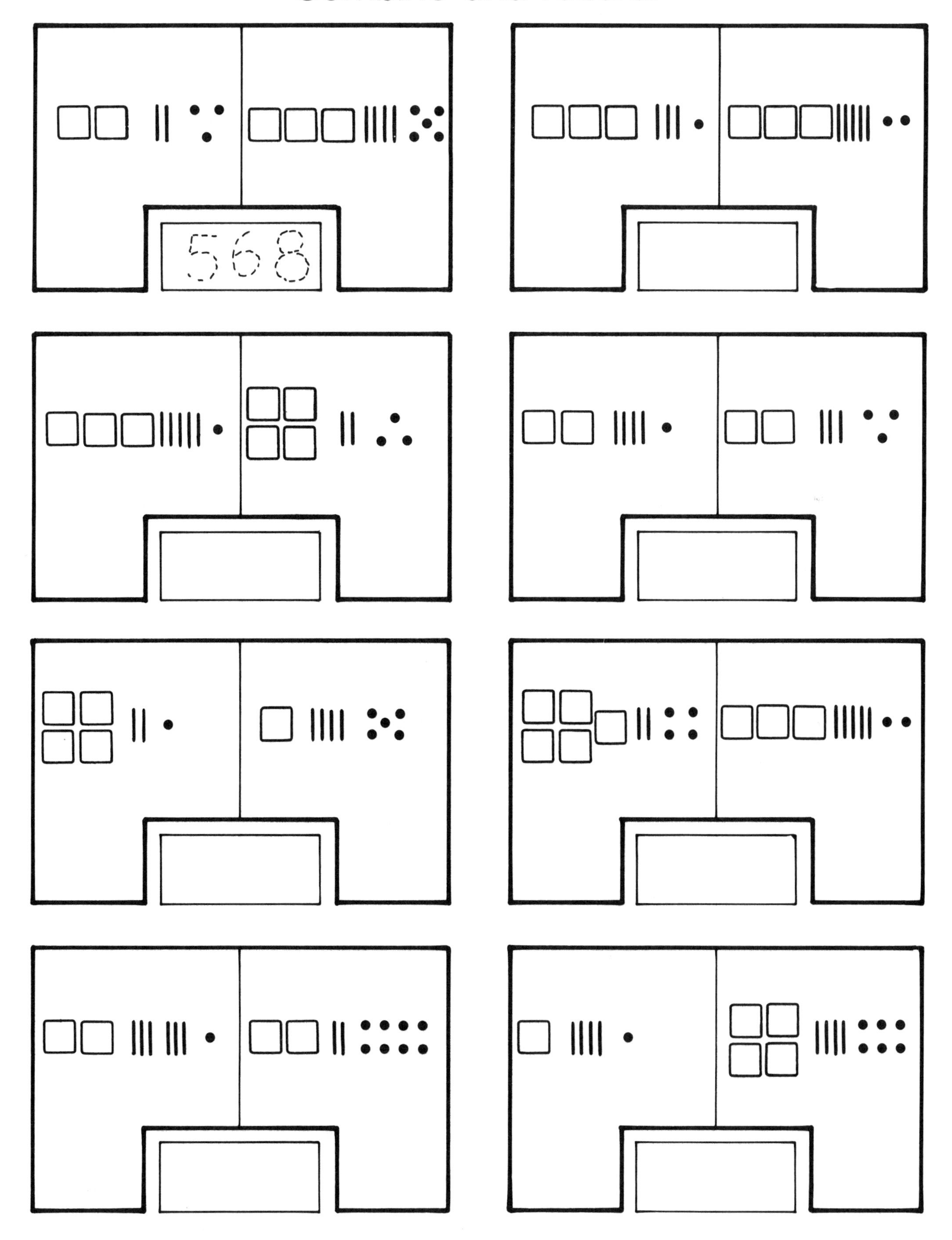

Combine and record.

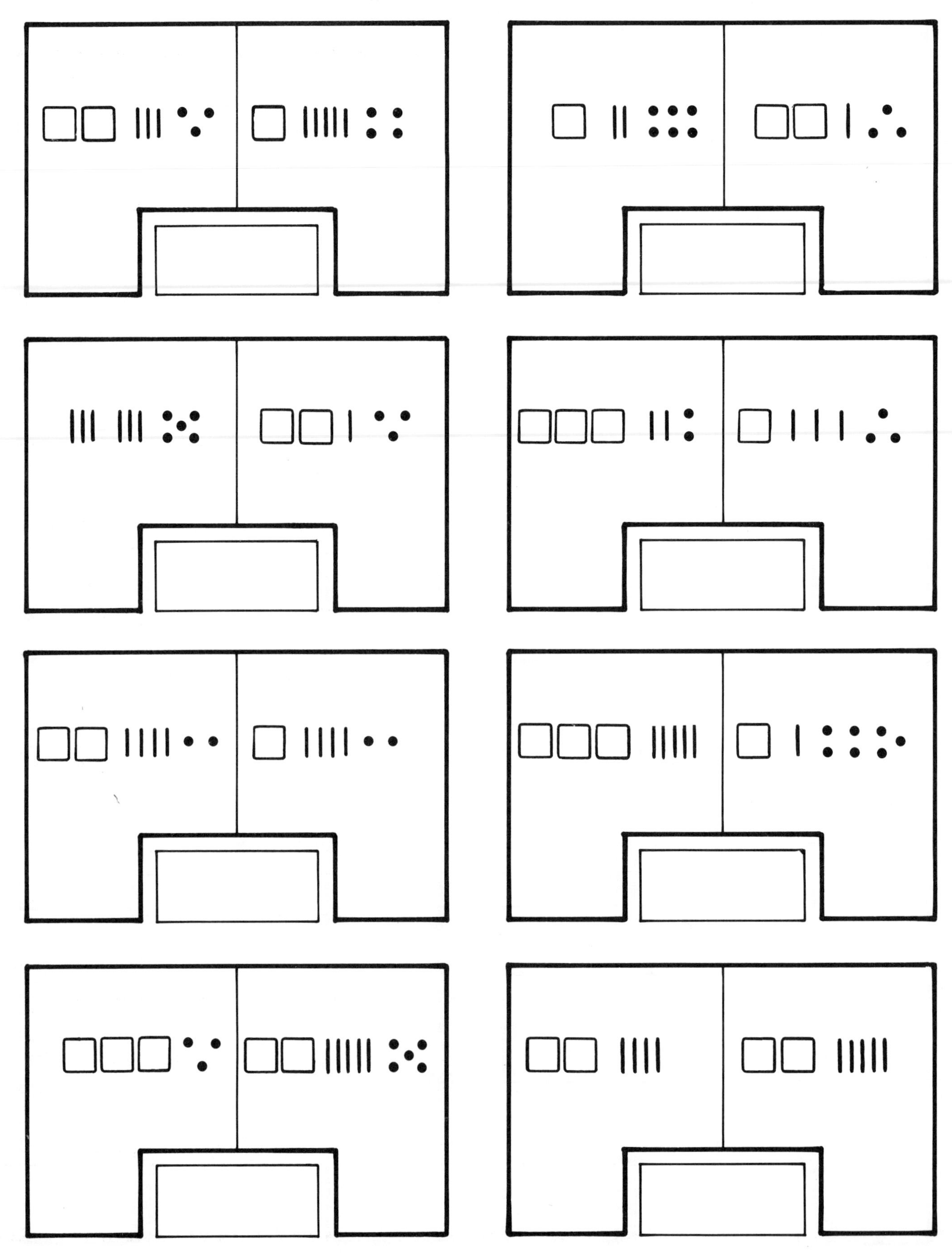

Combine and record.

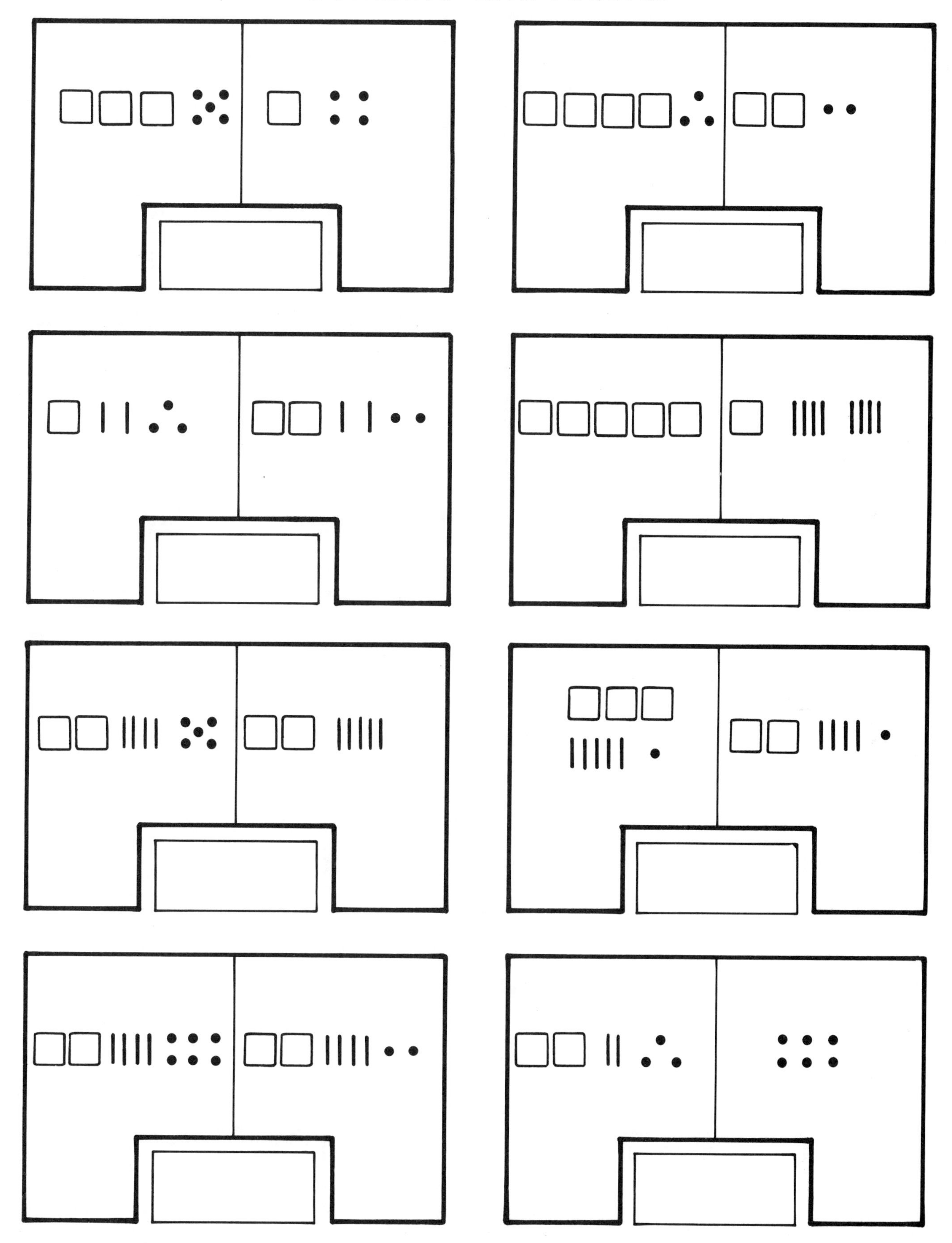

Combine and record.

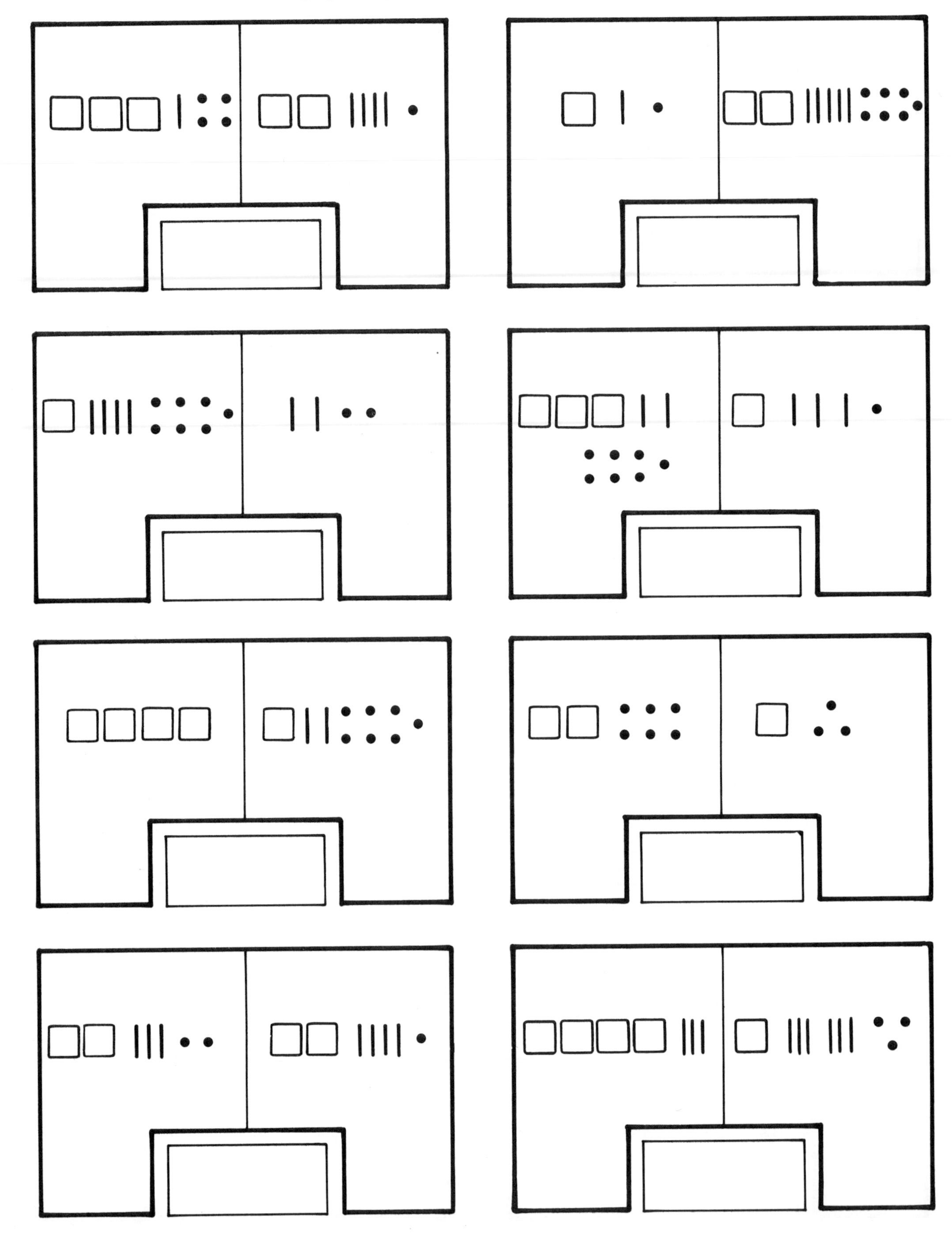

Combine and record.

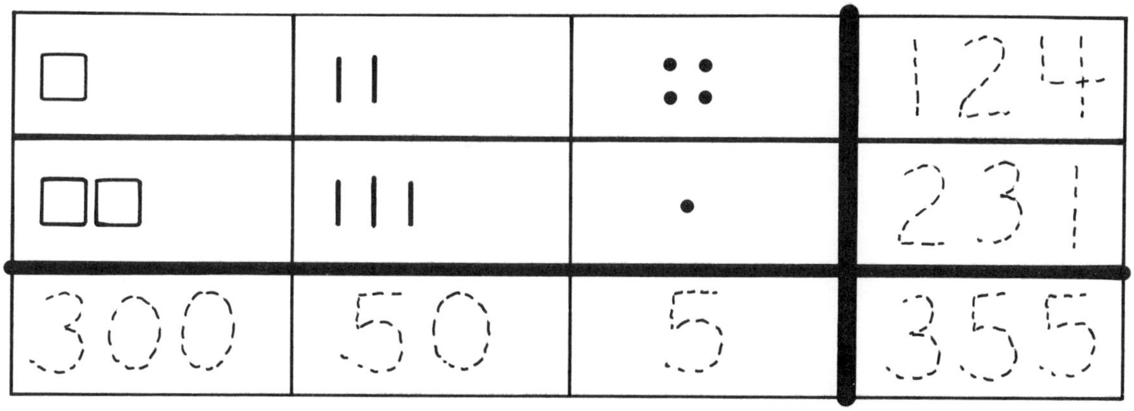

			124
			231
300	50	5	355

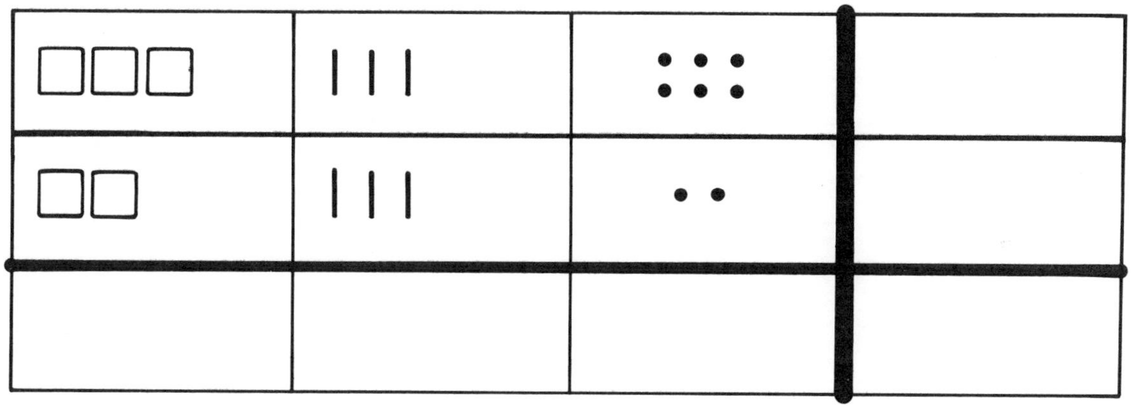

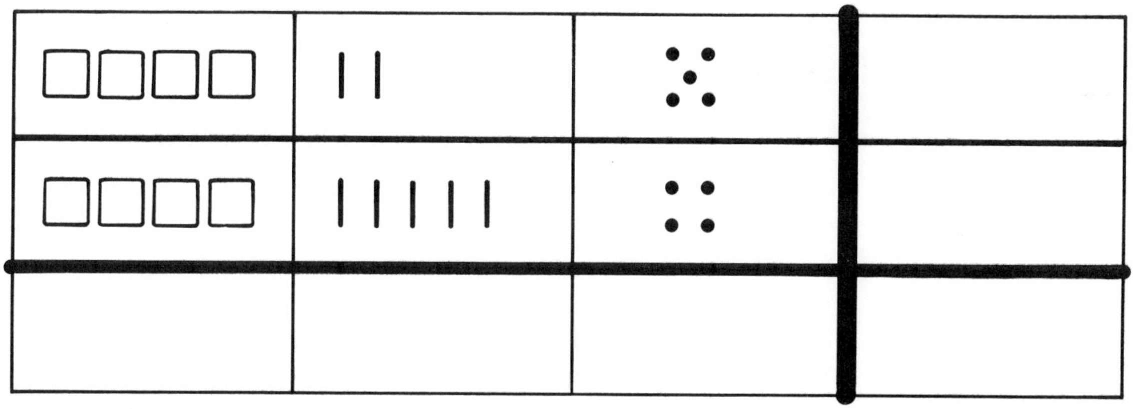

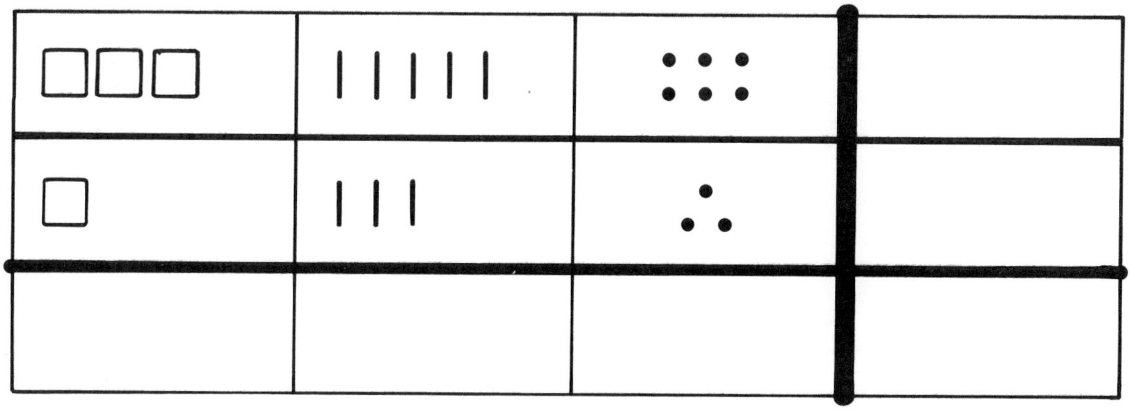

Combine and record.

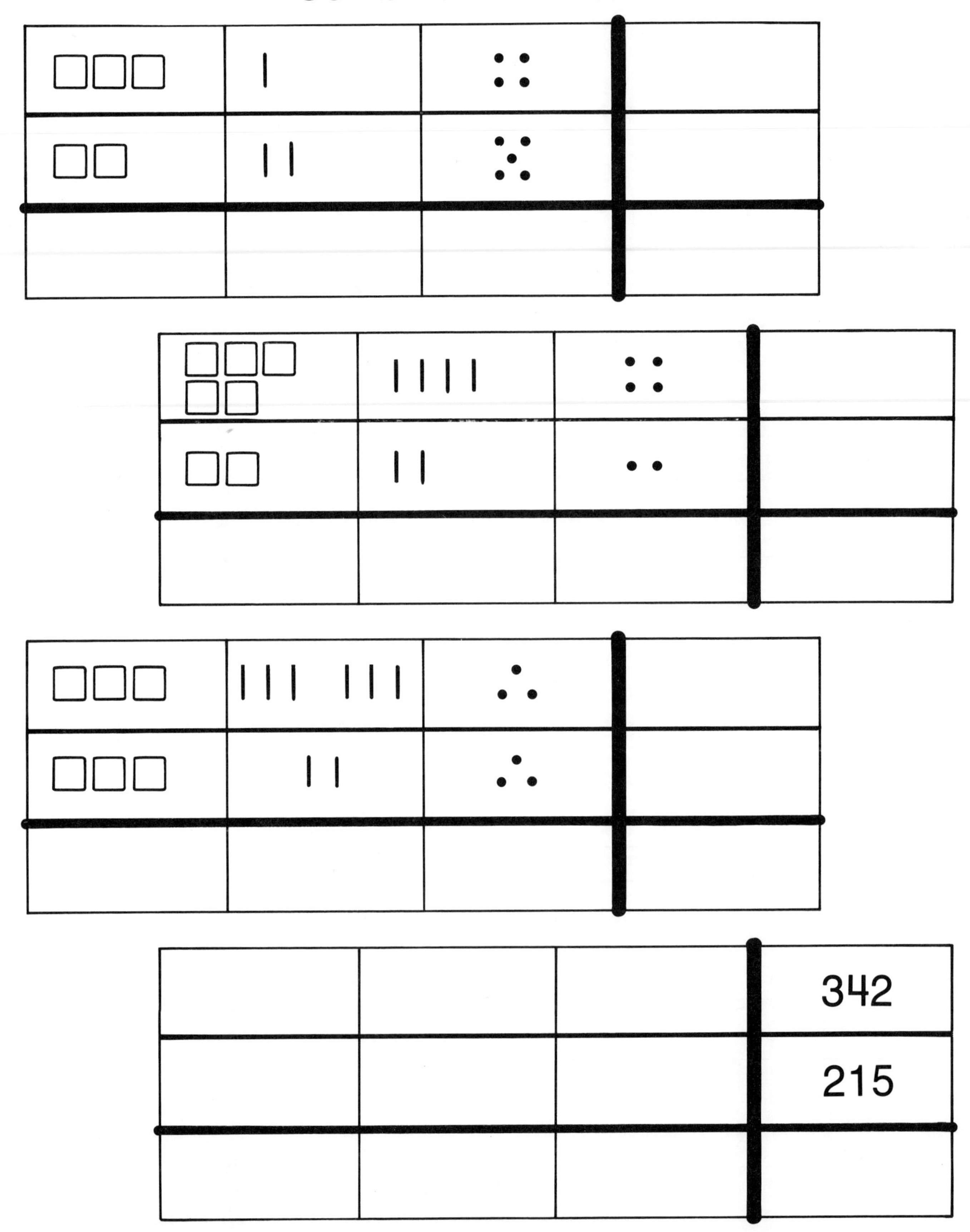

Combine and record.

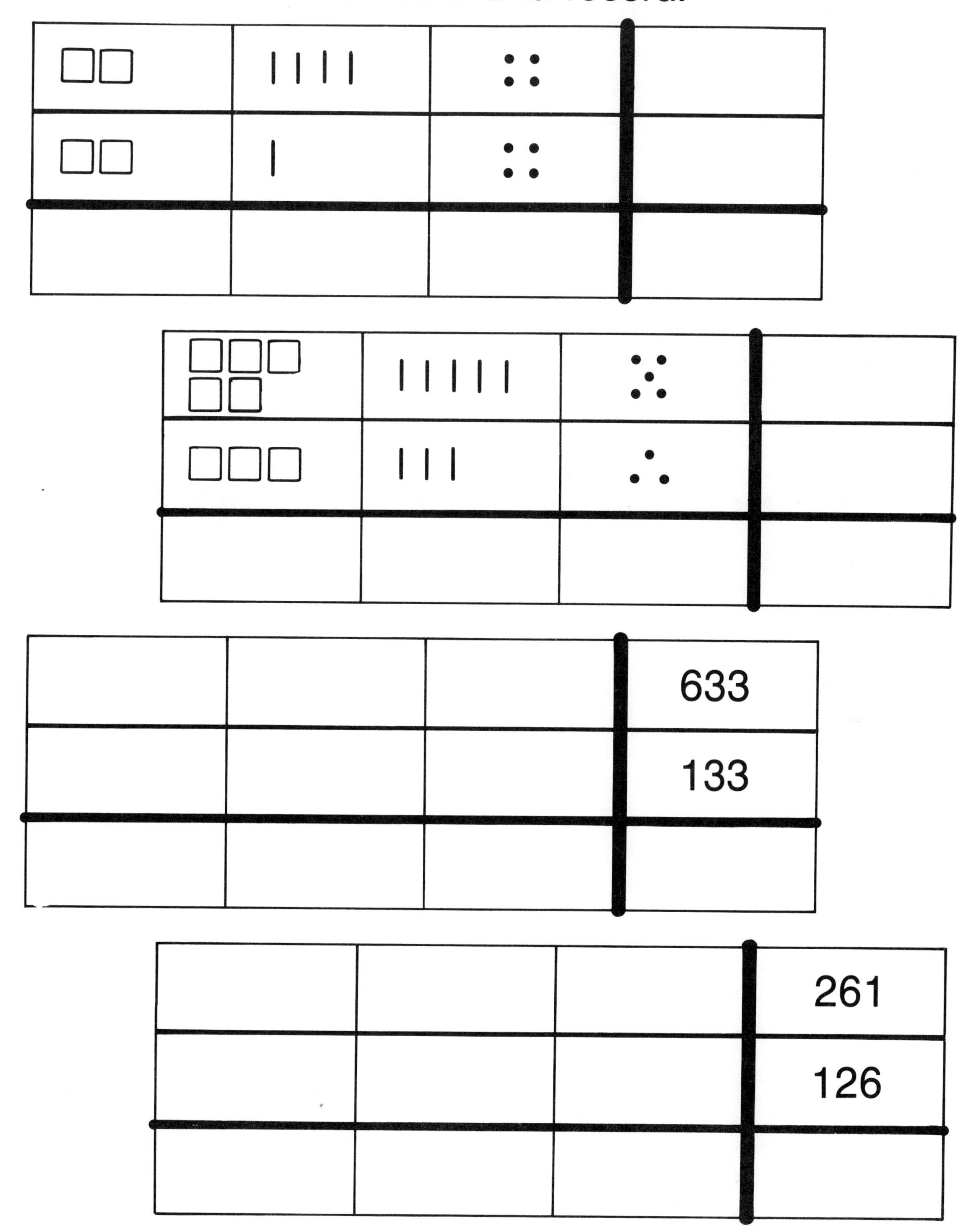

Color the ones, tens, and hundreds. Add.

	□	I	•
	3	2	5
+	1	2	3
	4	4	8

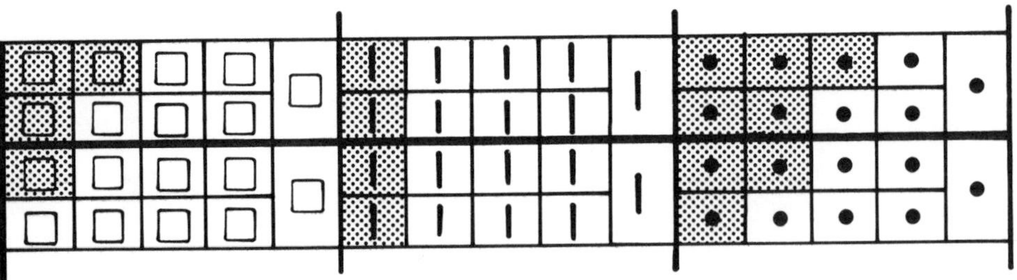

	□	I	•
	4	5	5
+	4	2	2

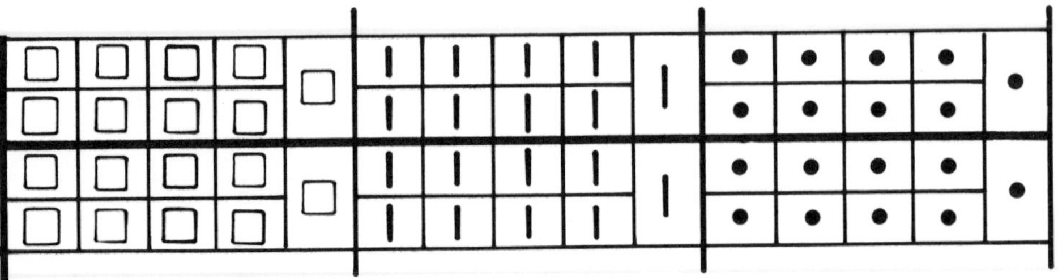

	□	I	•
	2	3	6
+	3	3	0

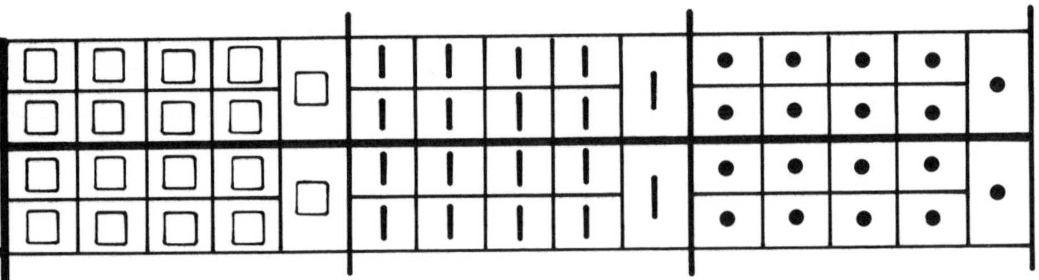

	□	I	•
	1	4	2
+	2	4	1

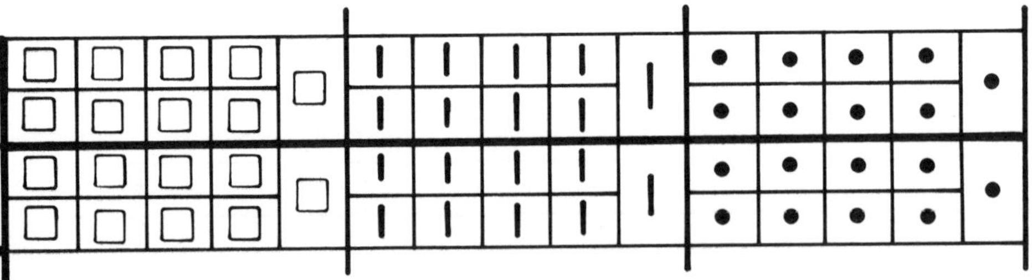

	□	I	•
	3	3	6
+	1	2	2

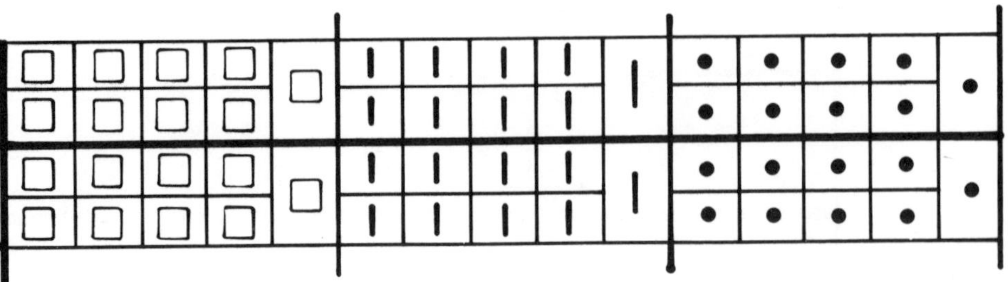

Color the ones, tens, and hundreds. Add.

	□	I	•
	3	2	1
+		2	5

	□	I	•
	2	3	6
+	1	3	1

	□	I	•
	3	0	0
+	1	7	2

	□	I	•
		3	7
+	4	0	1

	□	I	•
	2	5	9
+	3	2	0

Color the ones, tens, and hundreds. Add.

	□	I	•
	2	6	1
+	2	3	4

	□	I	•
	3	2	7
+	2	1	0

	□	I	•
	2	0	4
+	3	0	4

	□	I	•
	1	3	7
+	1	1	1

	□	I	•
	4	7	7
+	2	0	0

Color the ones, tens, and hundreds. Add.

	□	I	•
	3	4	0
+	2	2	3

	□	I	•
	1	2	5
+	1	3	3

	□	I	•
	4	3	4
+	2	1	0

	□	I	•
	2	5	3
+	1	2	2

	□	I	•
	3	1	6
+	1	2	3

Combine and record.

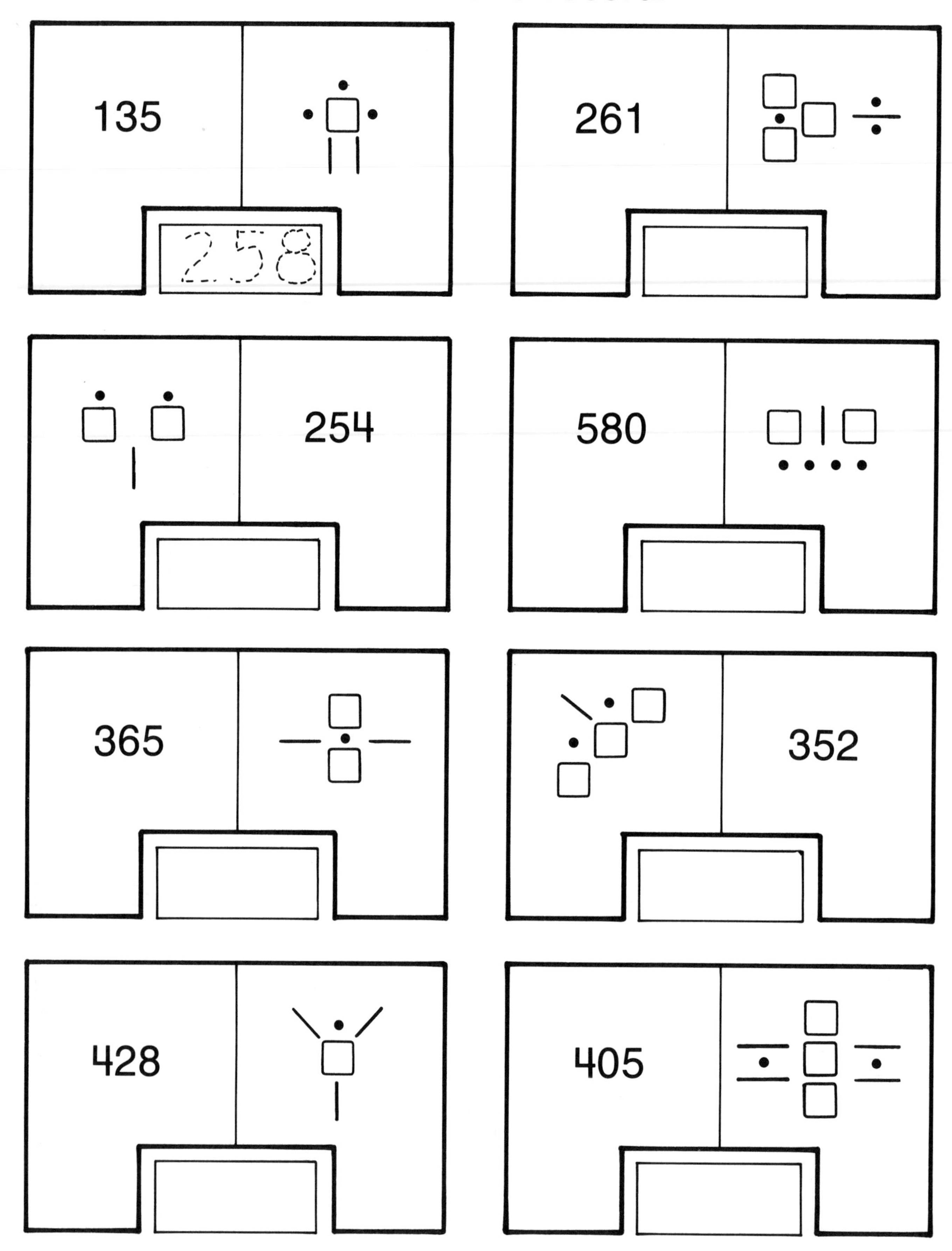

Combine and record.

231	352	444
127	171	305
216	260	423
68	335	517
370	408	34

Complete each problem.

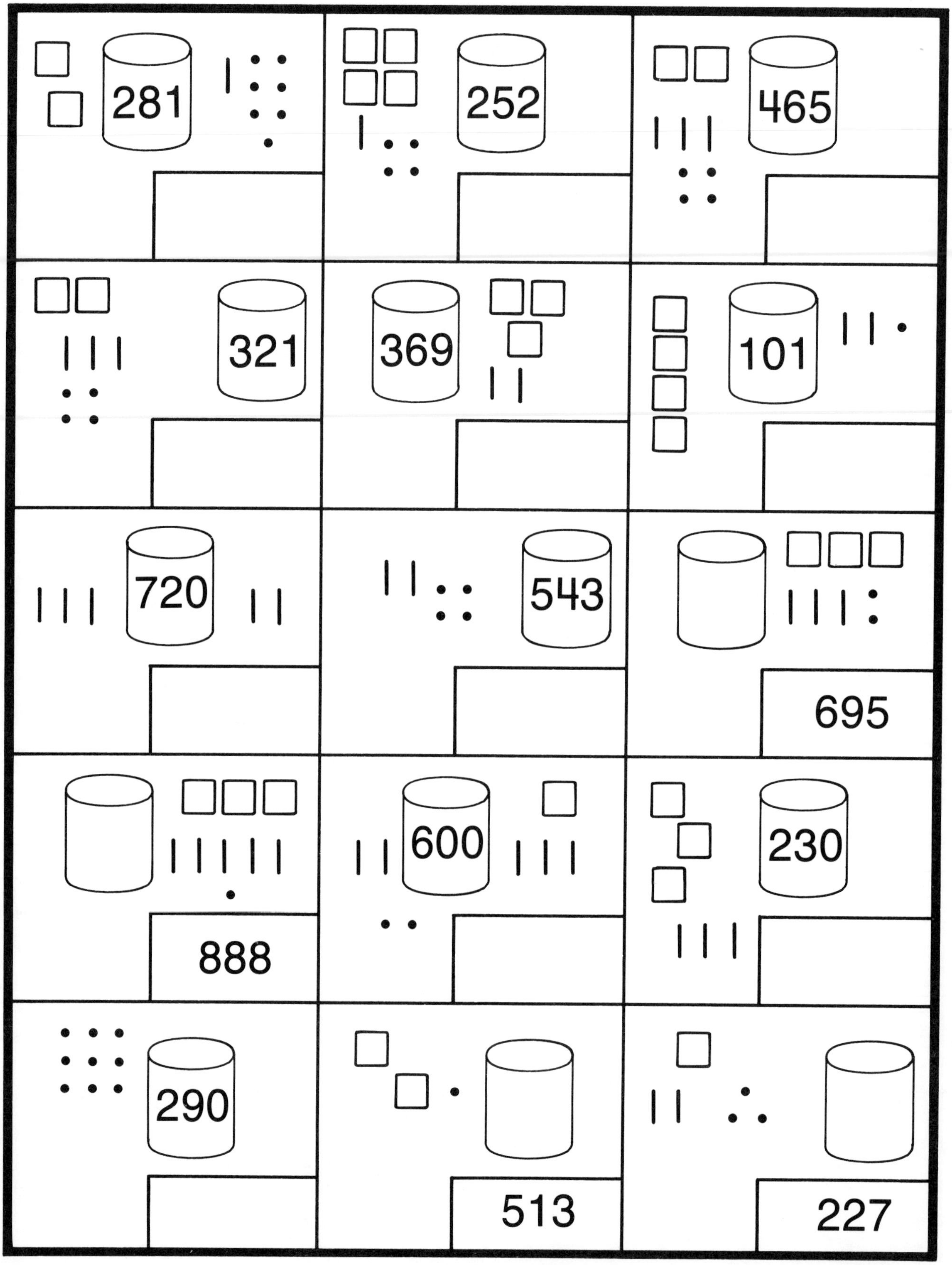

281	252	465
321	369	101
720	543	695
888	600	230
290	513	227

Combine and record.

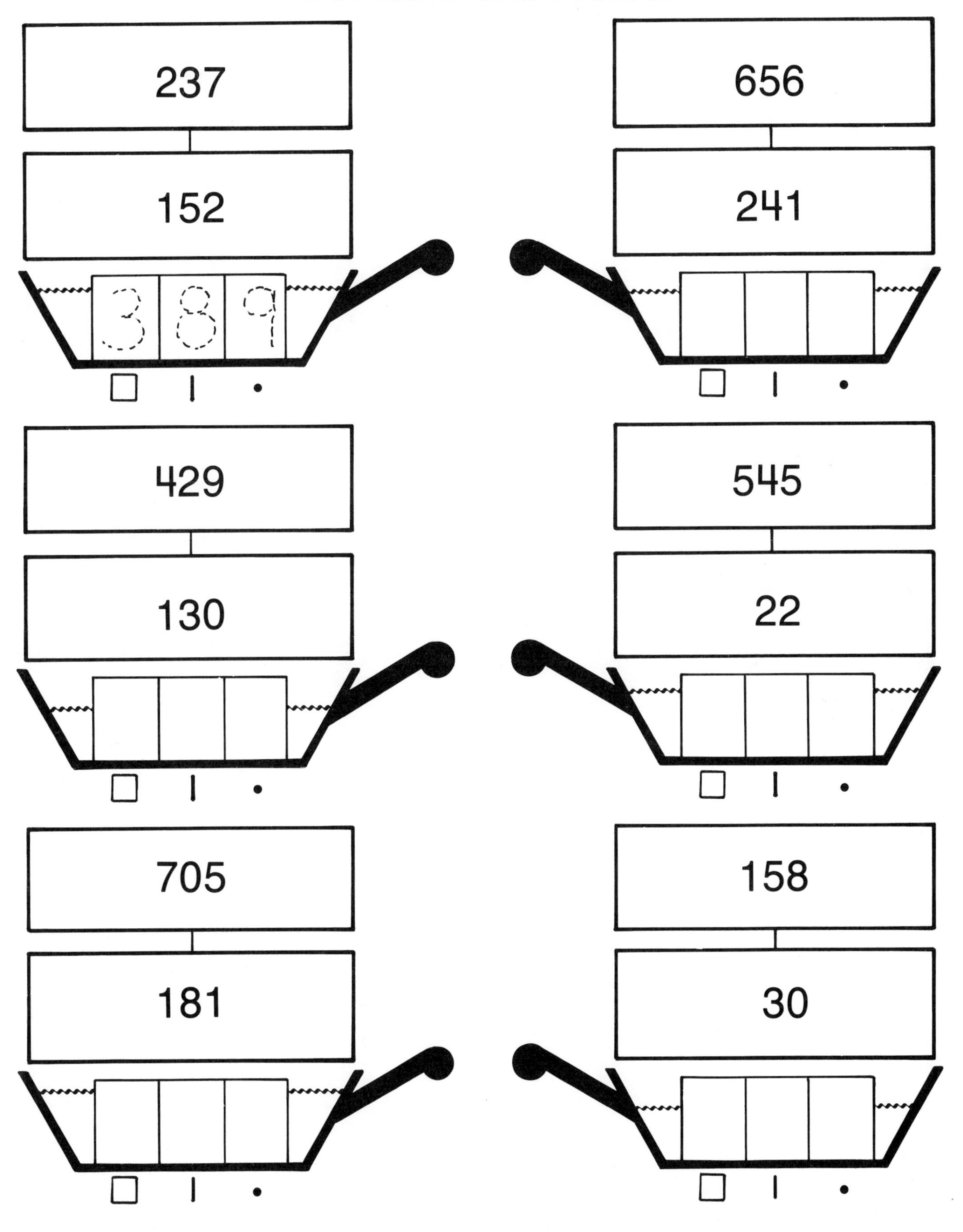

Combine and record. Trade if necessary.

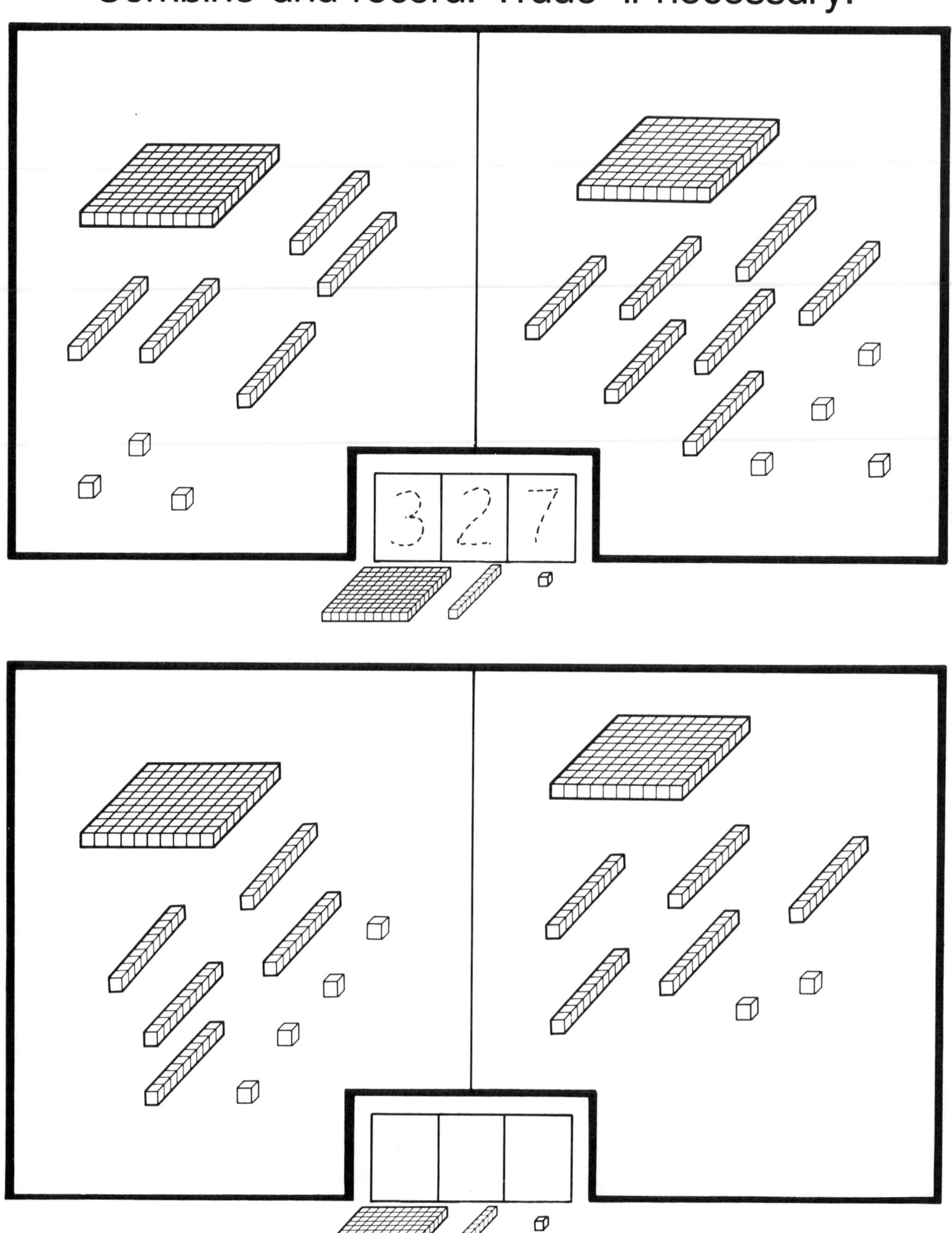

Combine and record. Trade if necessary.

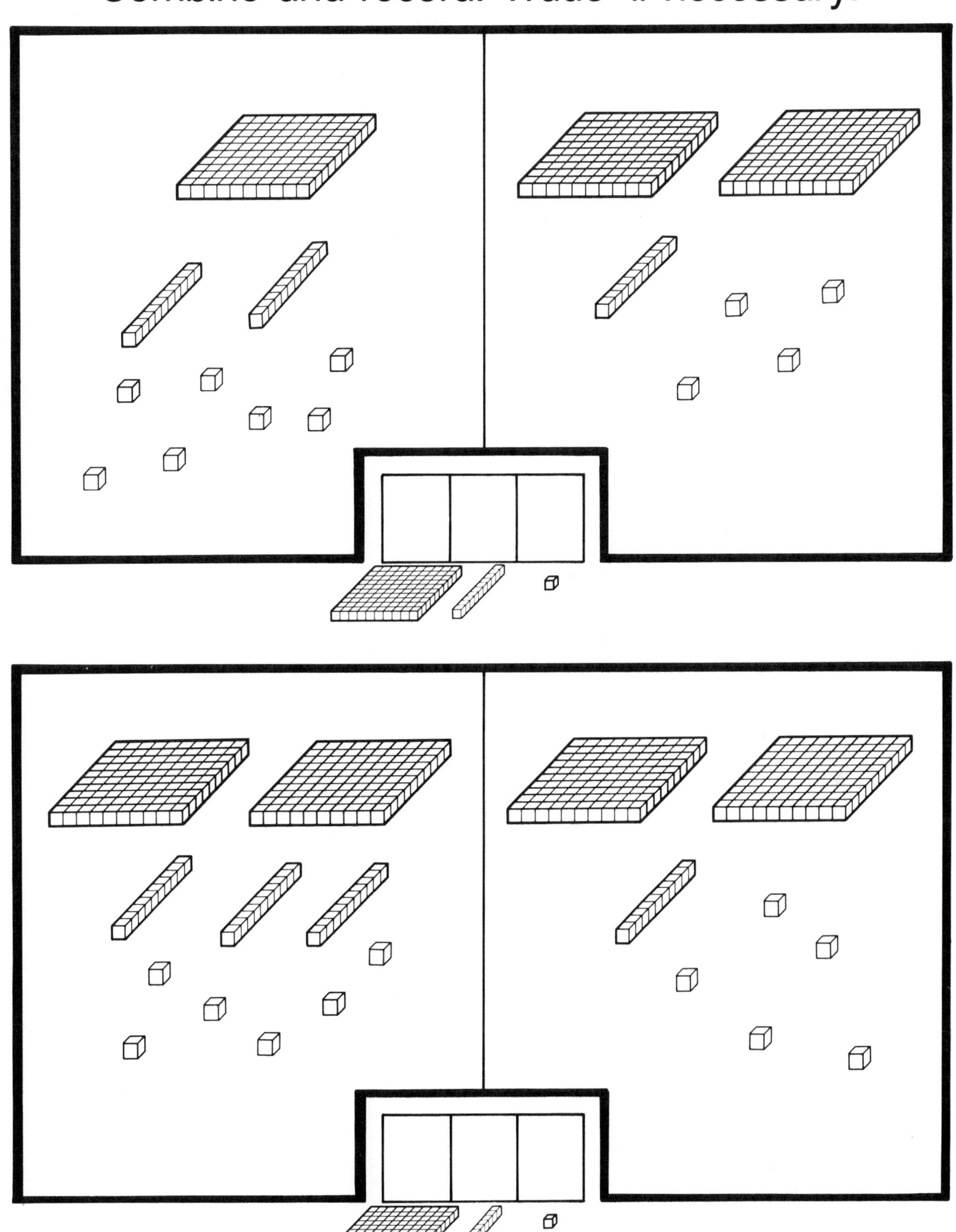

Combine and record. Trade if necessary.

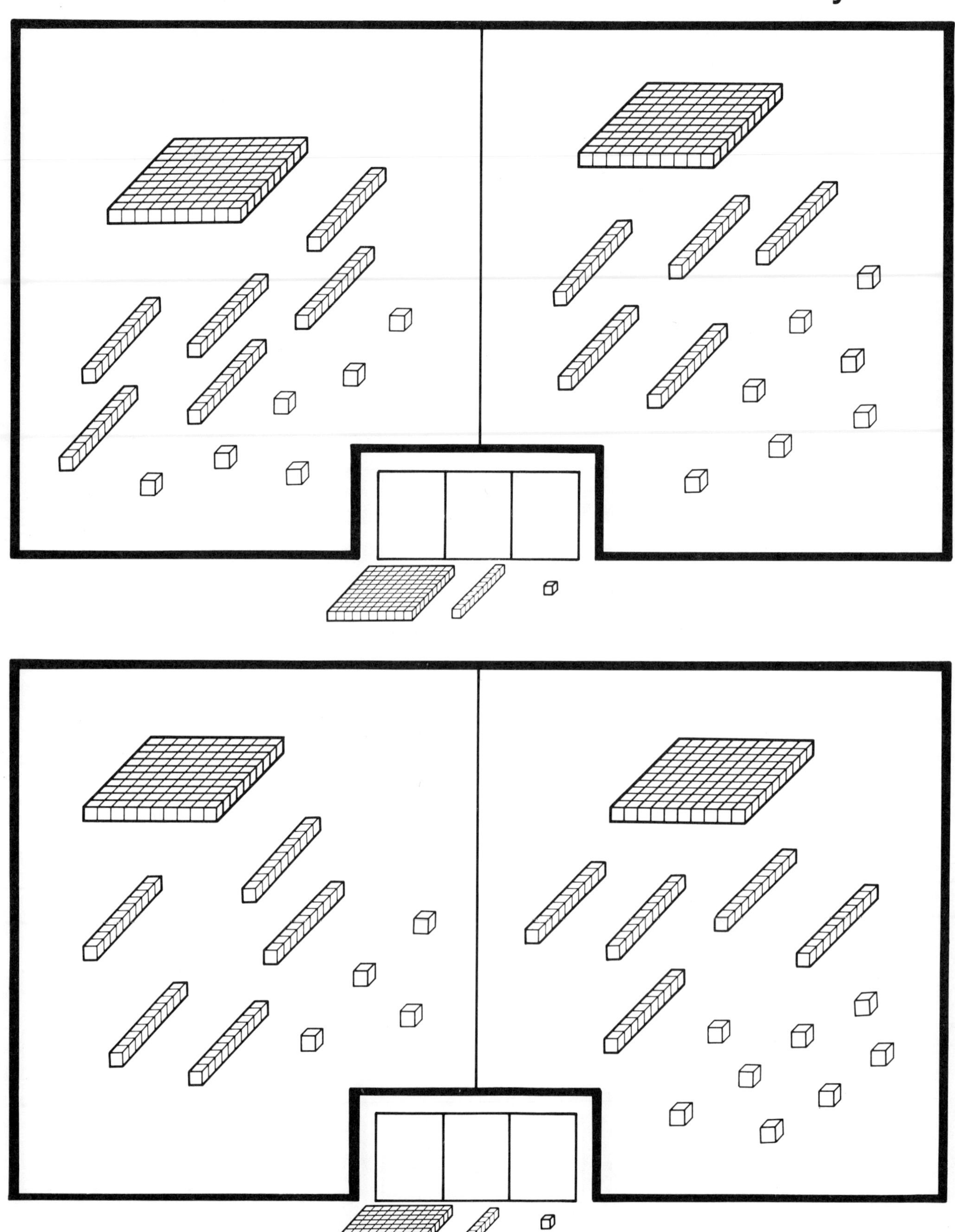

Combine and record. Trade if necessary.

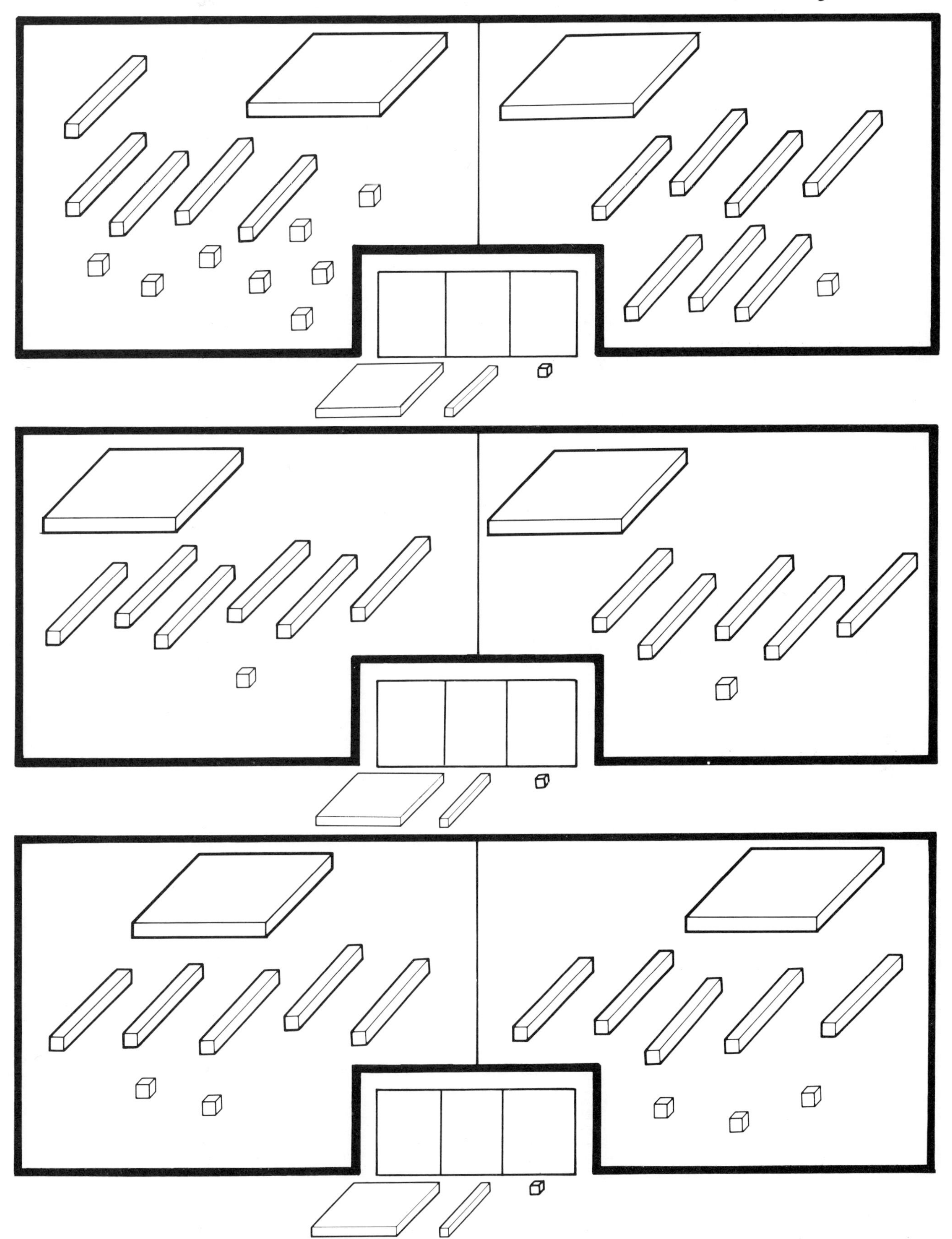

Combine and record. Trade if necessary.

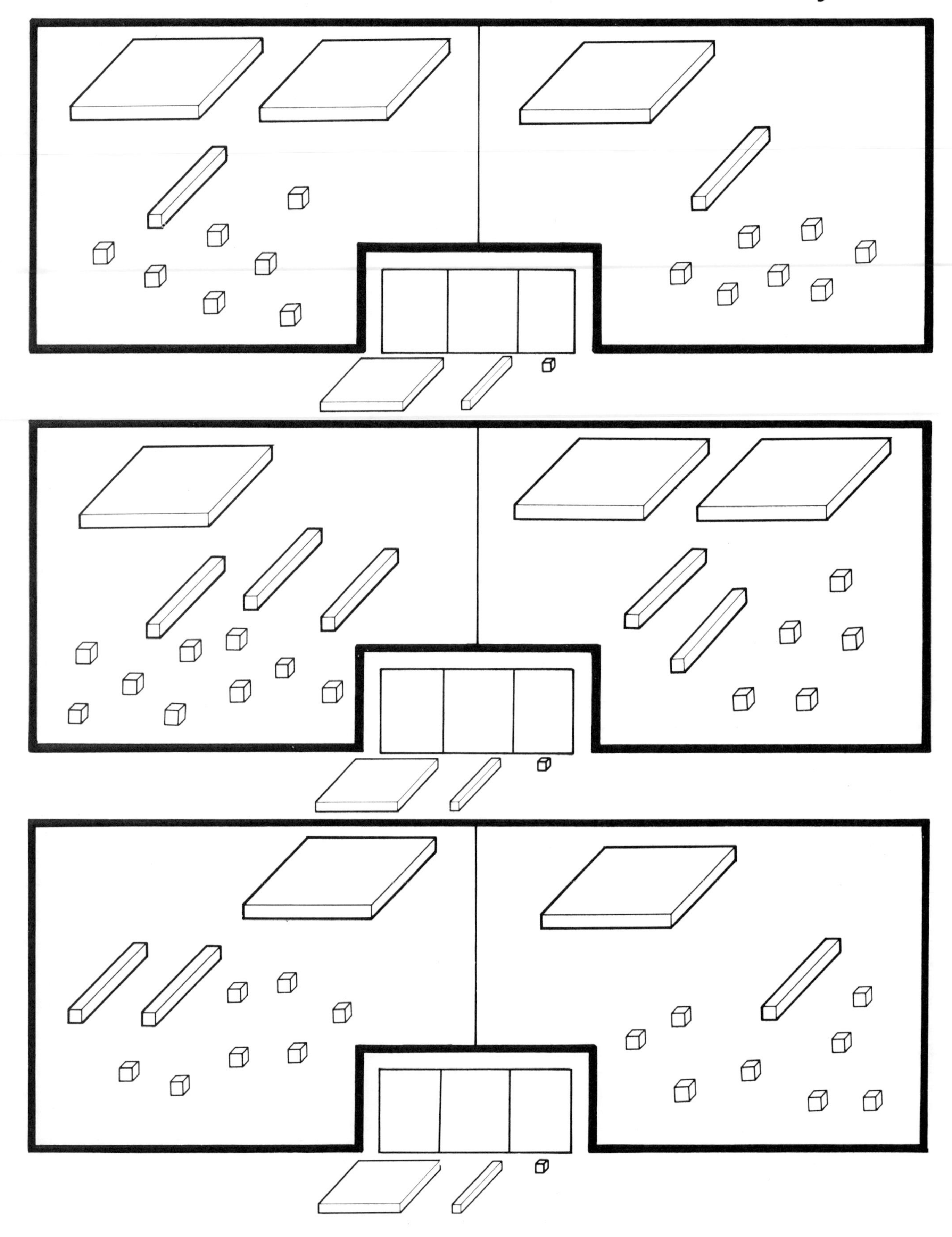

Combine and record. Trade if necessary.

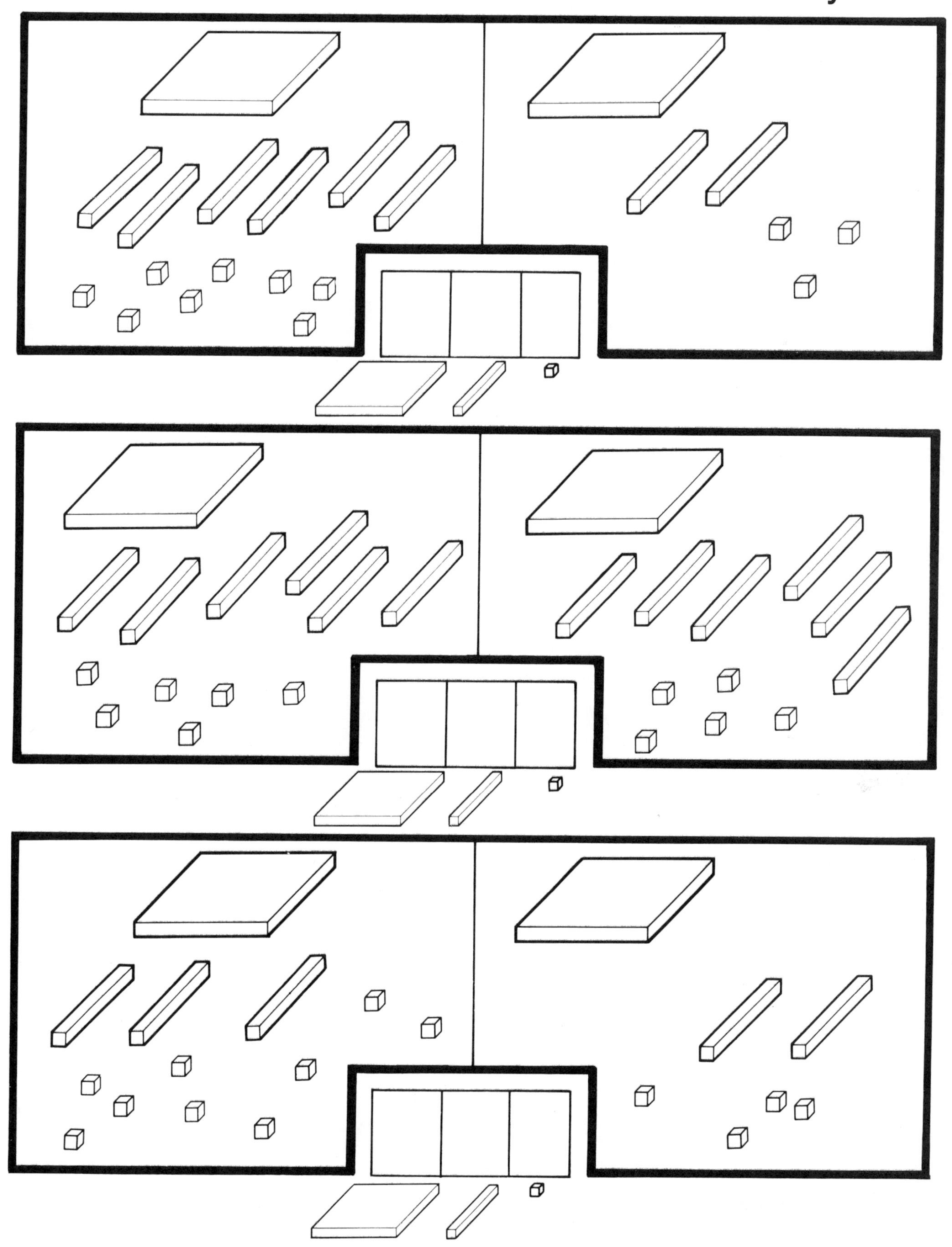

Combine and record. Trade if necessary.

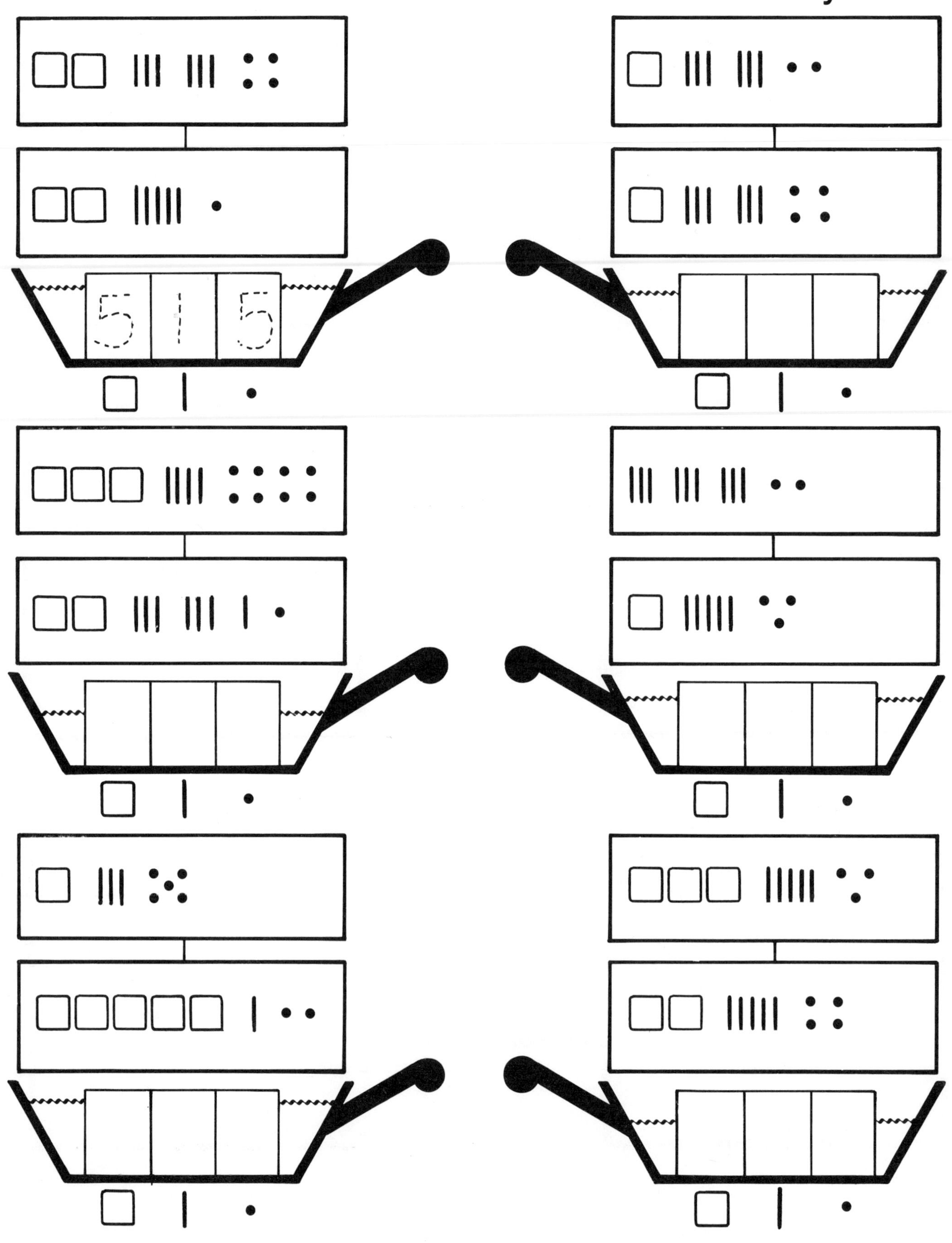

Combine and record. Trade if necessary.

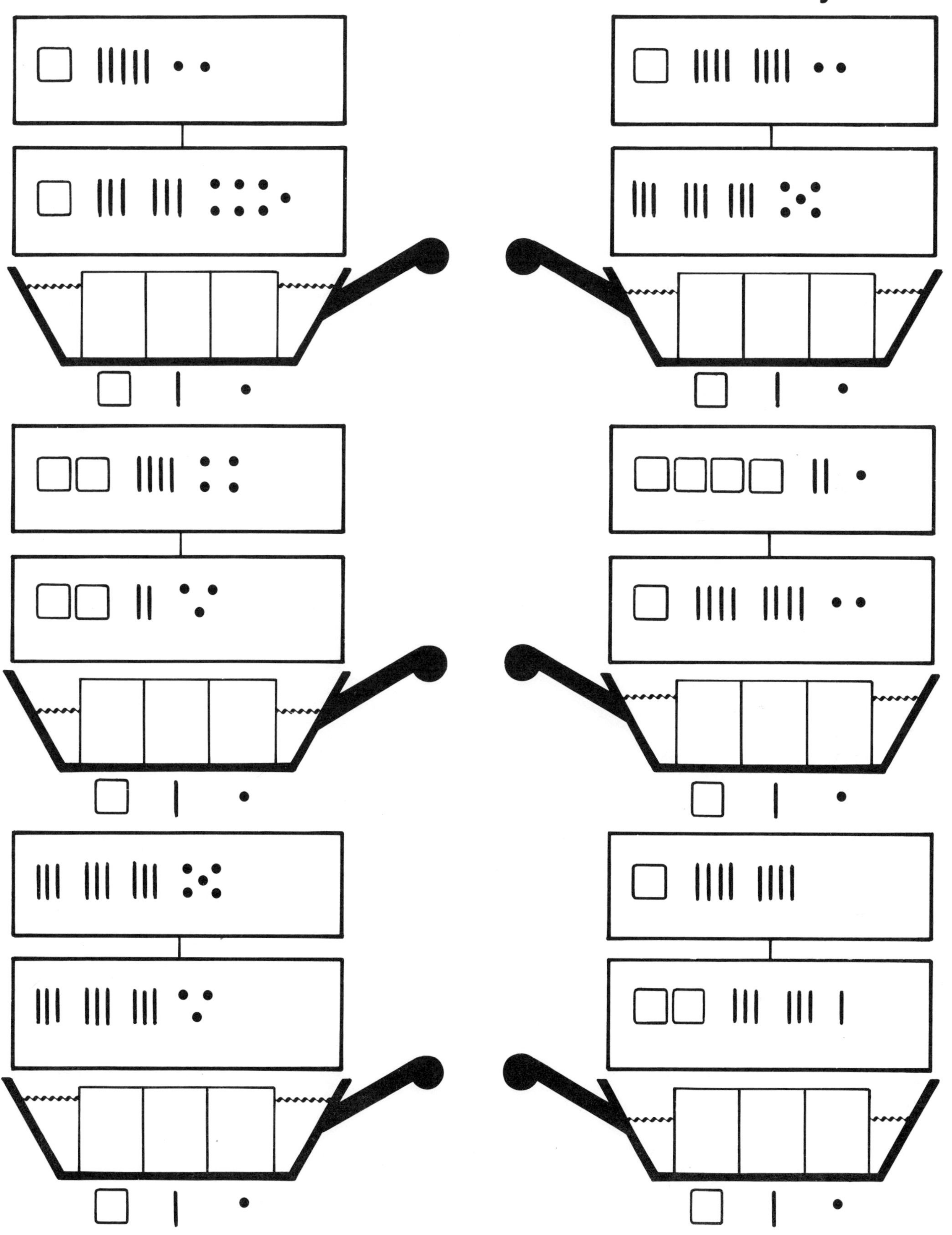

Combine and record. Trade if necessary.

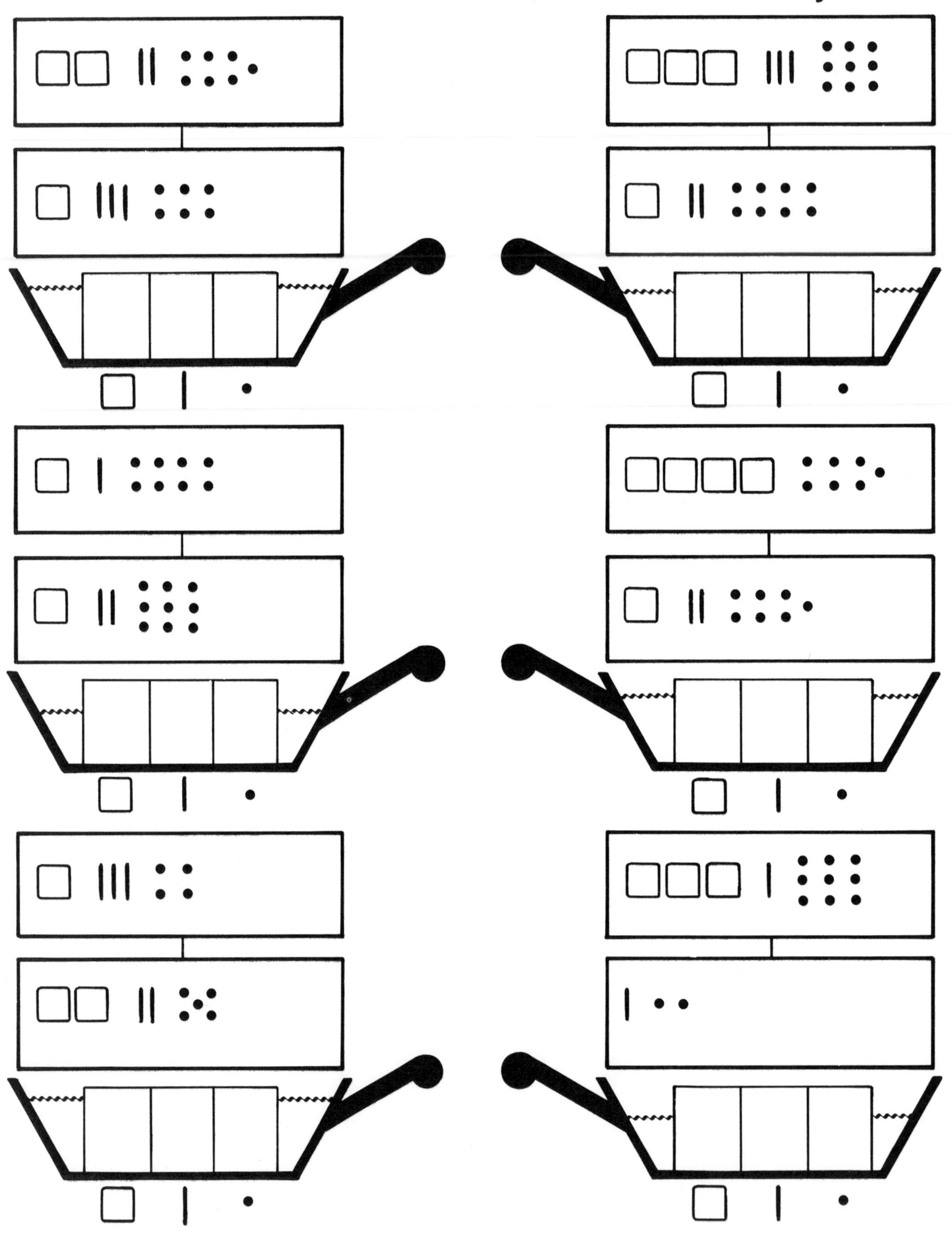

Combine and record. Trade if necessary.

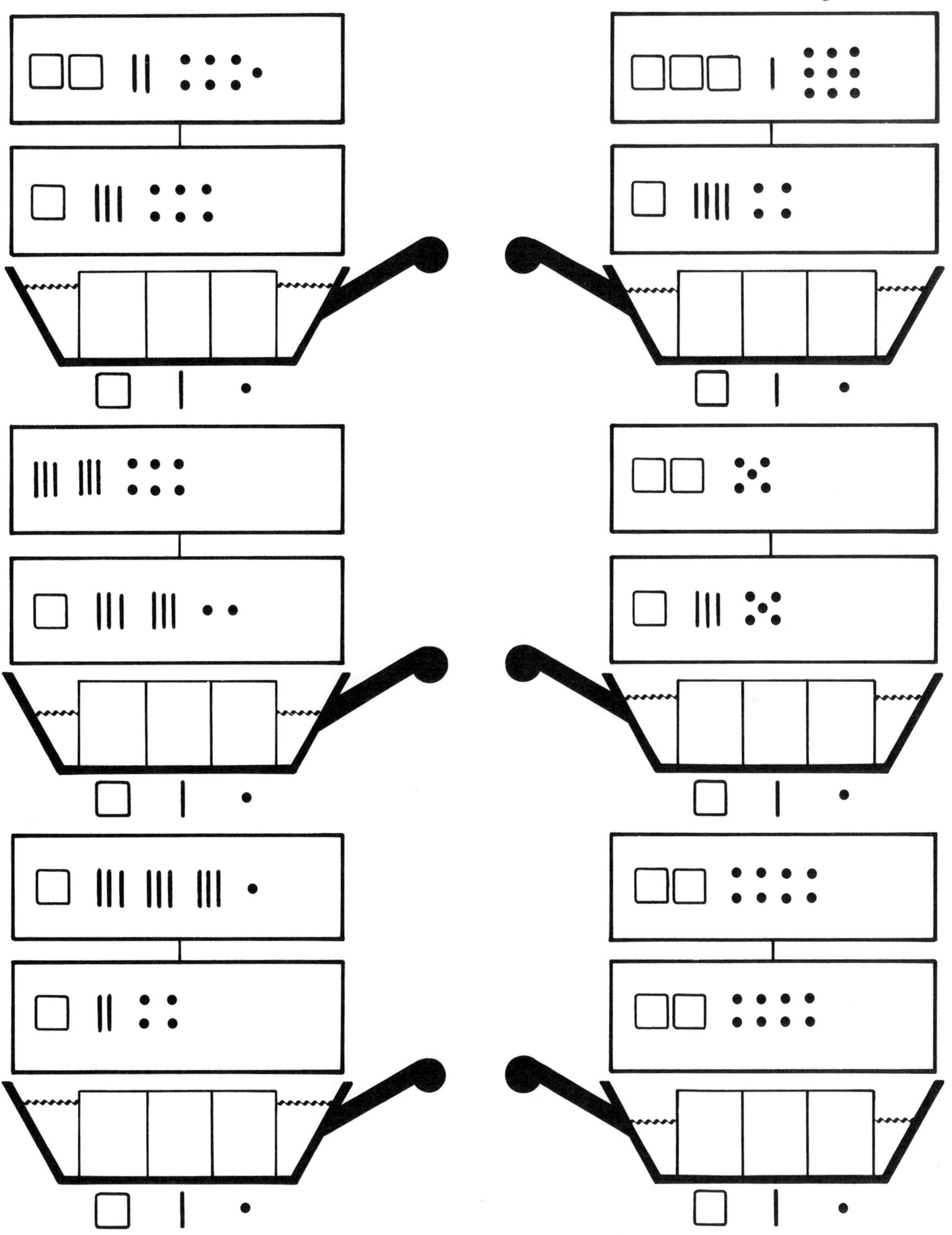

Combine and record. Trade if necessary.

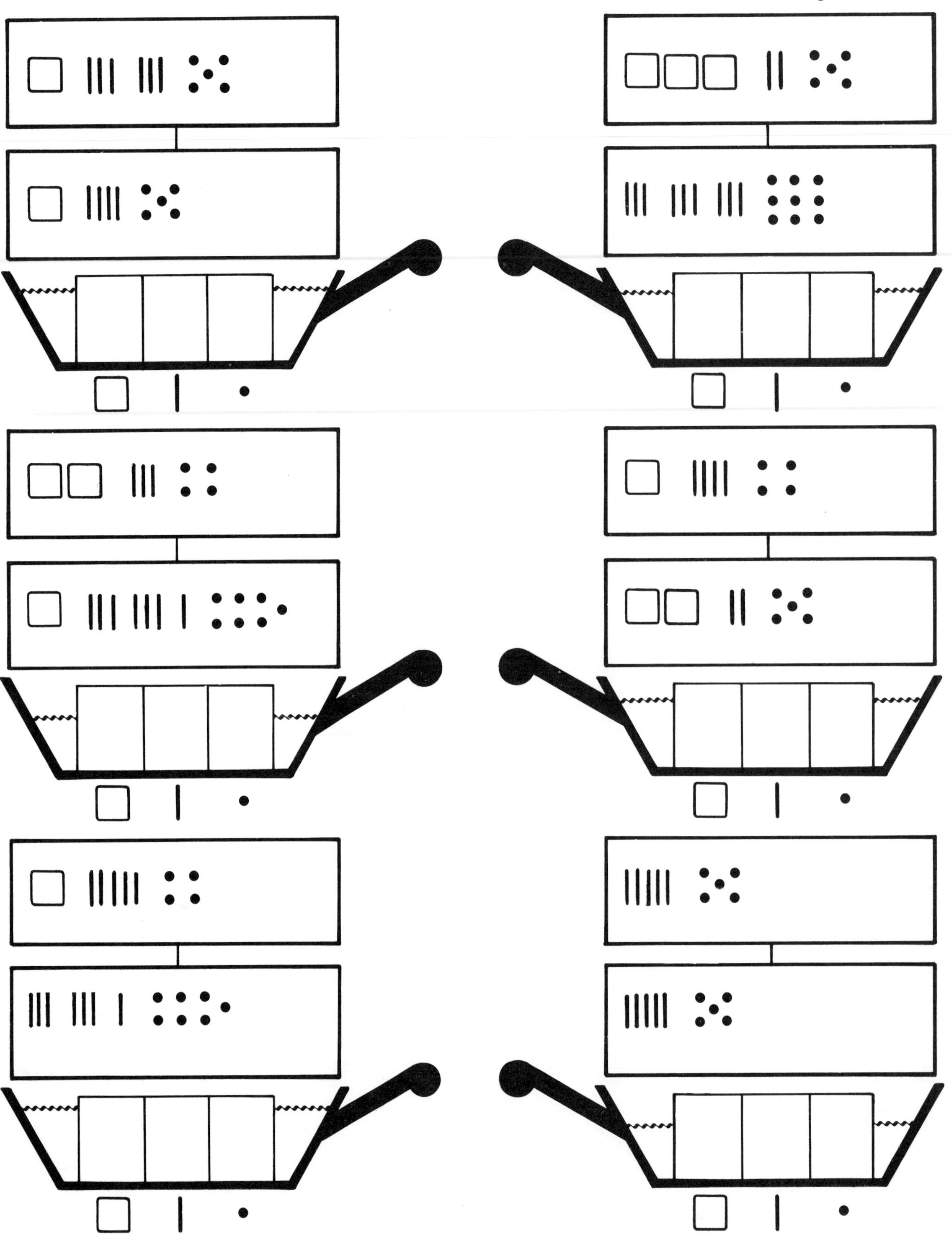

Add. Trade if necessary.

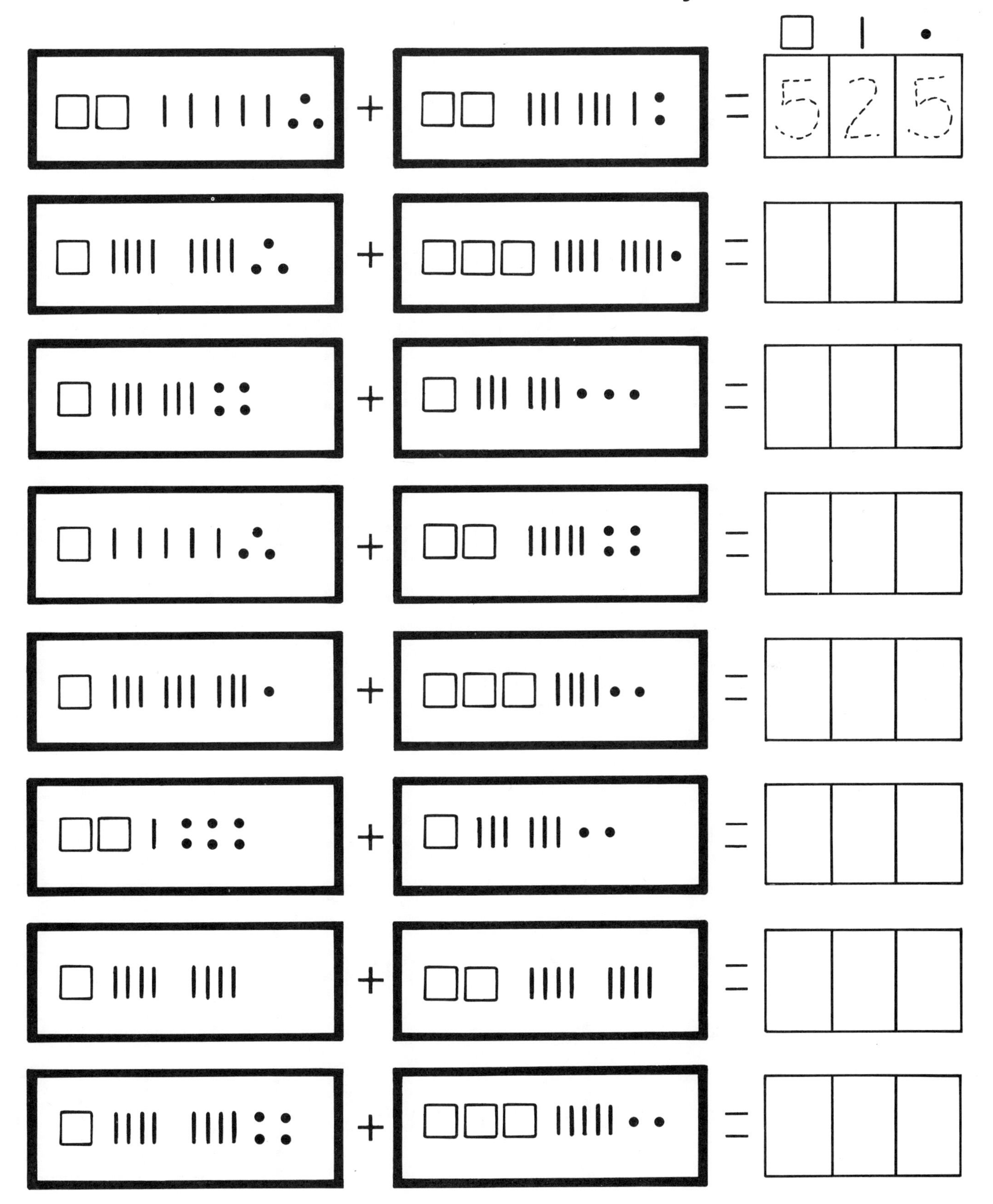

Add. Trade if necessary.

Add. Trade if necessary.

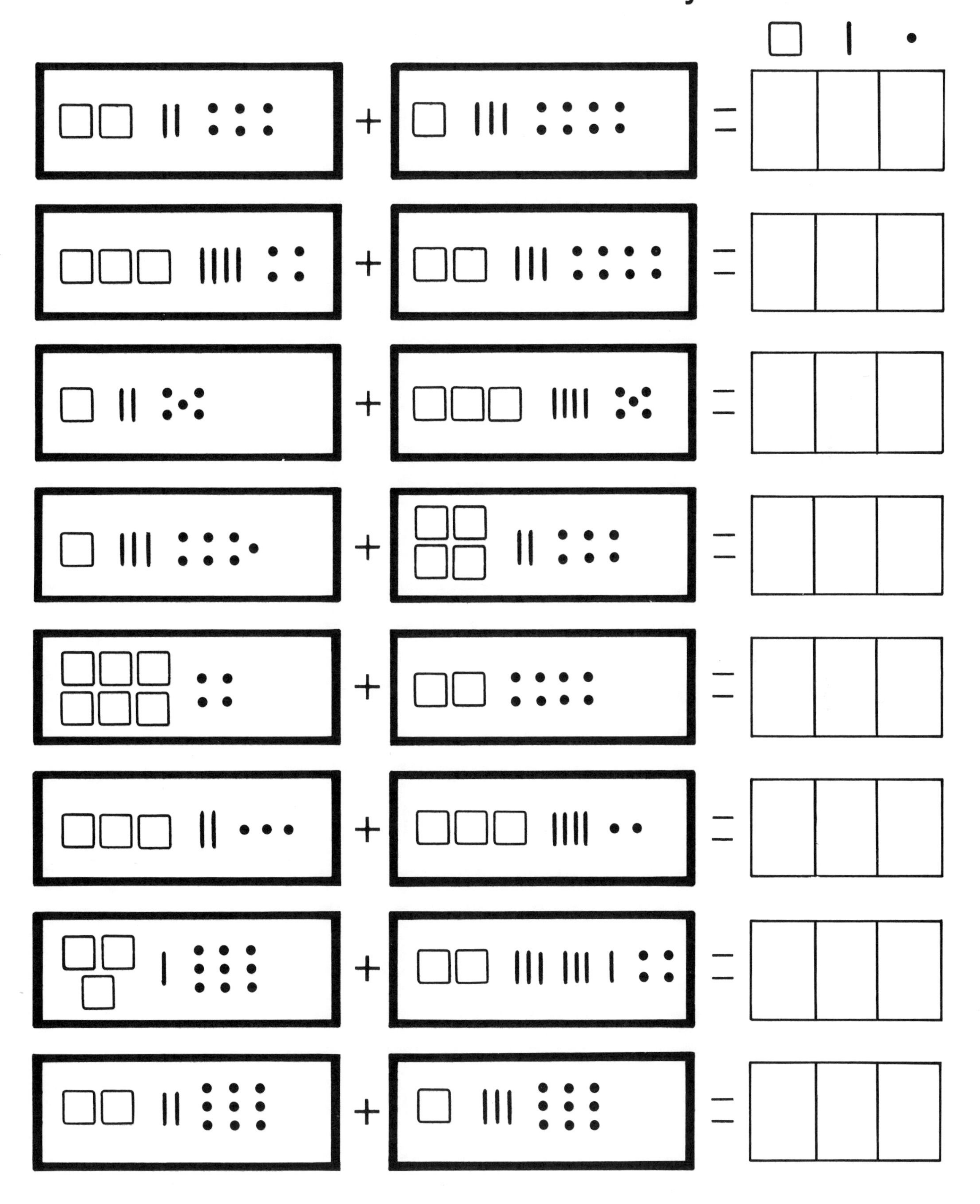

Add. Trade if necessary.

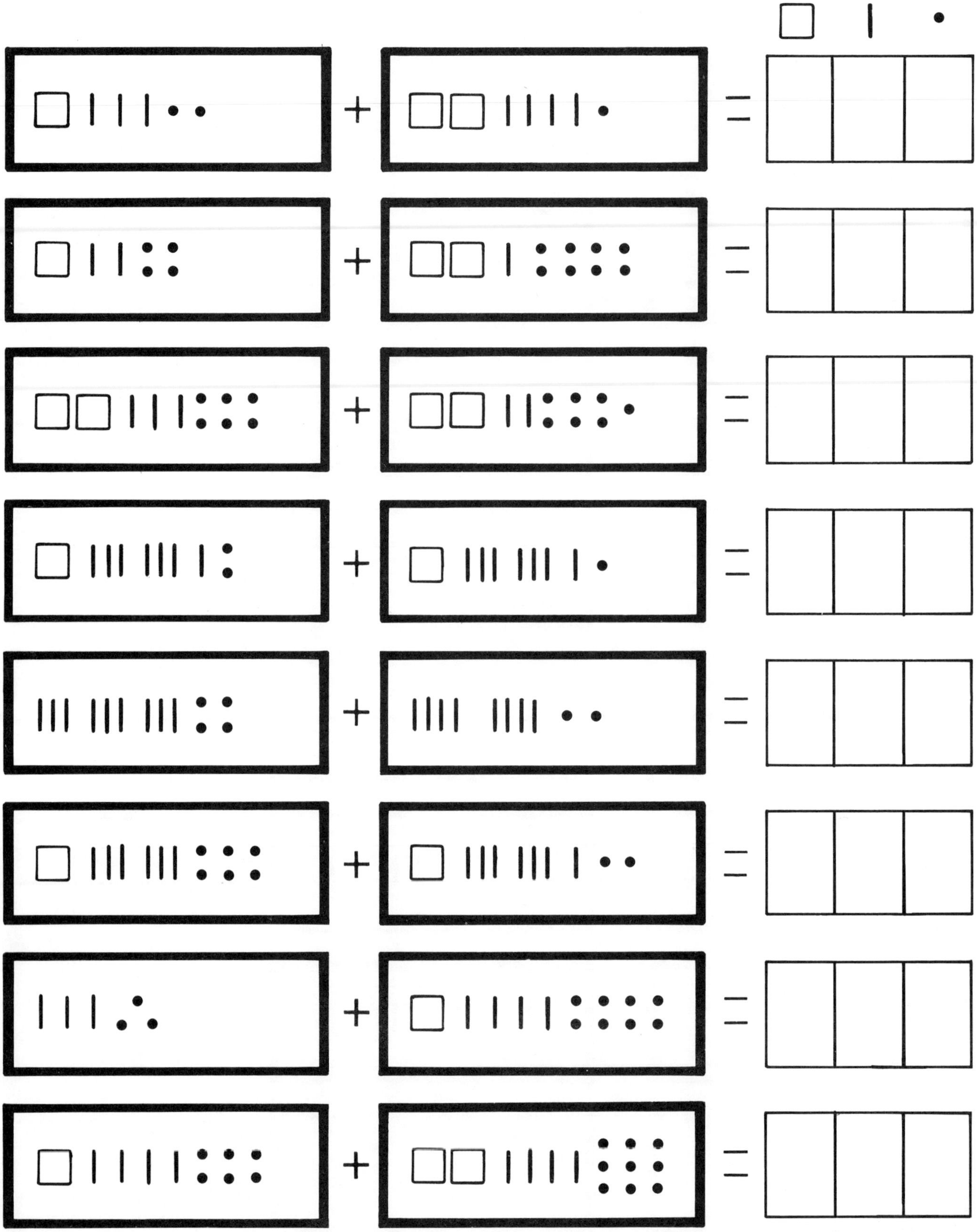

Add. Trade if necessary.

Combine and record.

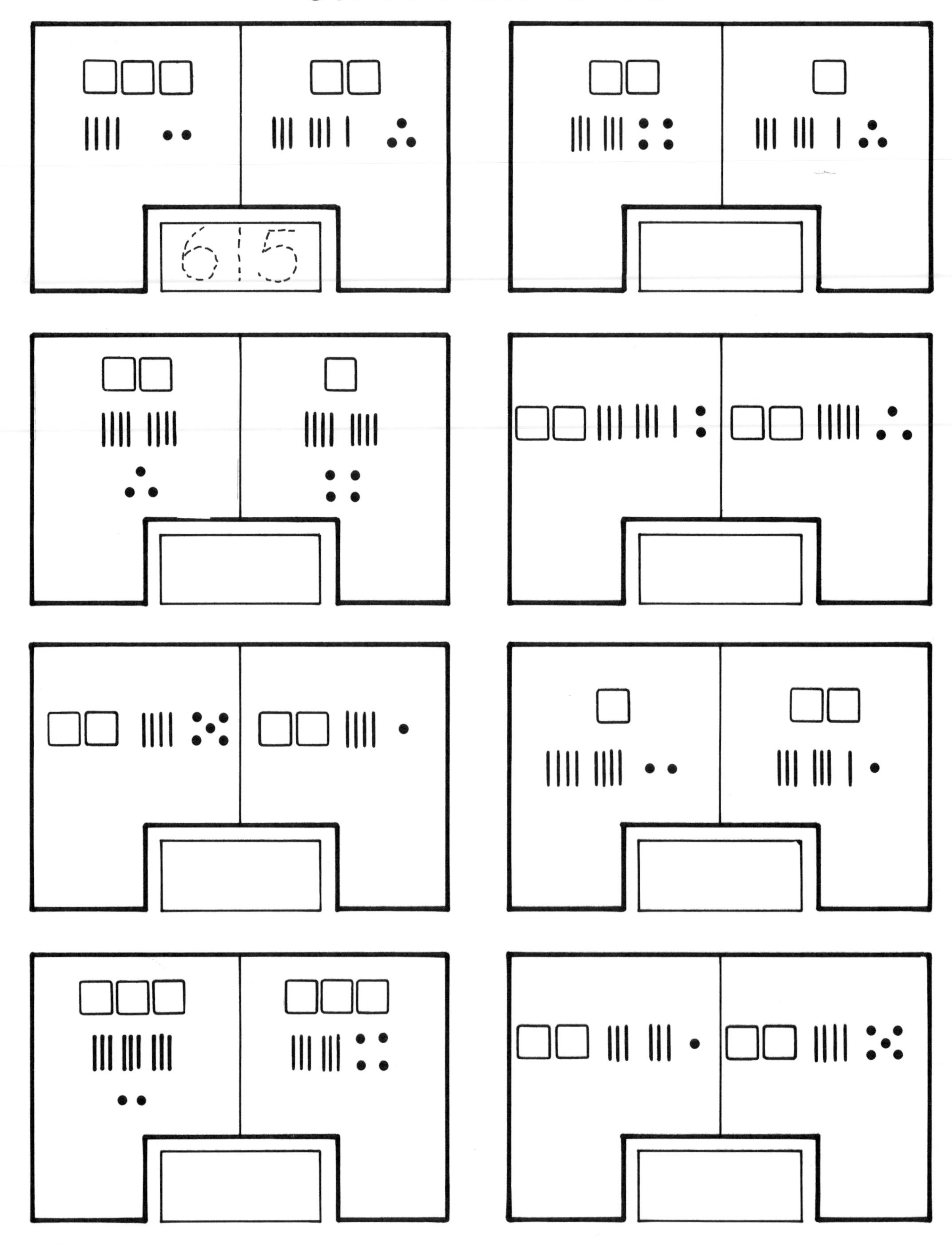

Combine and record.

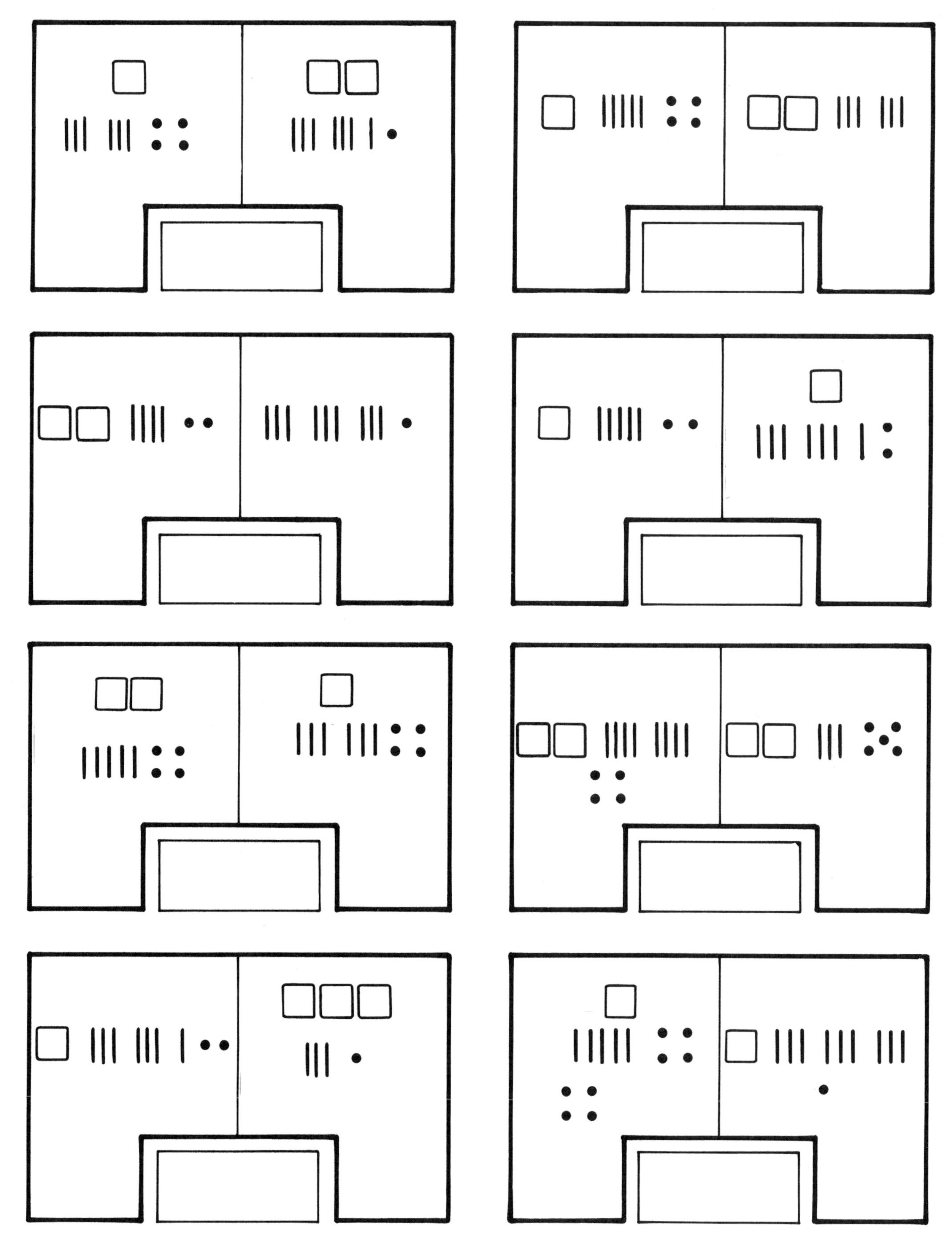

Combine and record.

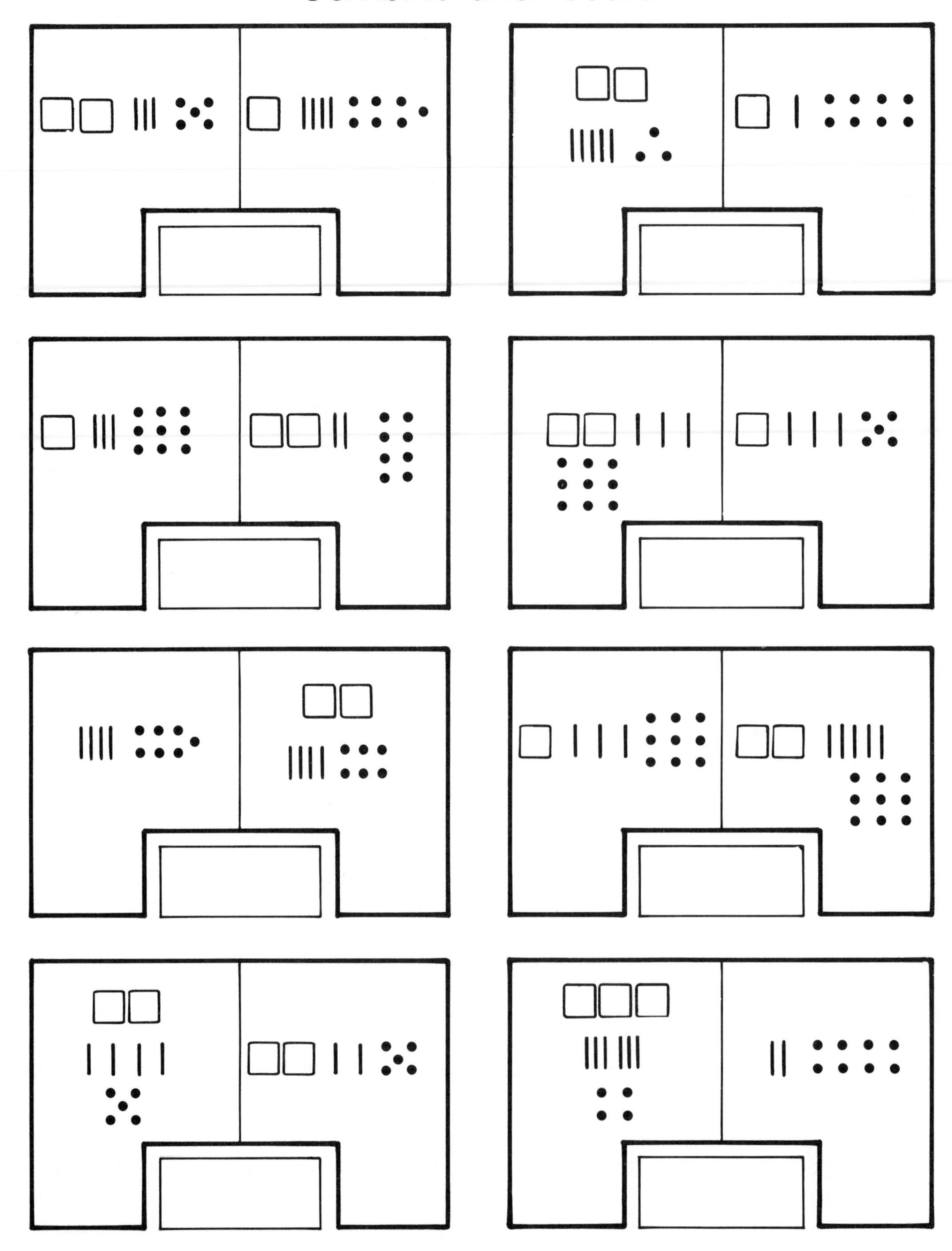

Combine and record.

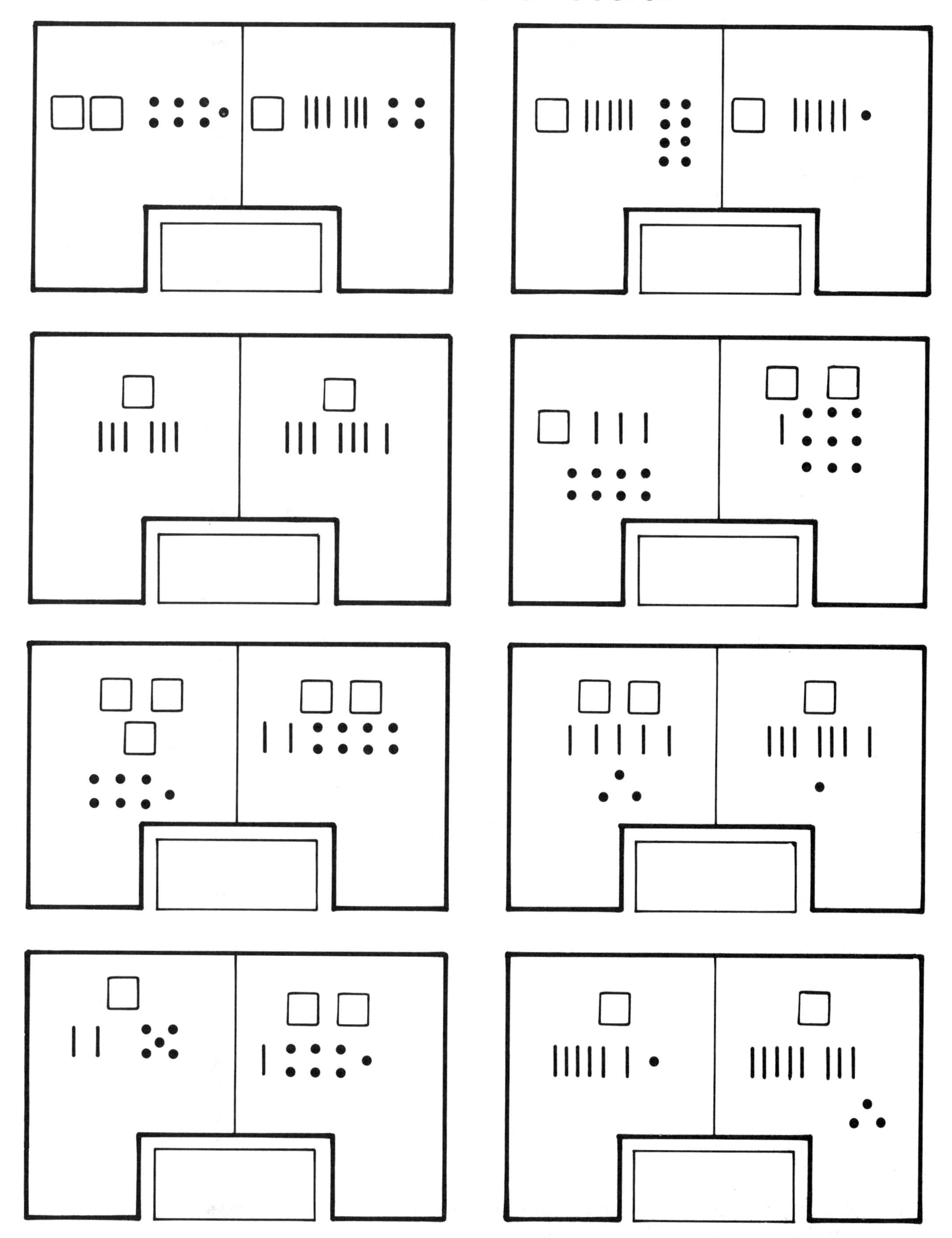

Combine and record.

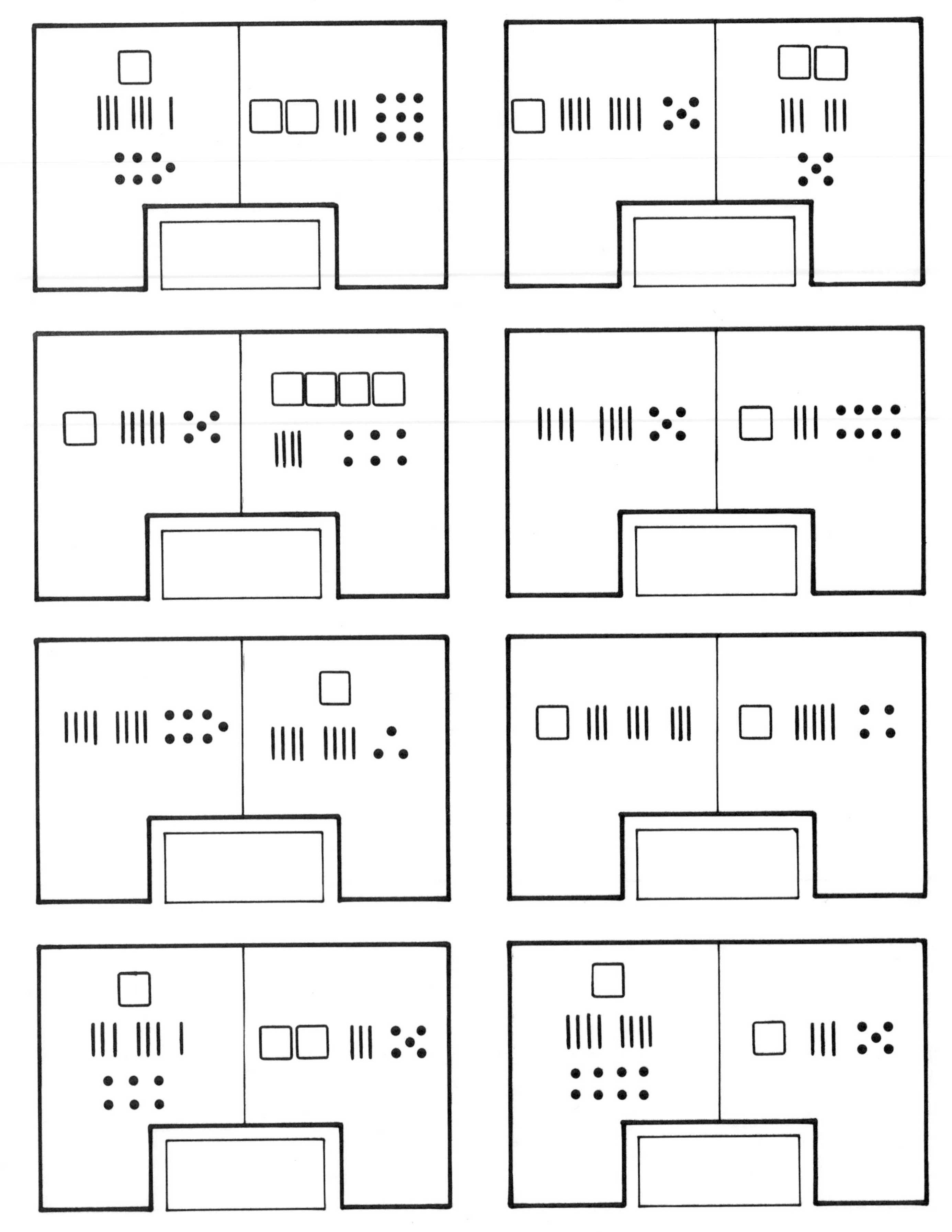

Combine and record.

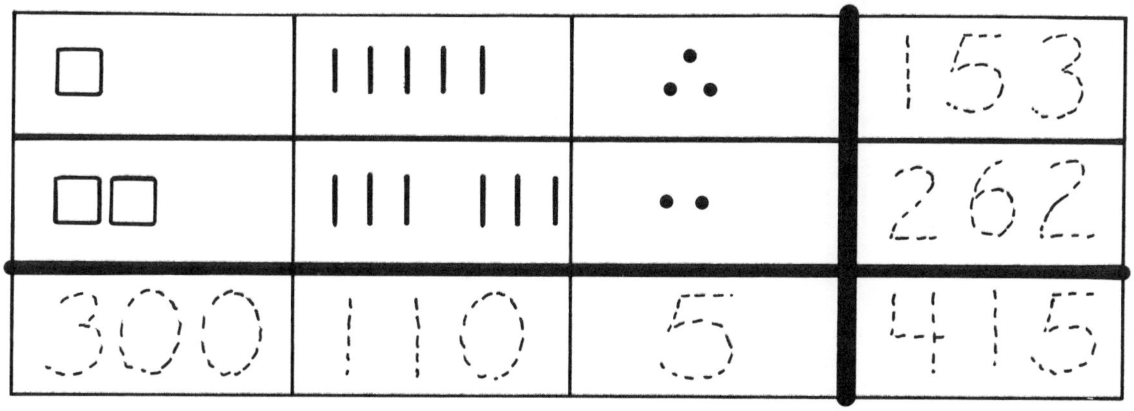

			153
			262
300	110	5	415

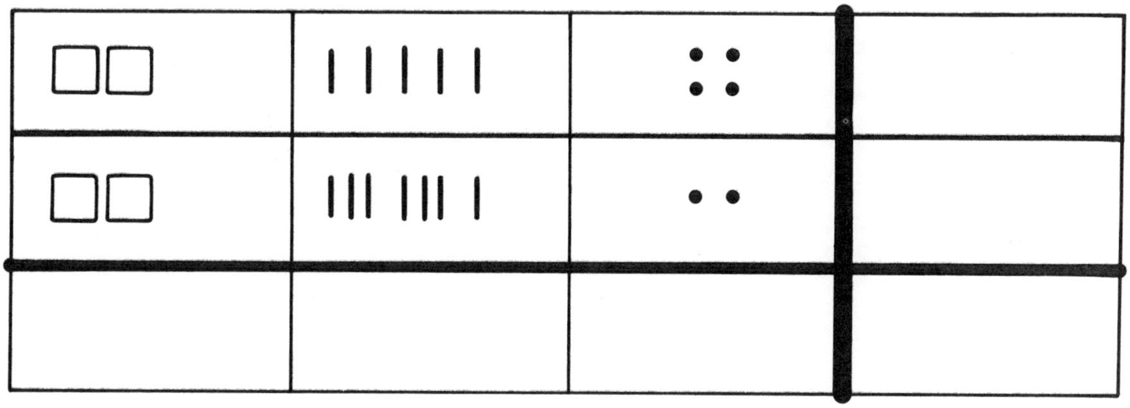

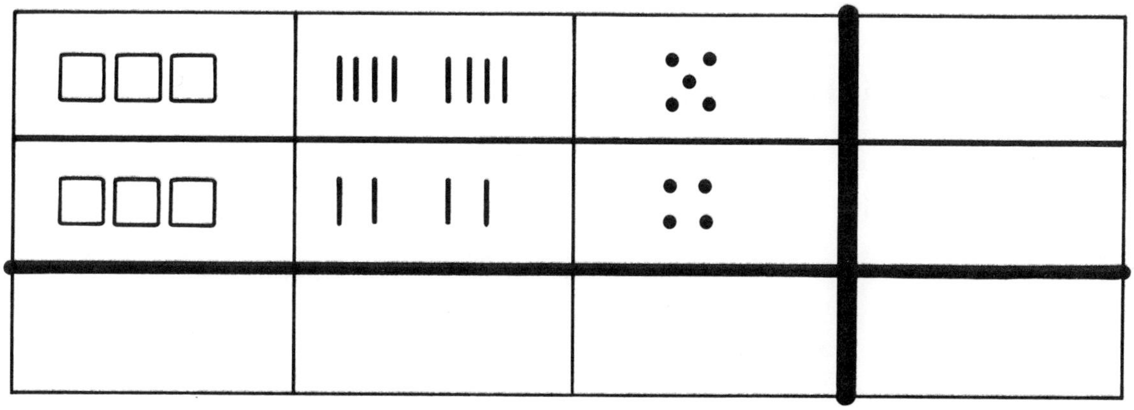

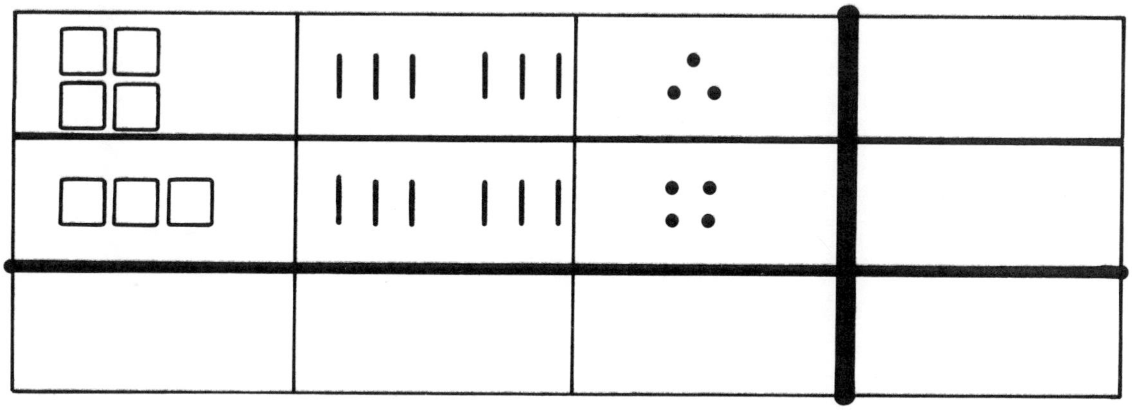

Combine and record.

			267
			252

Combine and record.

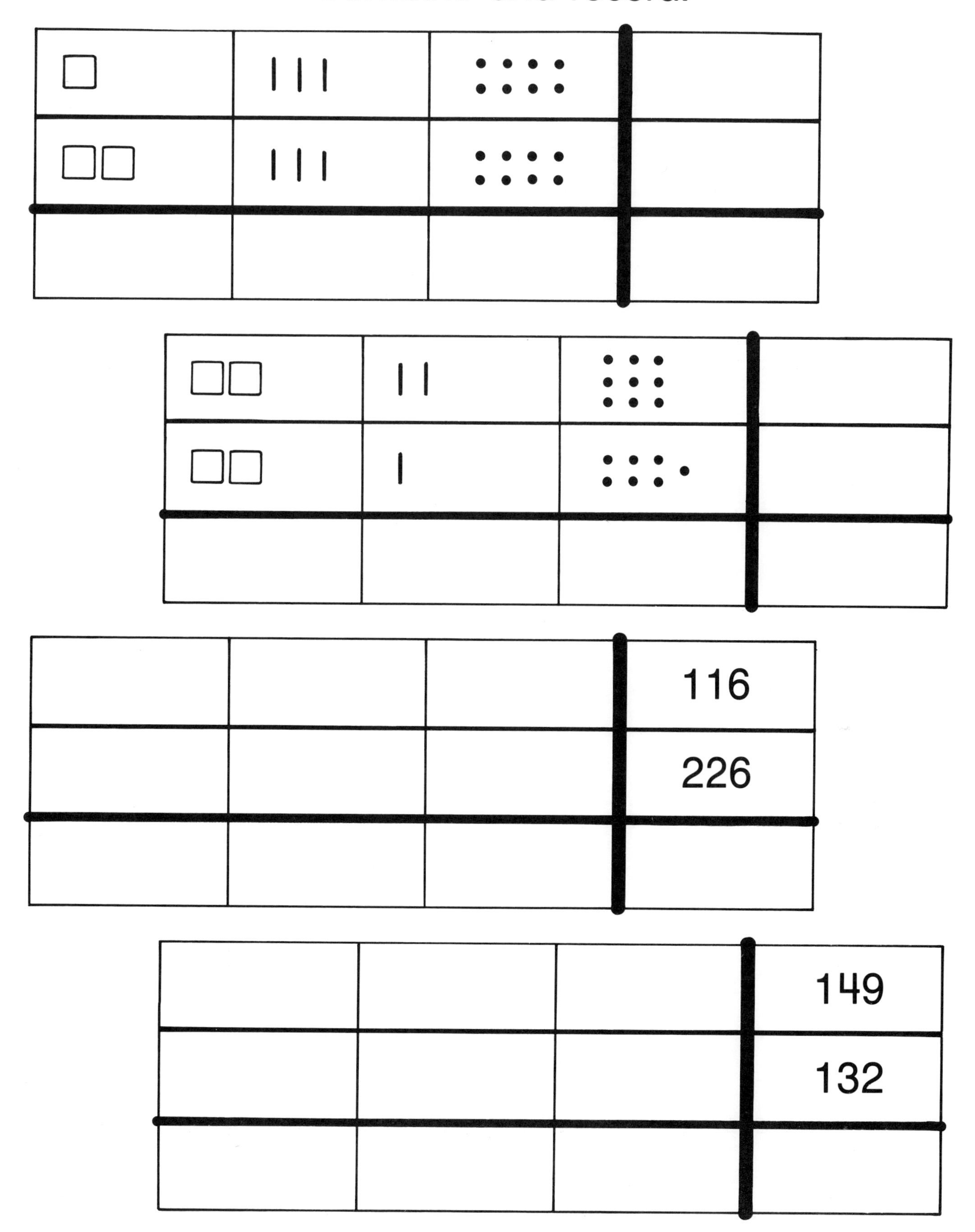

Combine and record.

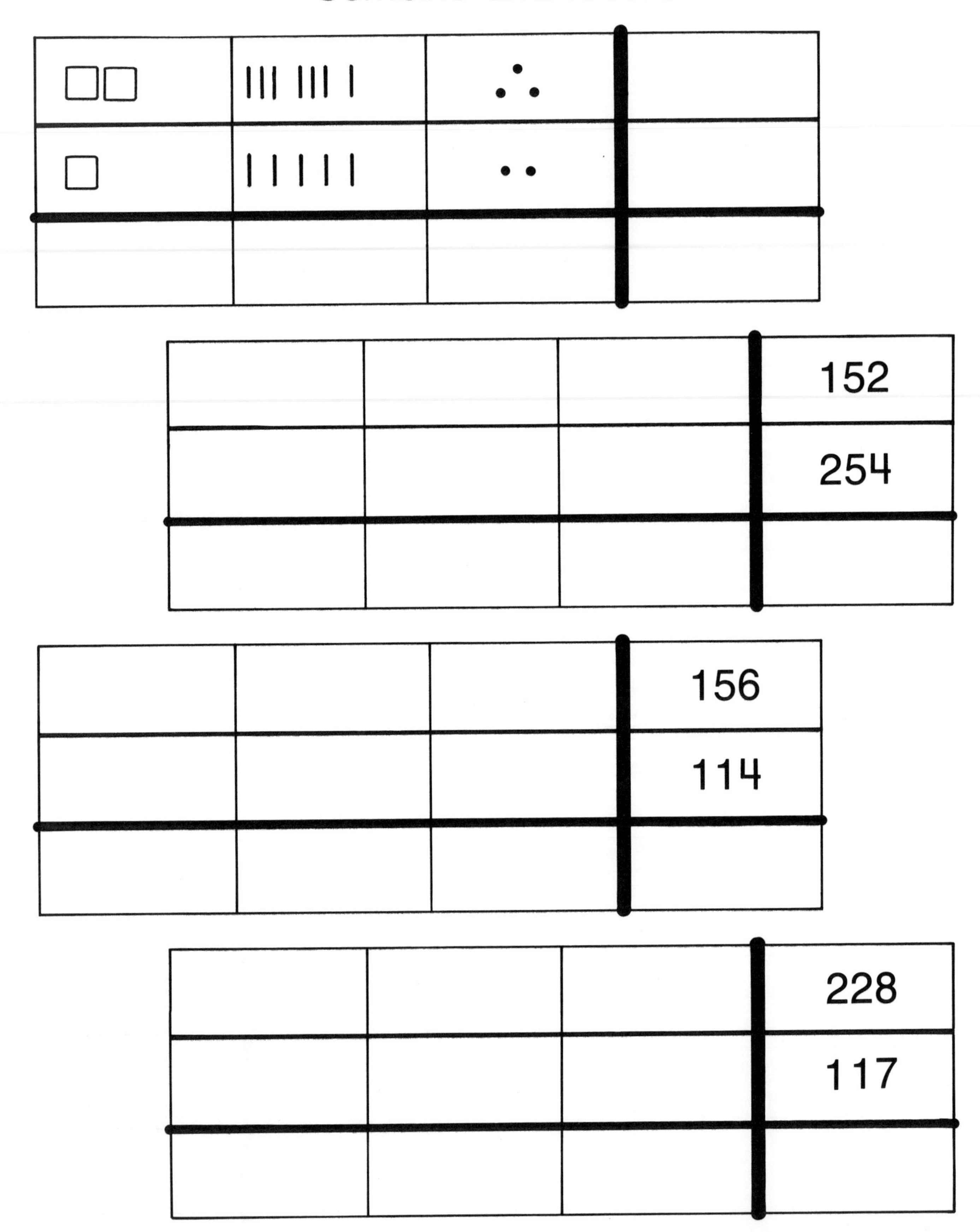

Combine and record.

Combine and record.

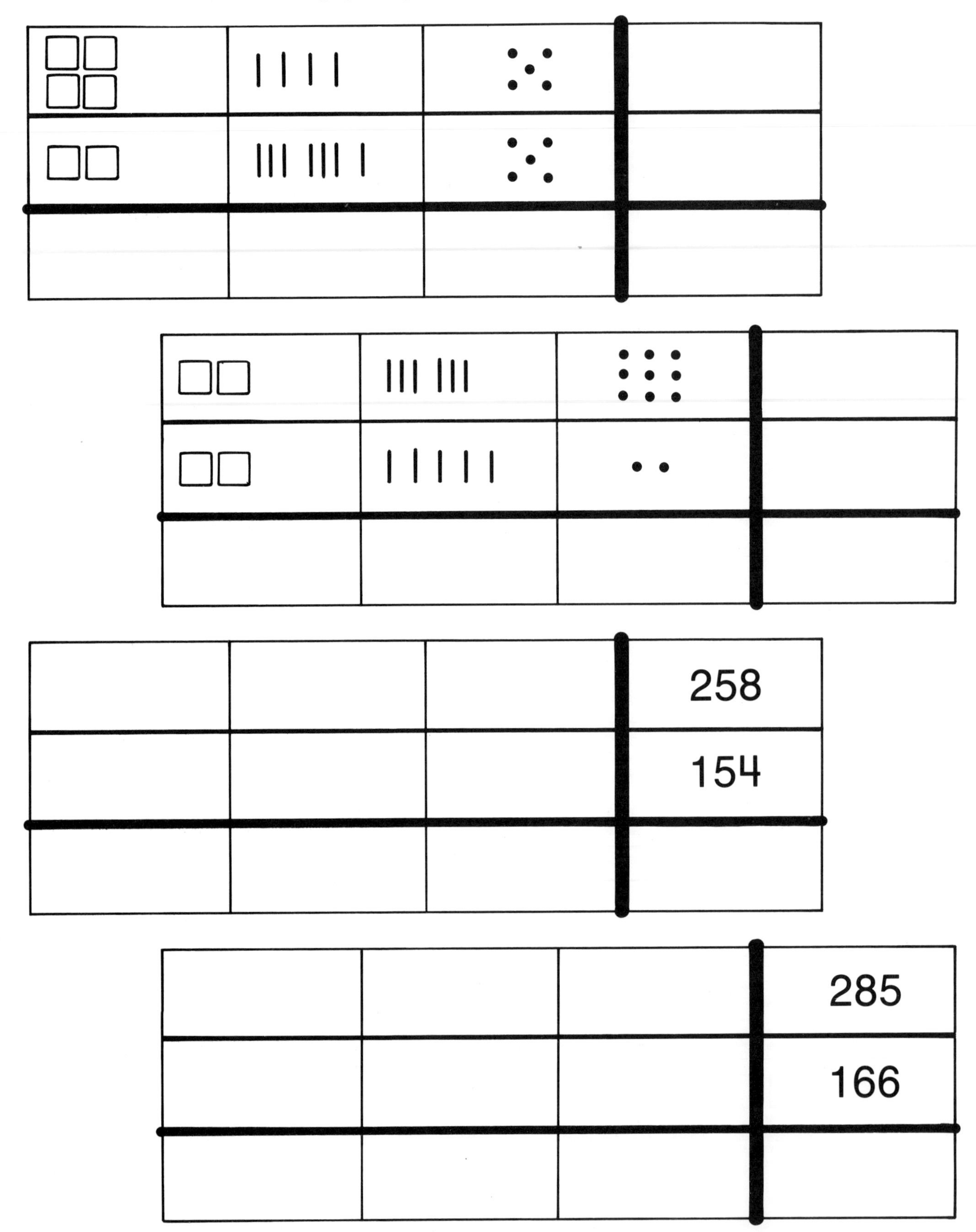

Color the ones, tens, and hundreds. Add.

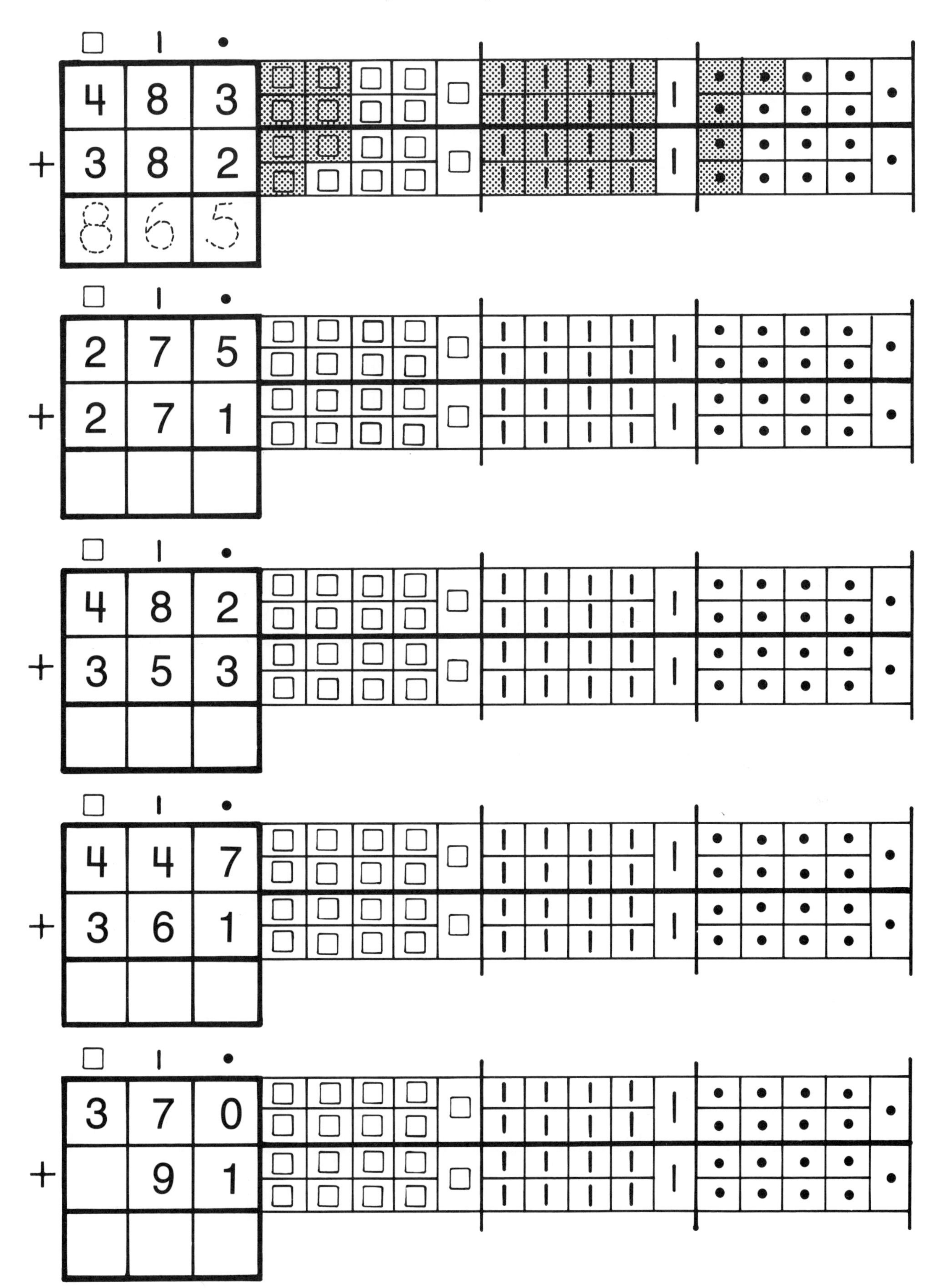

Color the ones, tens, and hundreds. Add.

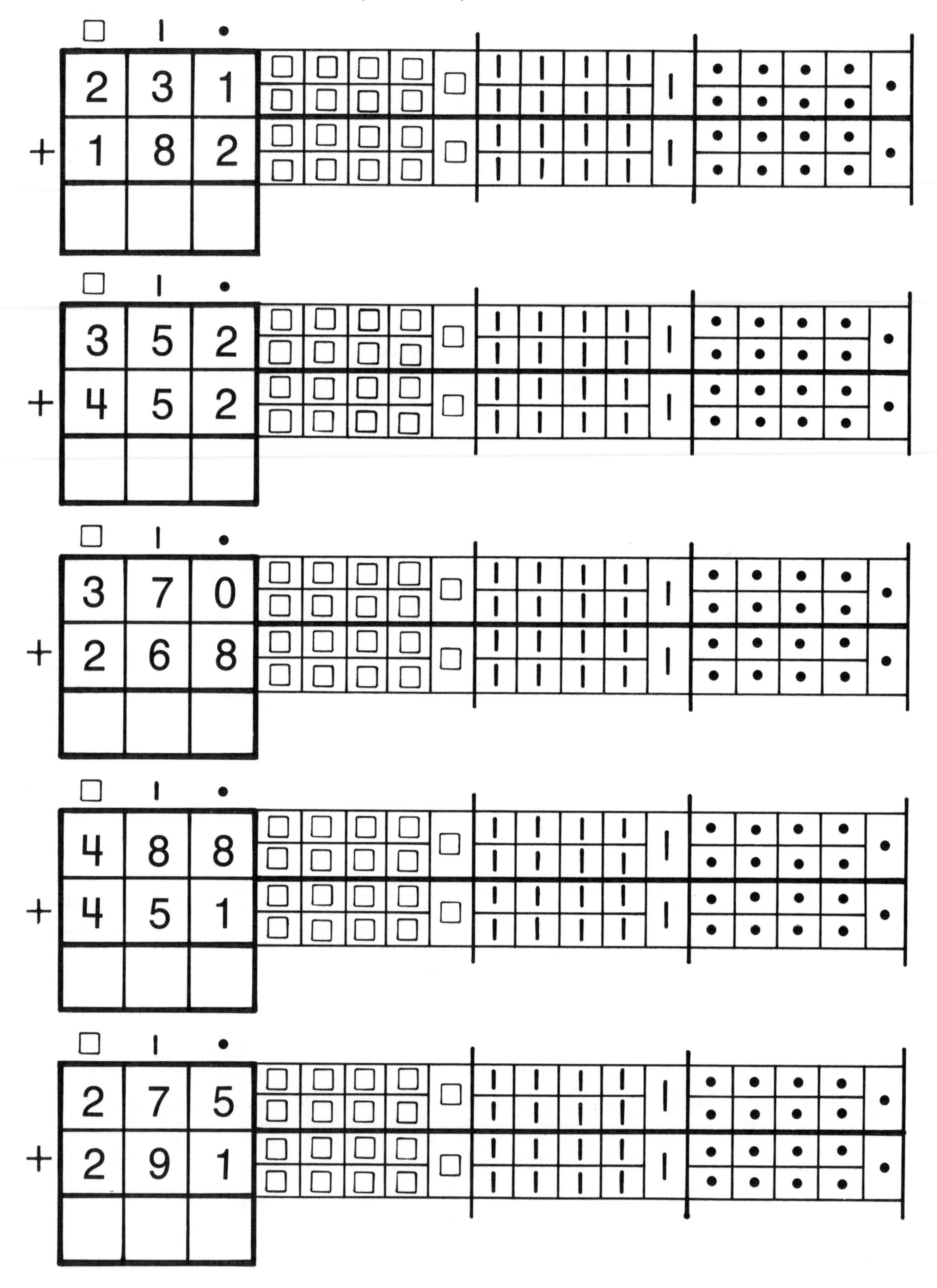

Color the ones, tens, and hundreds. Add.

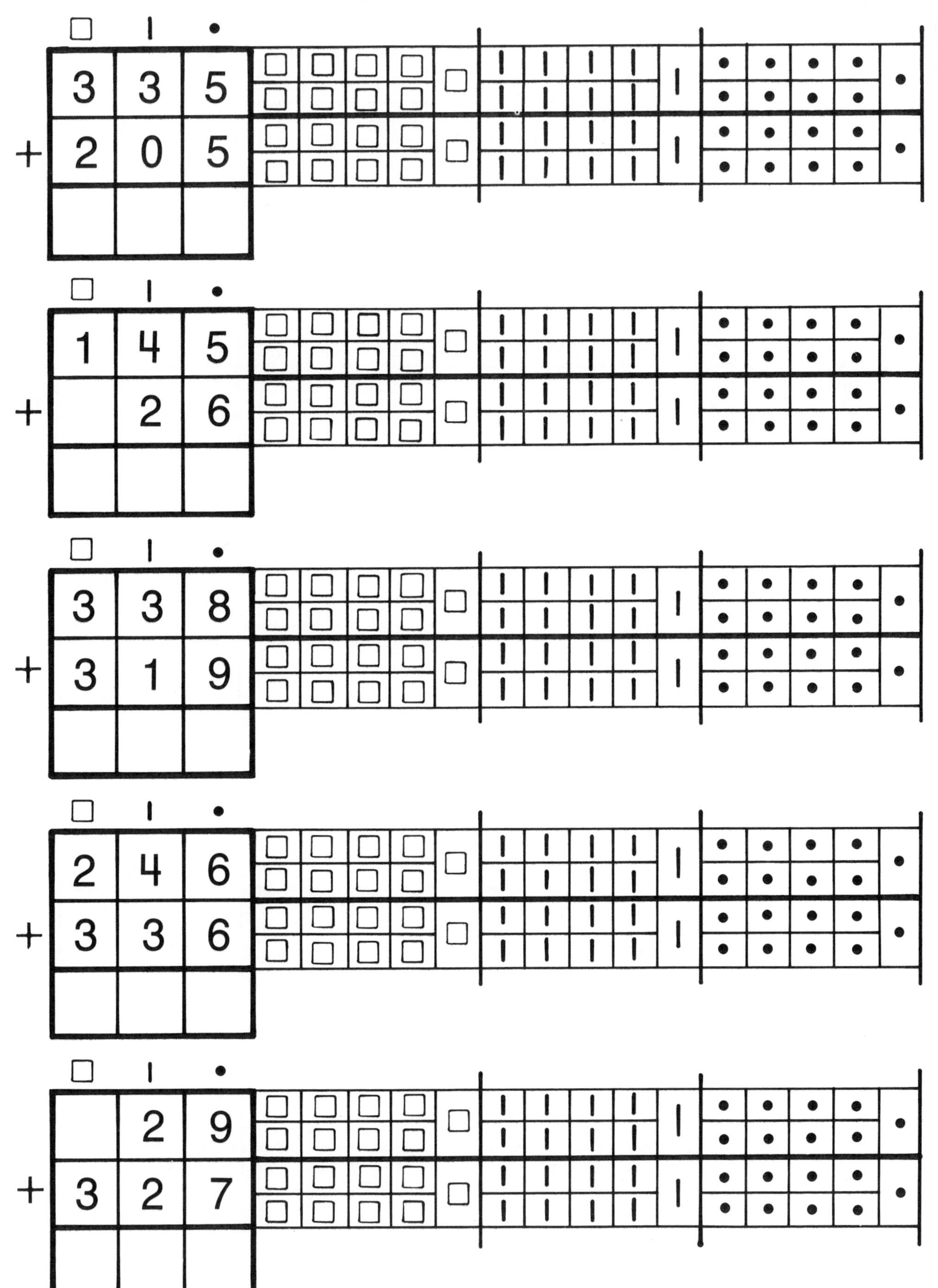

Color the ones, tens, and hundreds. Add.

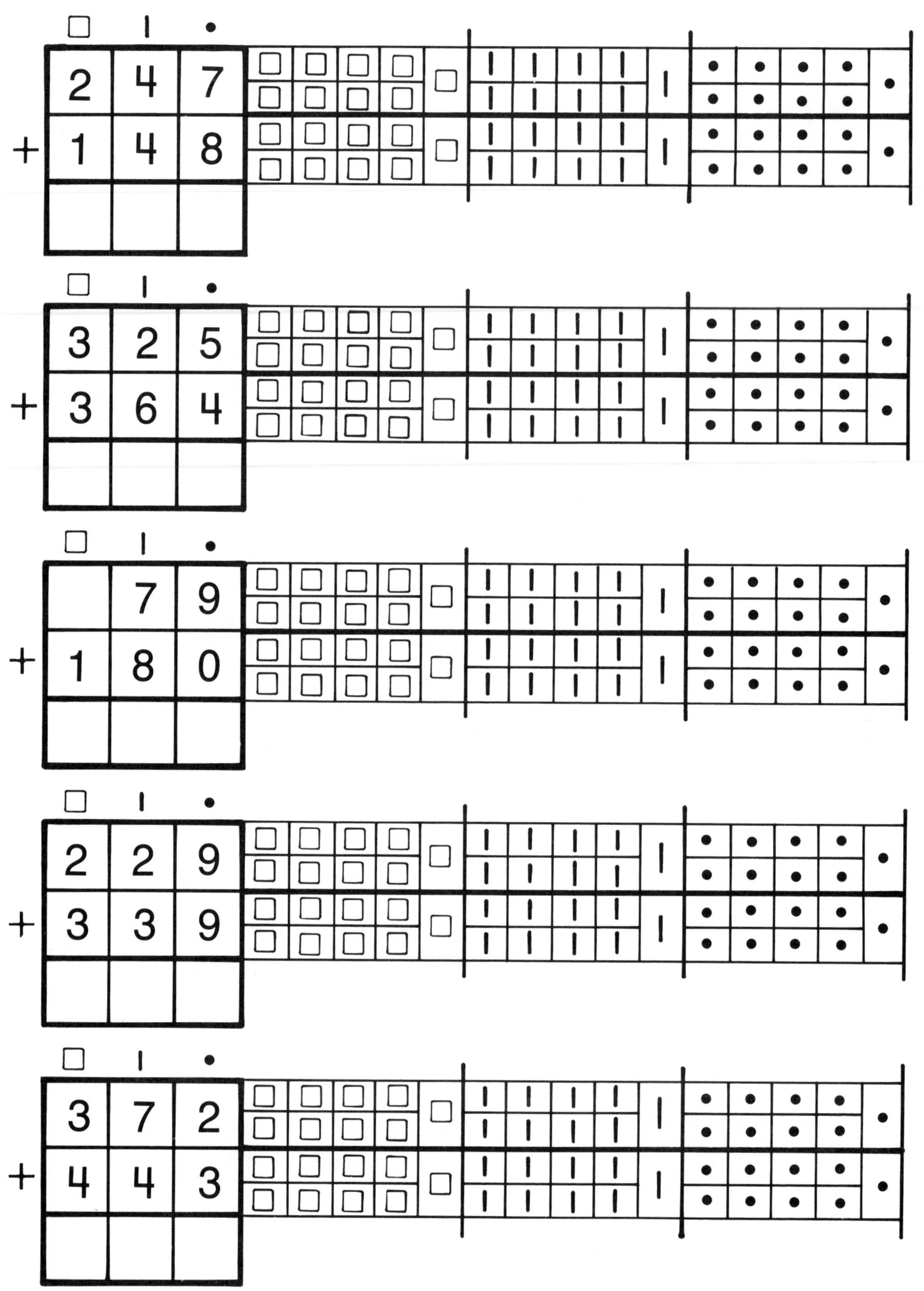

Color the ones, tens, and hundreds. Add.

	□	I	•
	4	8	8
+	4	7	7

	□	I	•
	3	5	9
+	3	5	2

	□	I	•
	4	4	9
+	2	7	2

	□	I	•
	2	7	2
+	3	8	5

	□	I	•
	4	9	6
+		9	9

Combine and record.

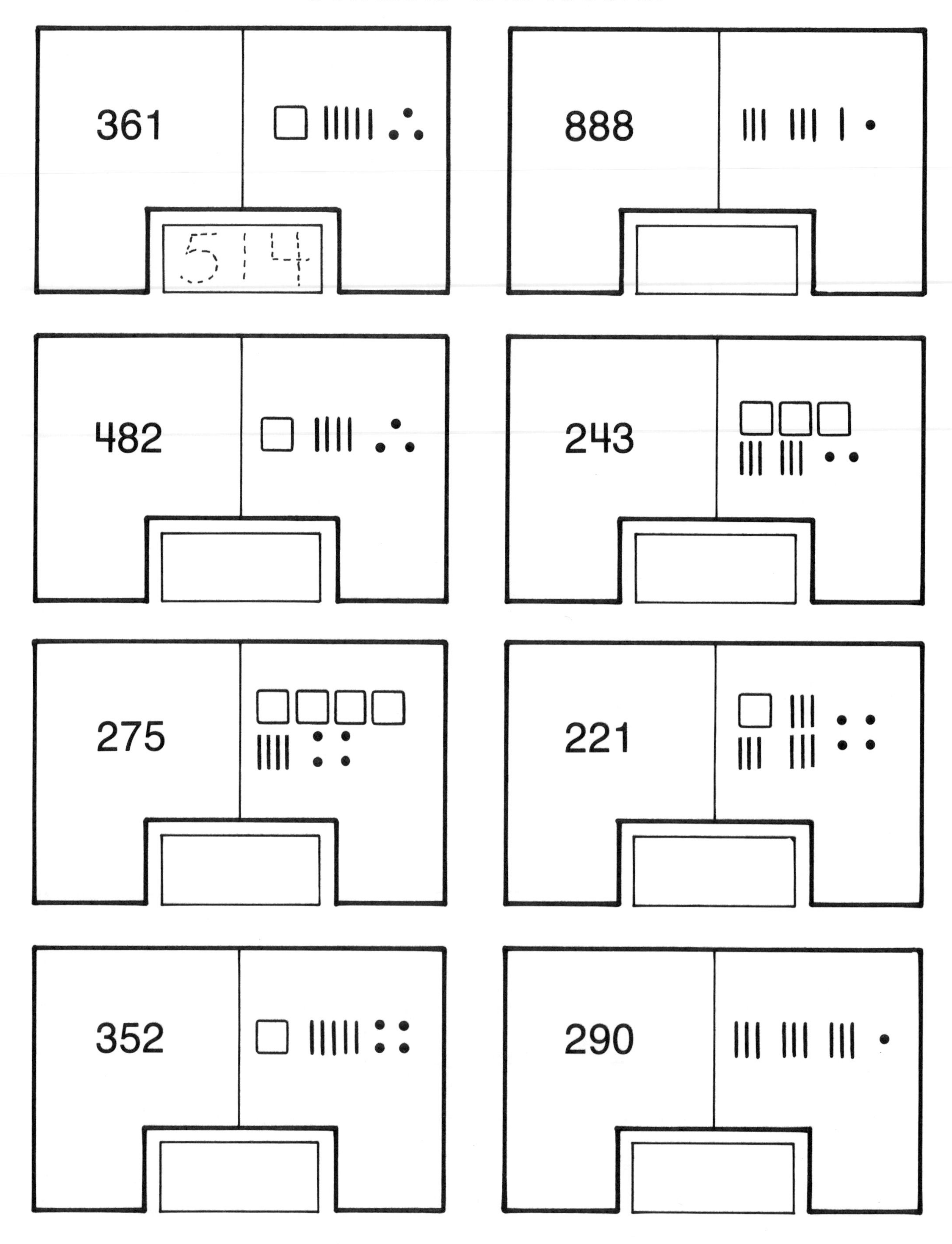

Combine and record.

141	424	135
328	838	224
468	165	538
239	428	487
216	347	708

Combine and record.

248	482	476
175	251	287
267	684	364
787	259	358
299	324	379

Combine and record. Trade if necessary.

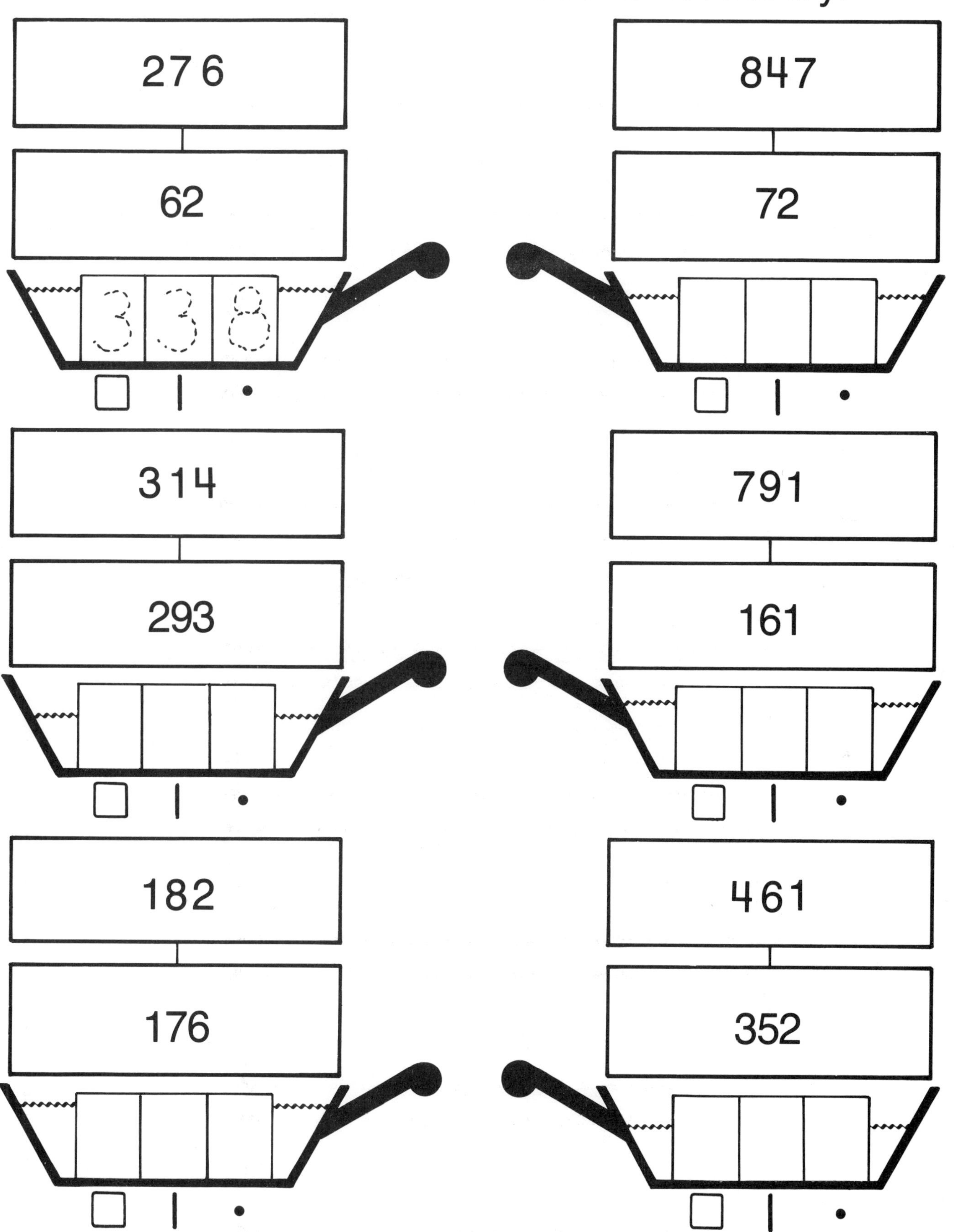

This is 1 thousand.

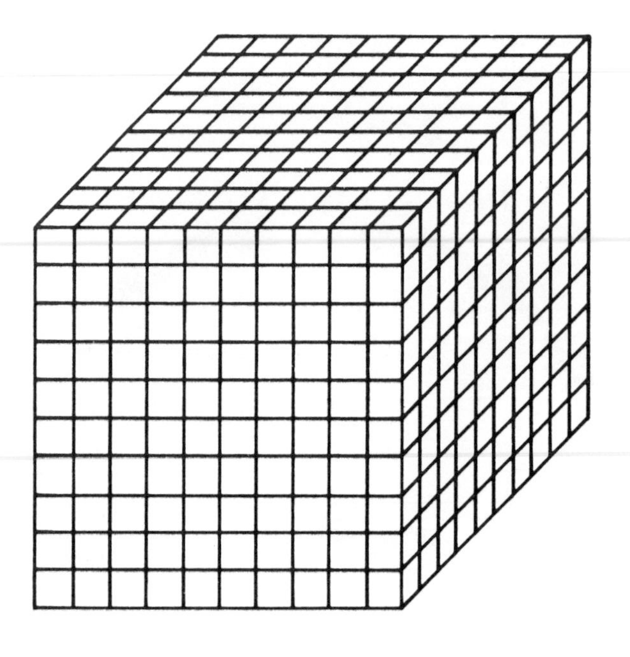

Combine and record.

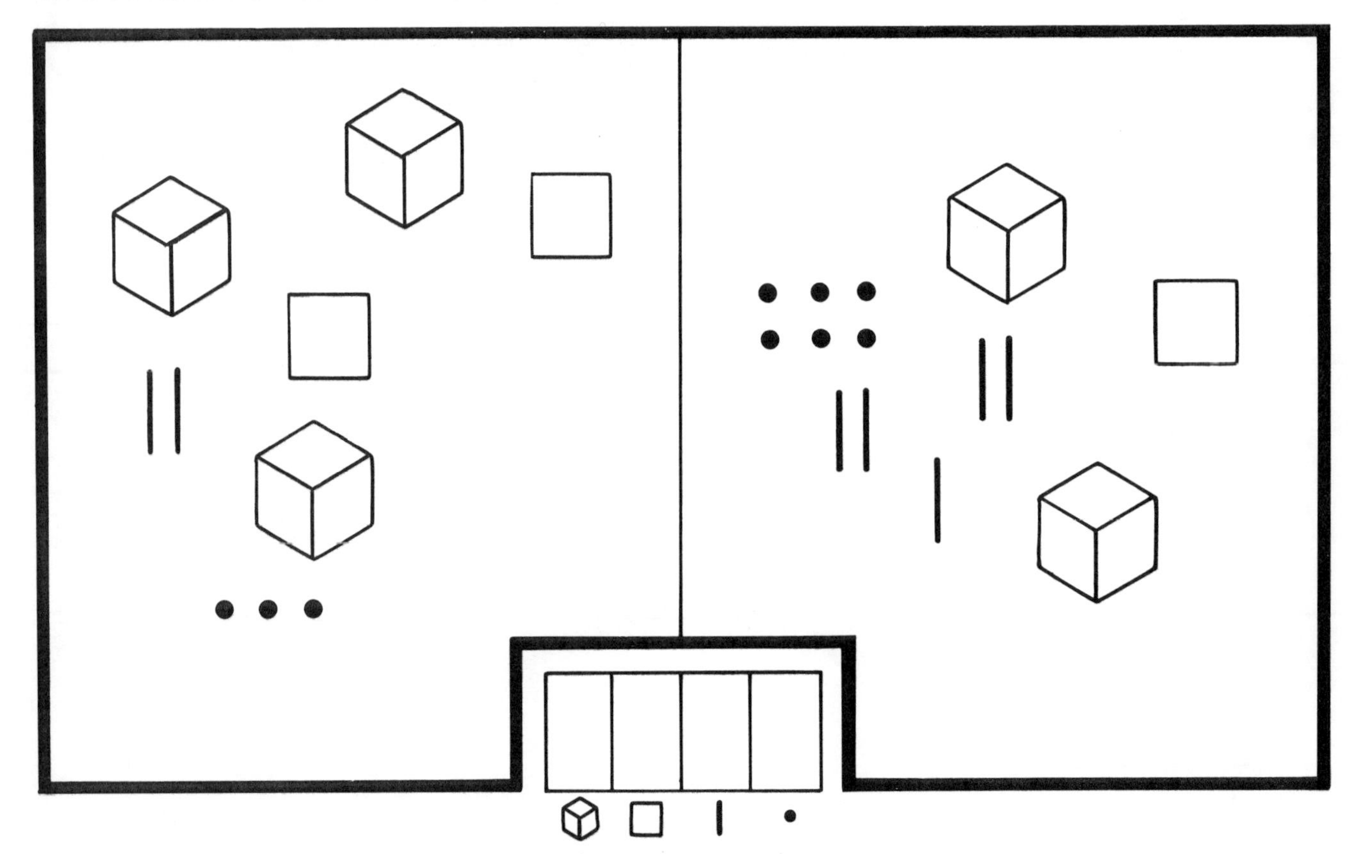

Combine and record.

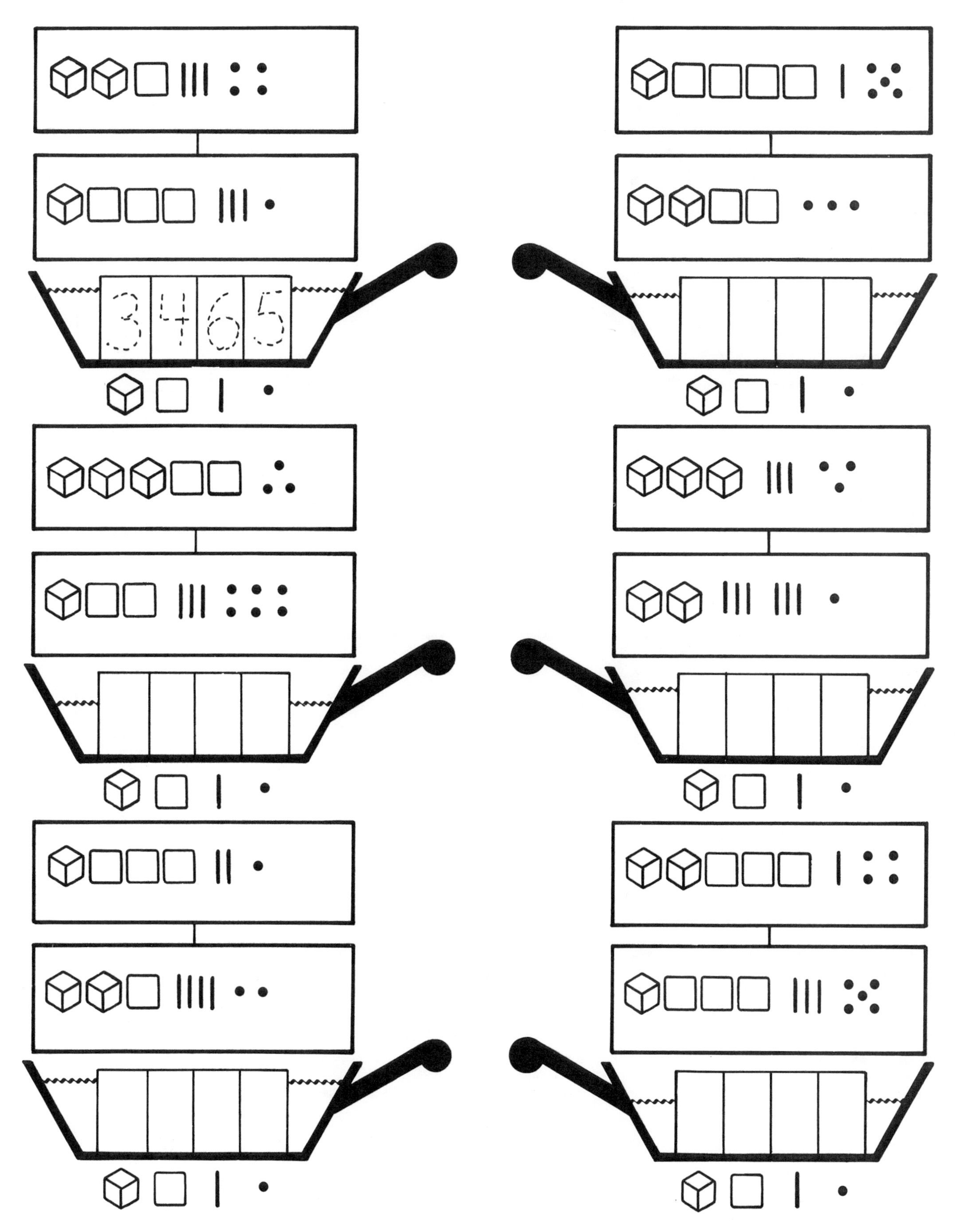

Add.

4 5 4 5

Add.

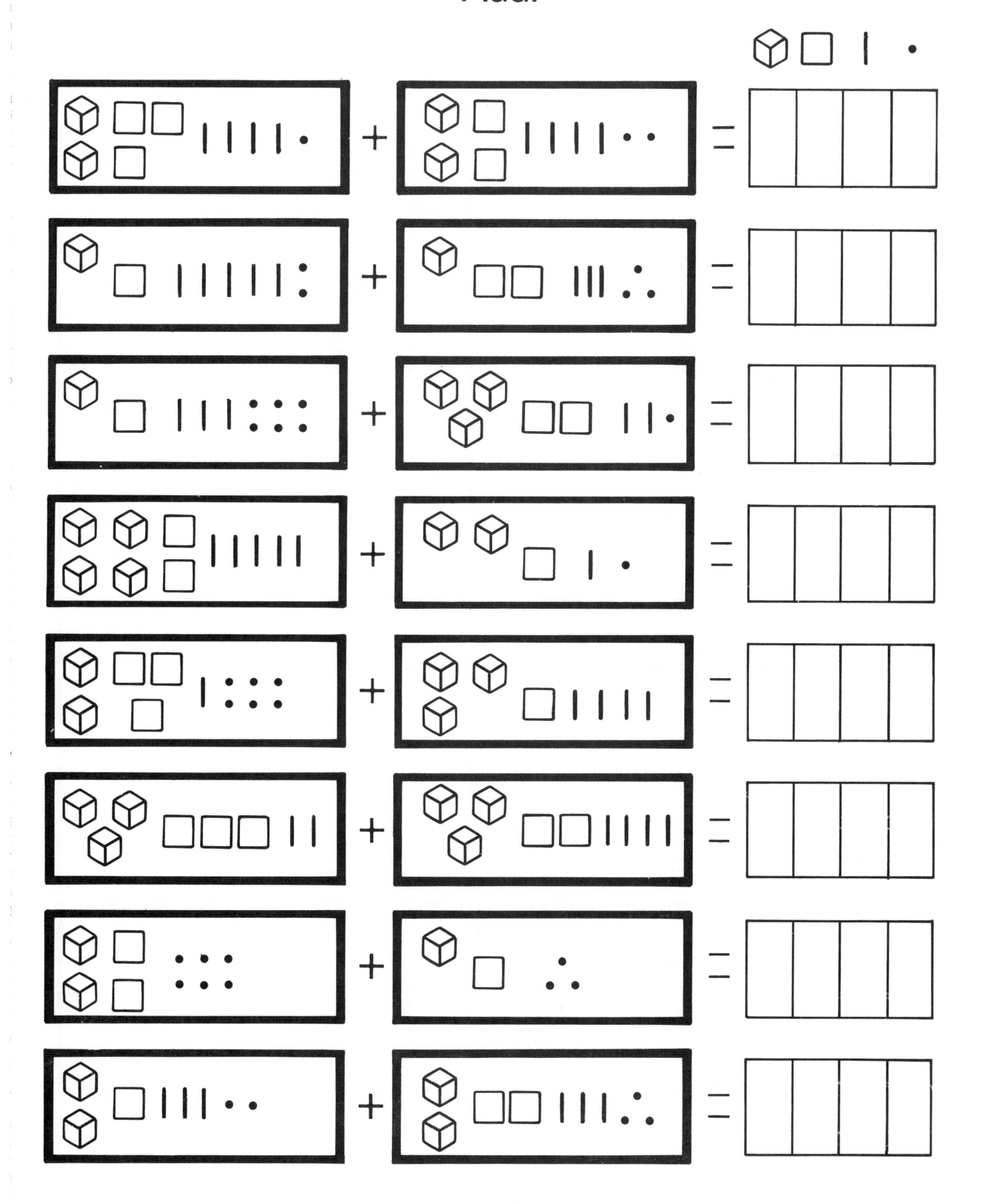

Combine and record.

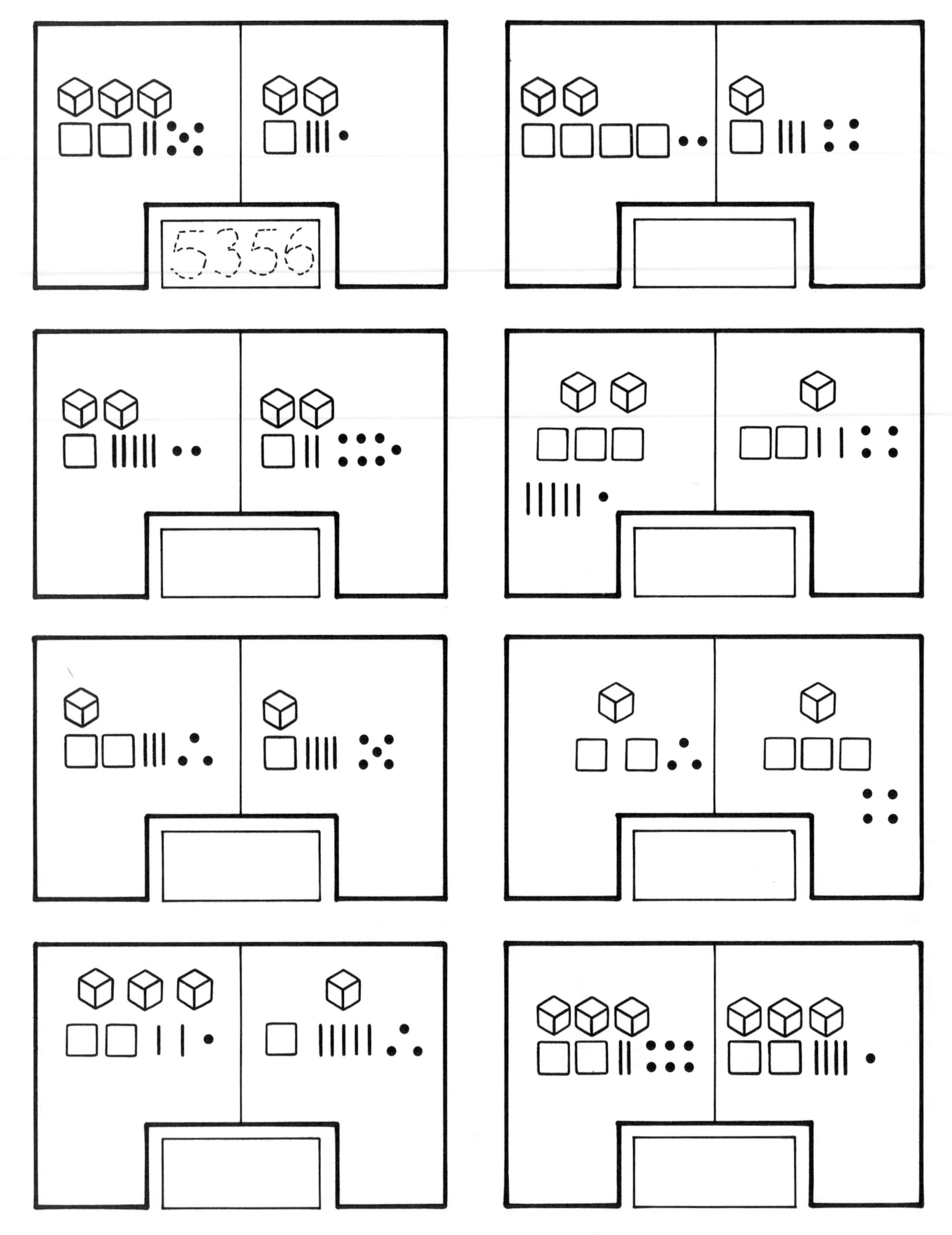

Combine and record.

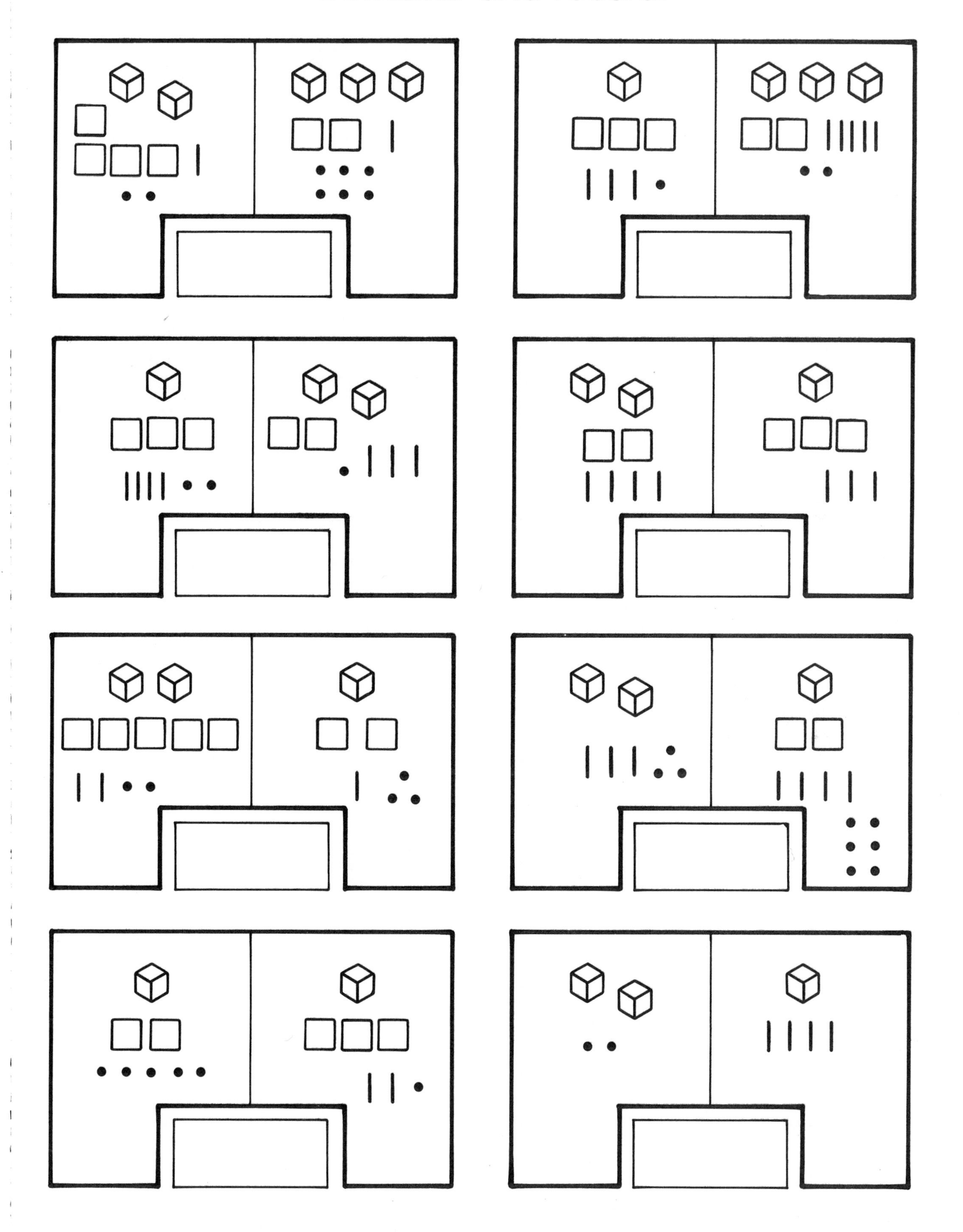

Color the ones, tens, hundreds, and thousands. Add.

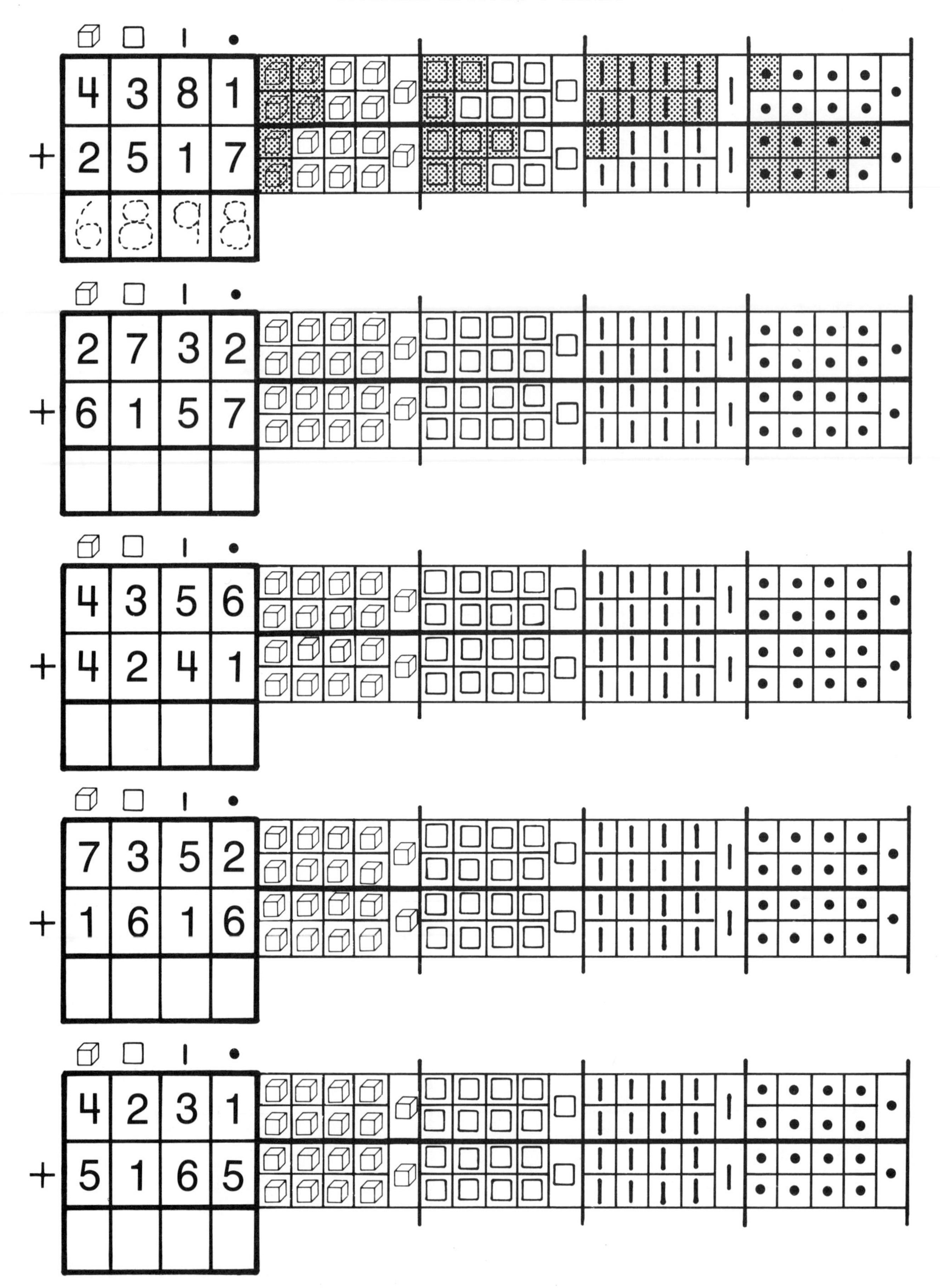

	4	3	8	1
+	2	5	1	7
	6	8	9	8

	2	7	3	2
+	6	1	5	7

	4	3	5	6
+	4	2	4	1

	7	3	5	2
+	1	6	1	6

	4	2	3	1
+	5	1	6	5

Color the ones, tens, hundreds, and thousands. Add.

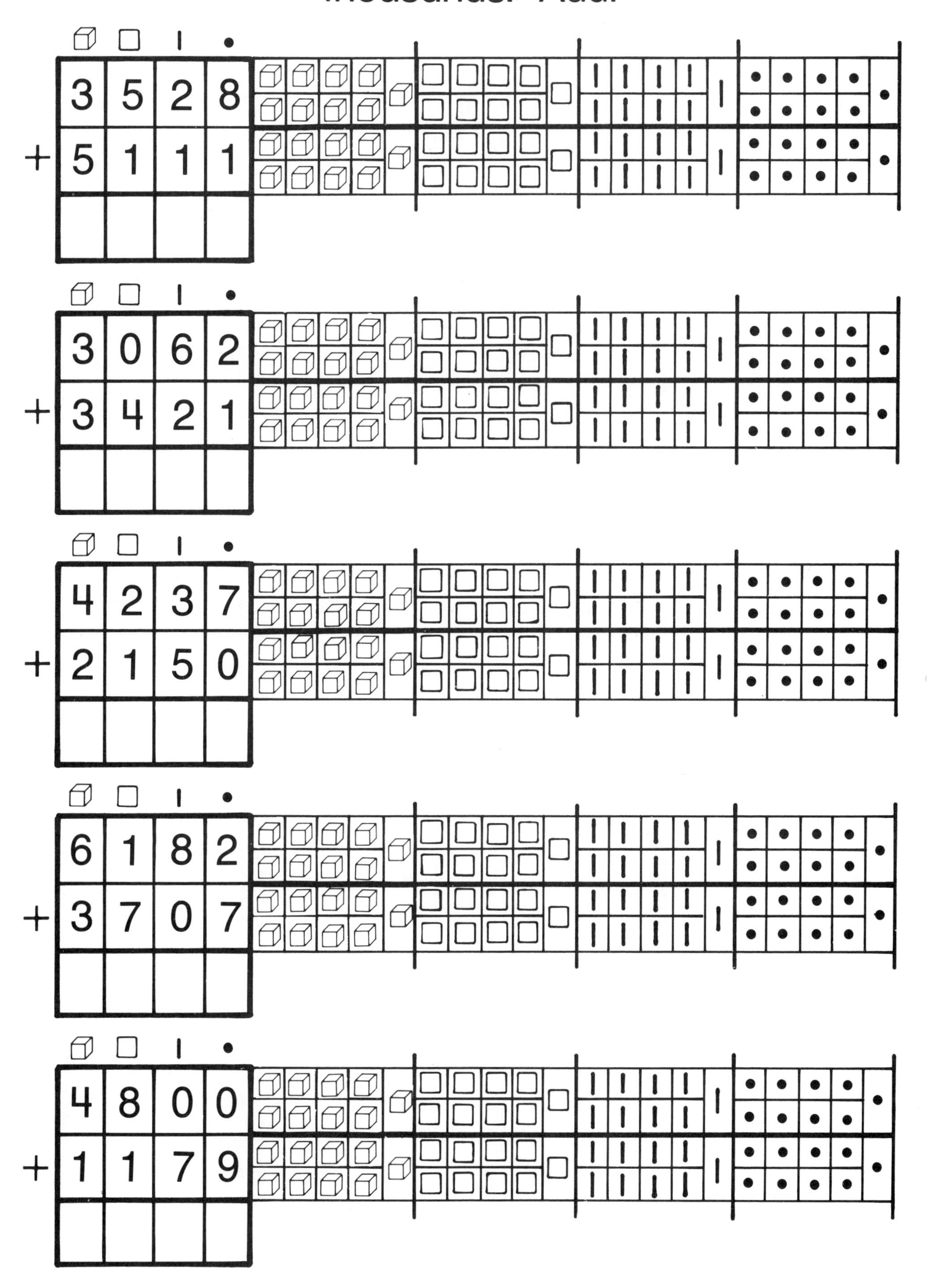

Color the ones, tens, hundreds, and thousands. Add.

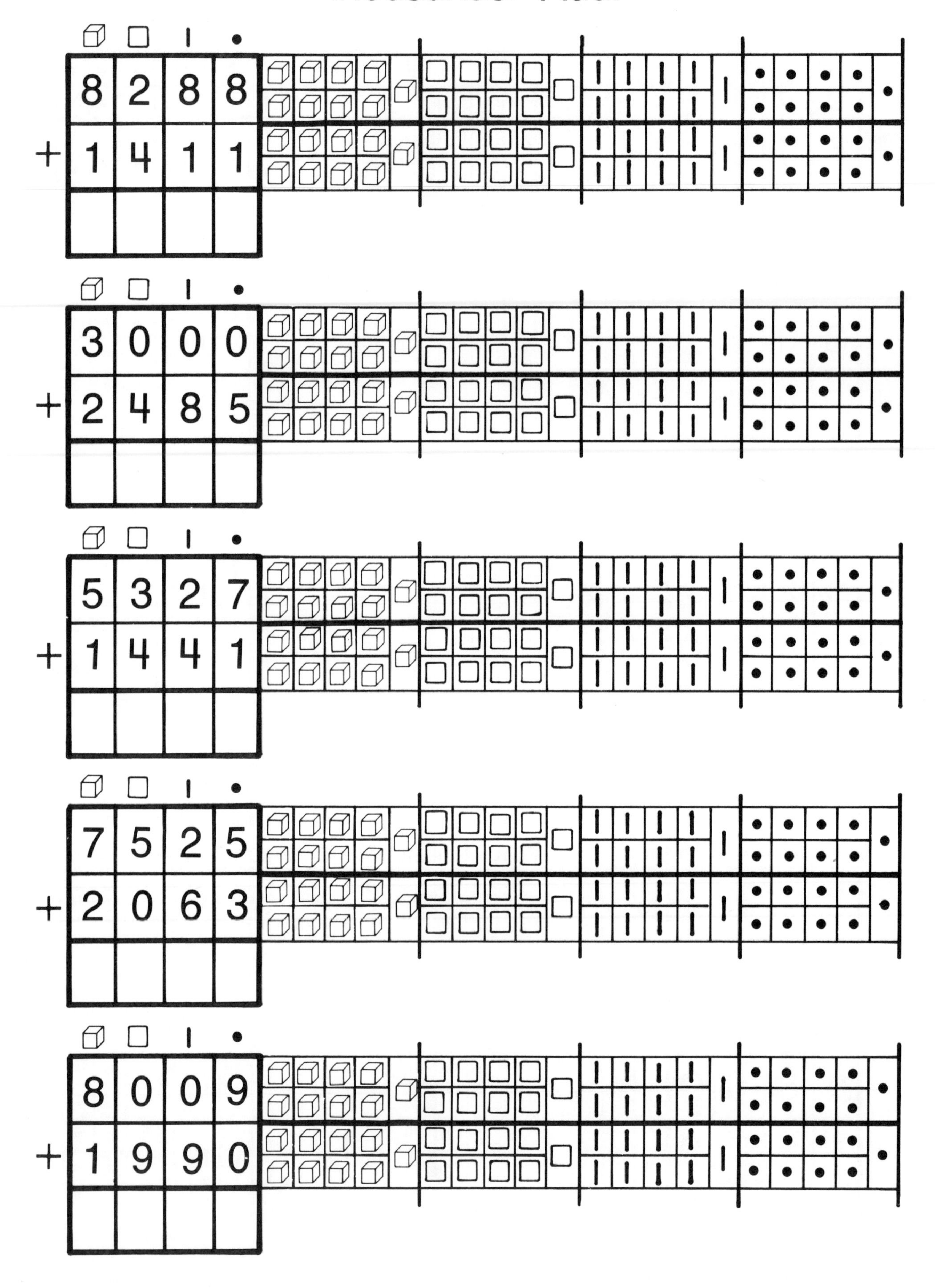

Combine and record.

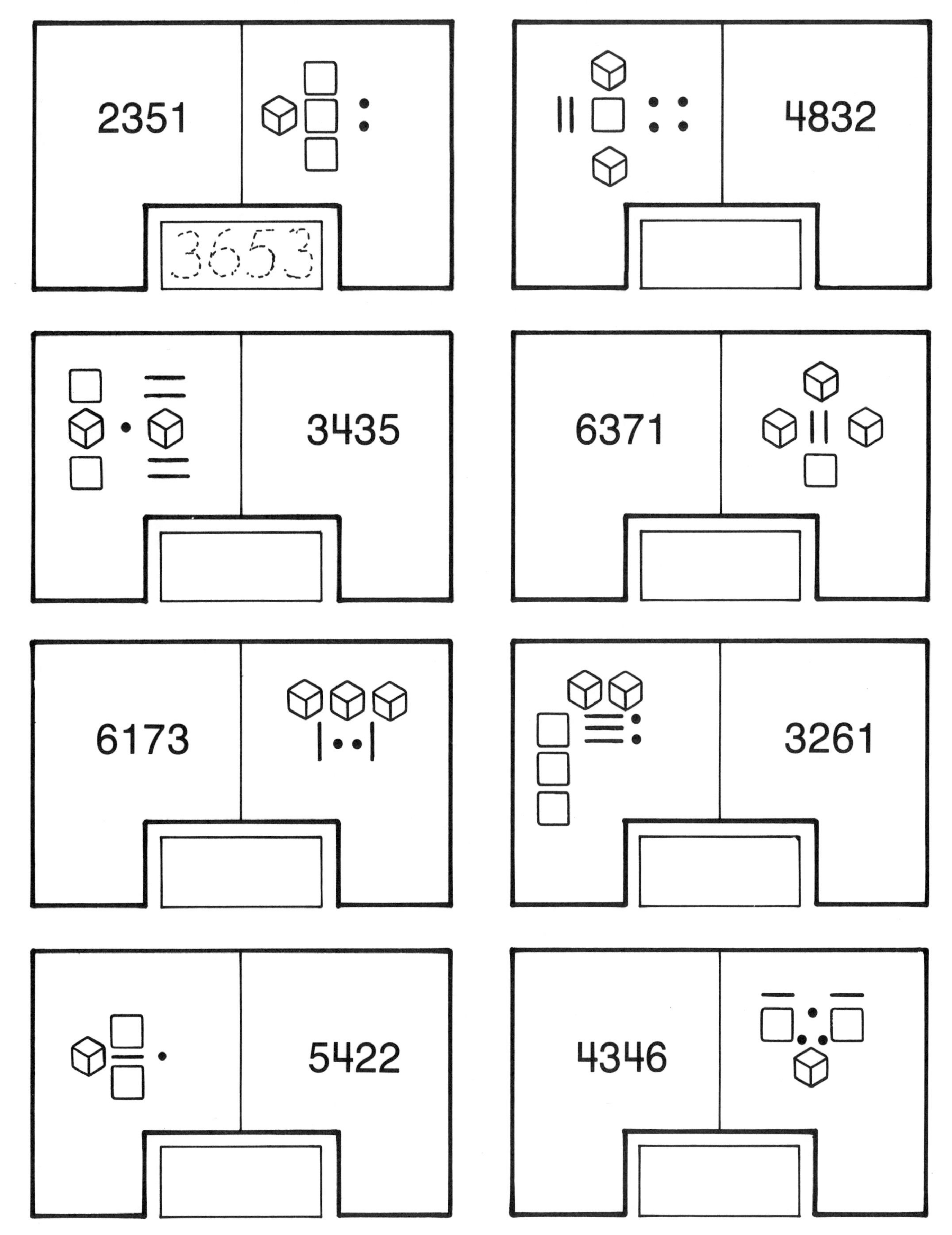

Complete each problem.

3242	4372	1523
4255	1006	2436 / 3436
6231	4222 / 4444	1200
1507	6821	3245
4633	2323 / 2555	5387

Combine and record.

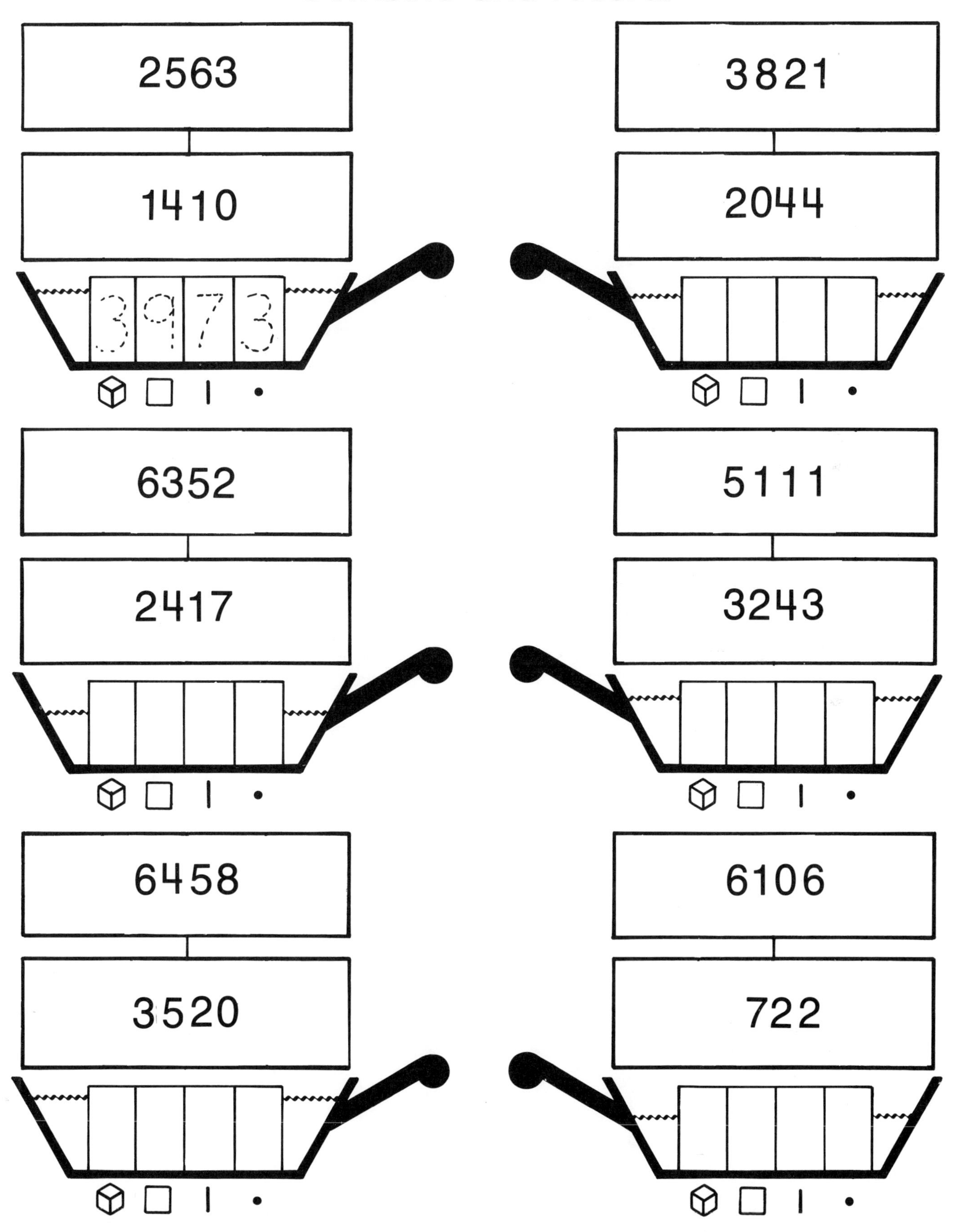

Add. Trade if necessary.

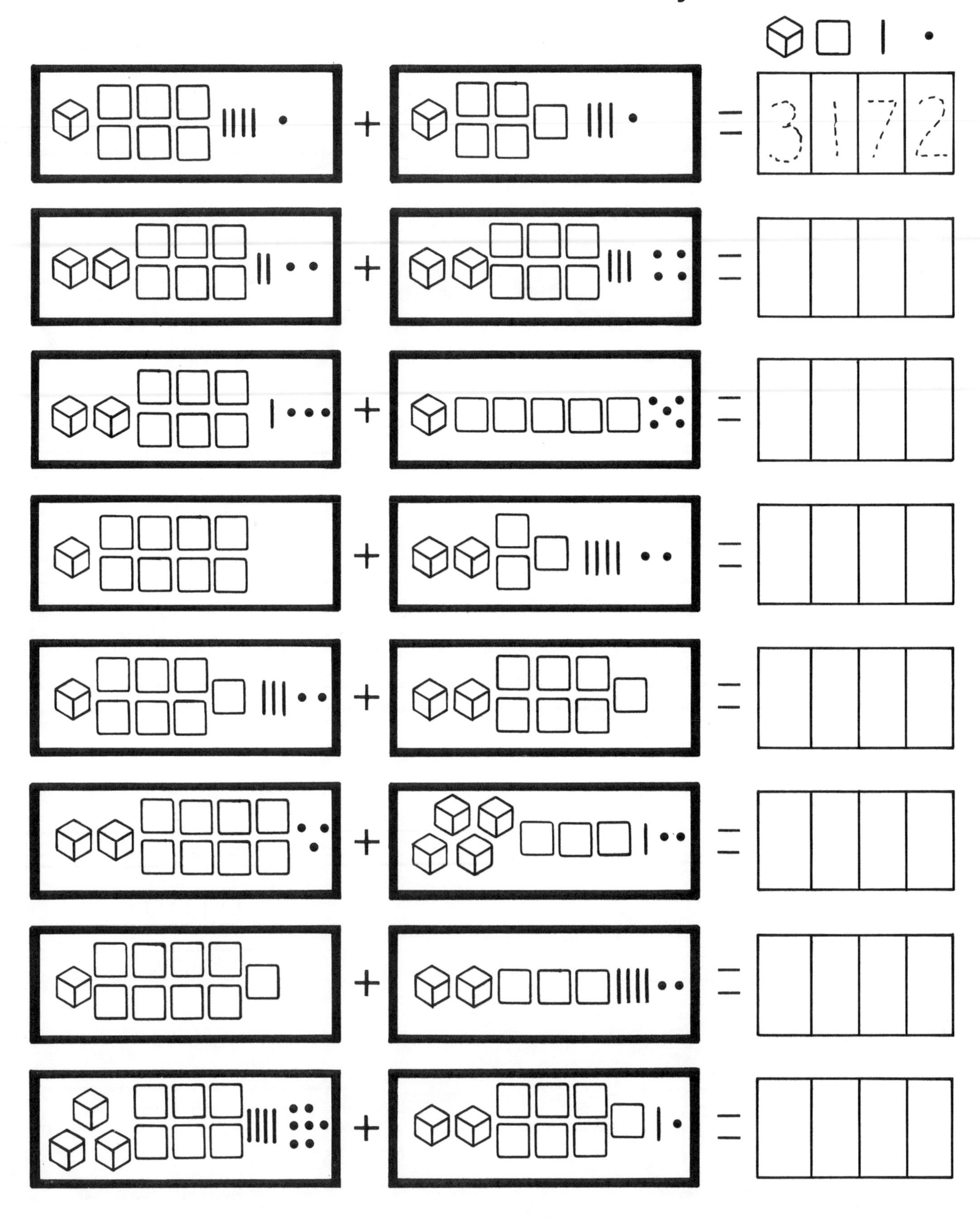

Add. Trade if necessary.

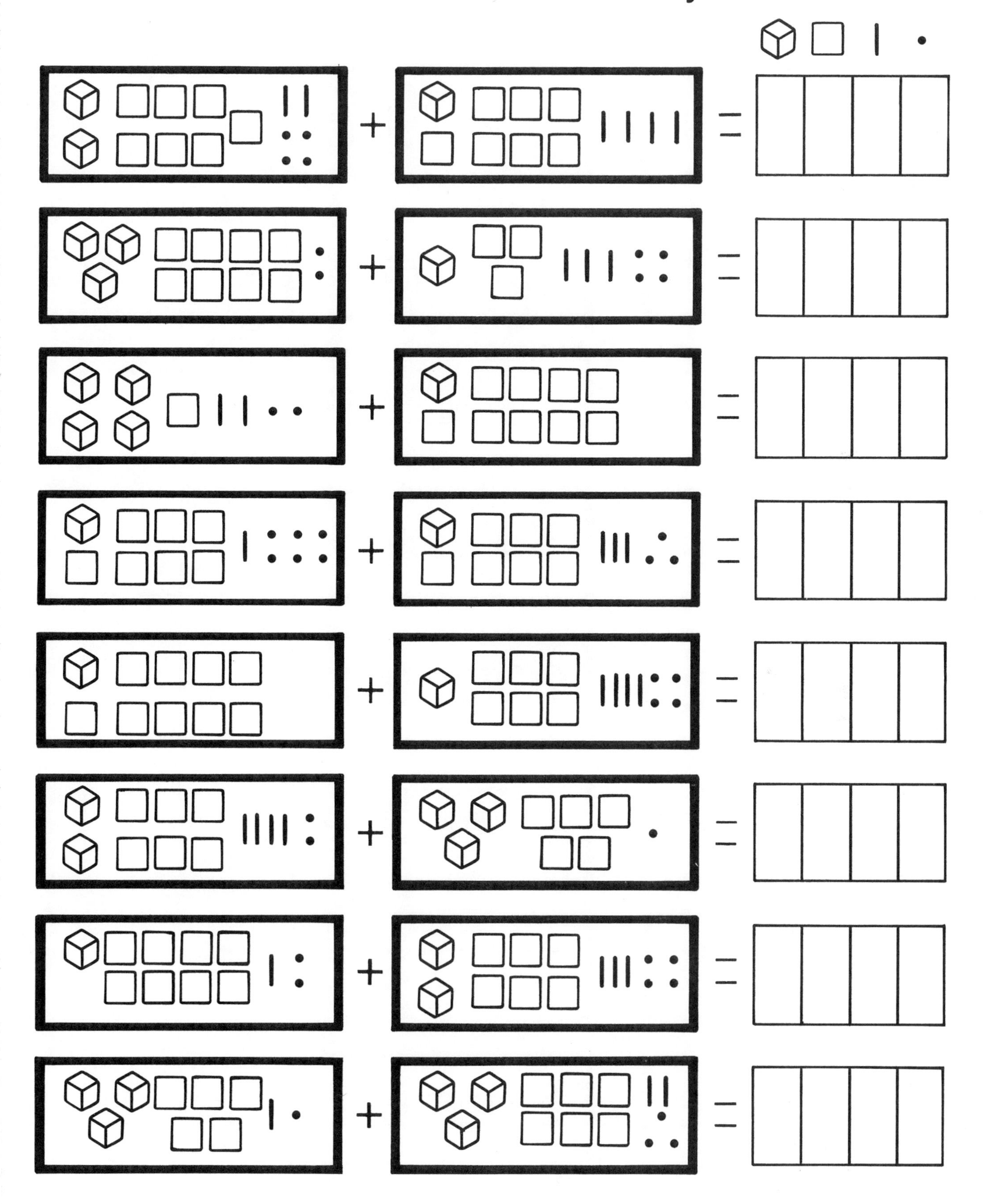

Add. Trade if necessary.

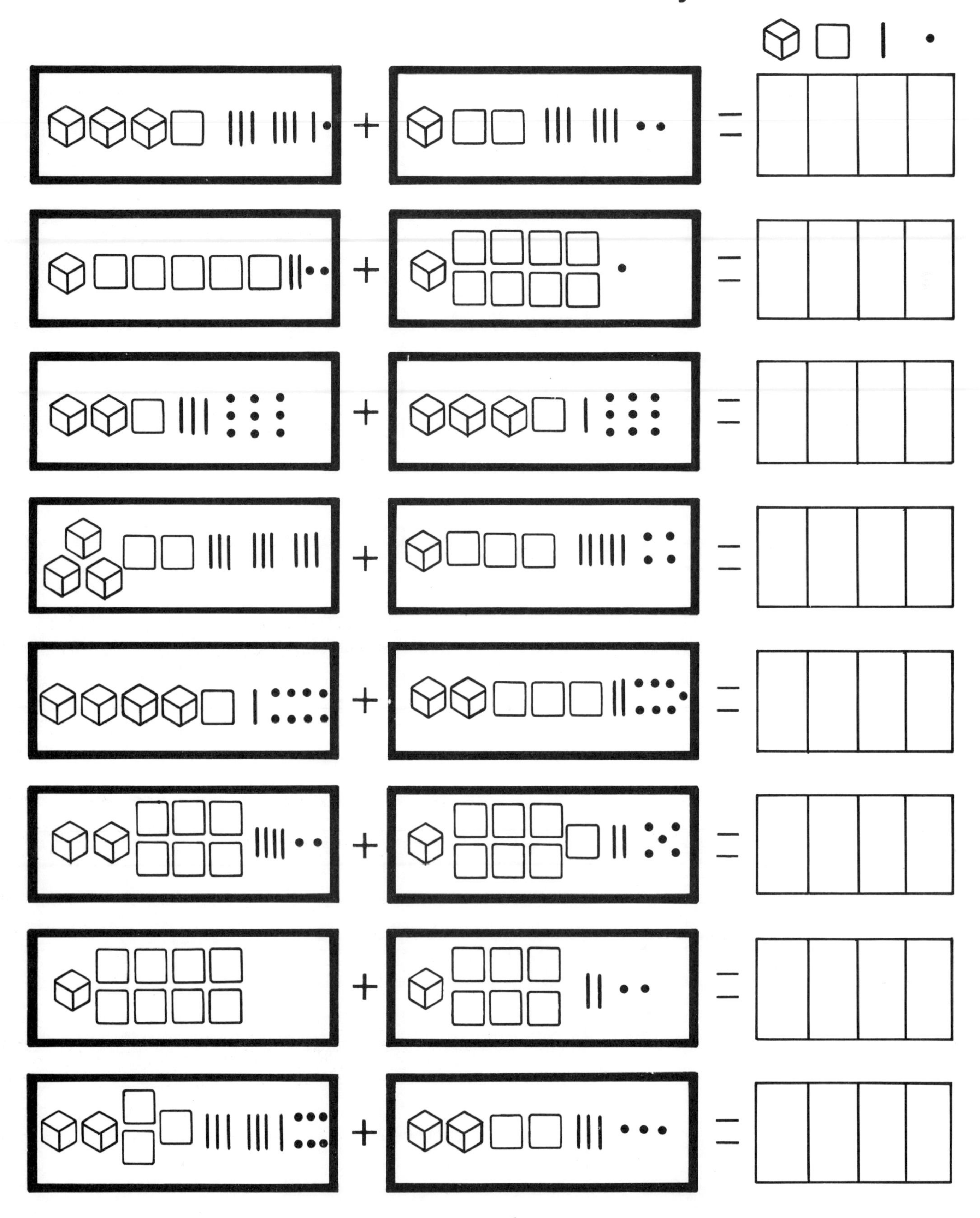

Add. Trade if necessary.

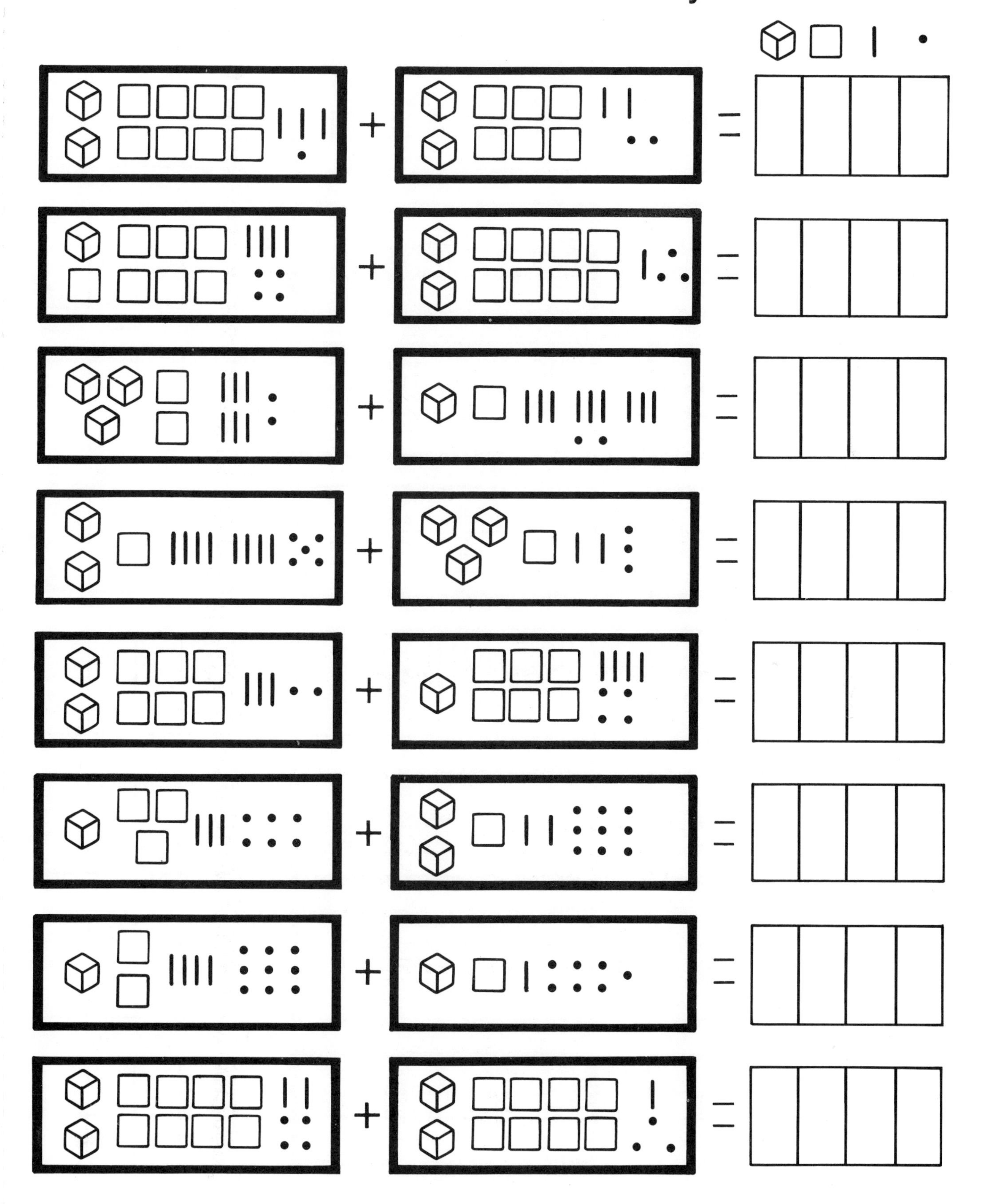

Add. Trade if necessary.

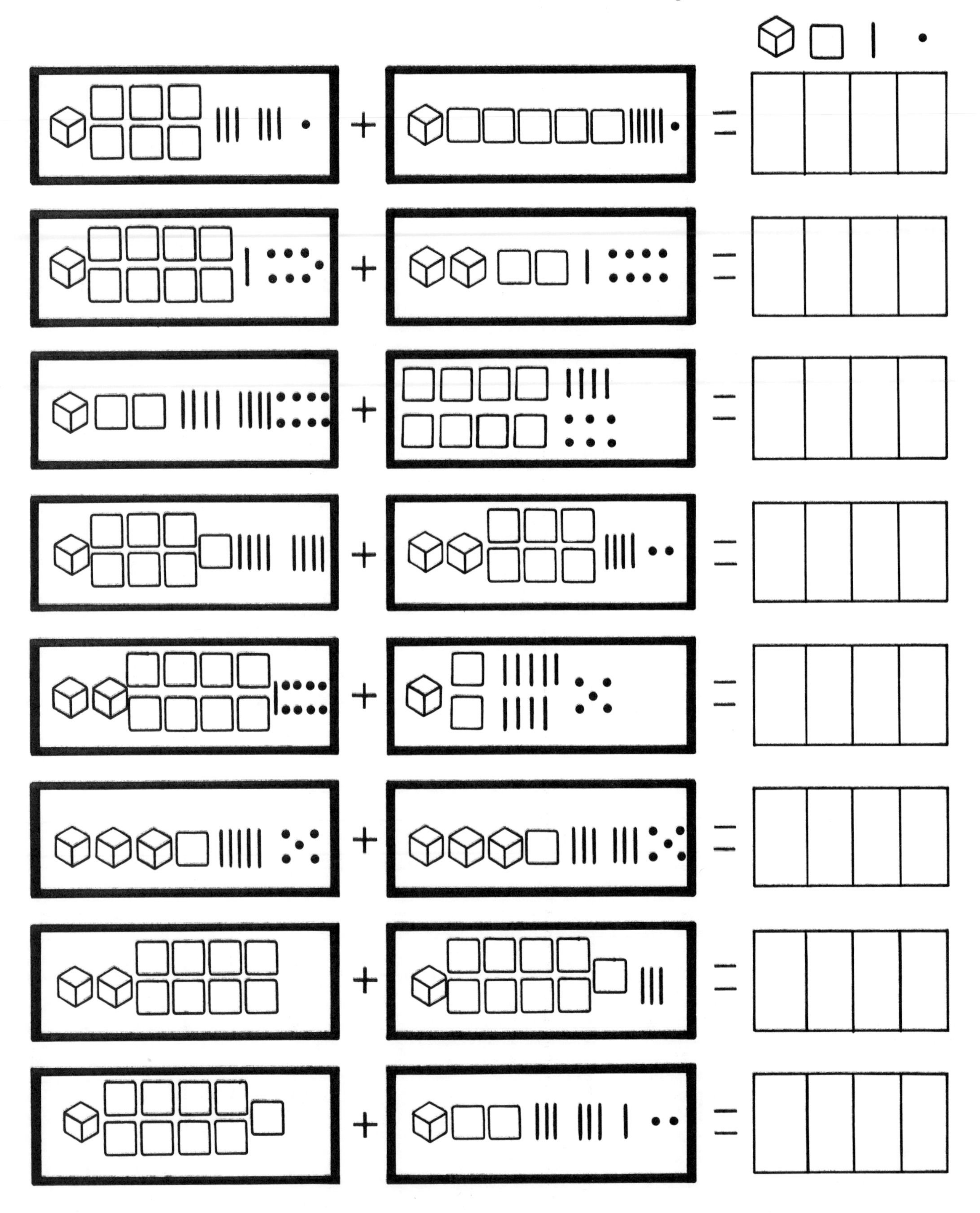

Combine and record.

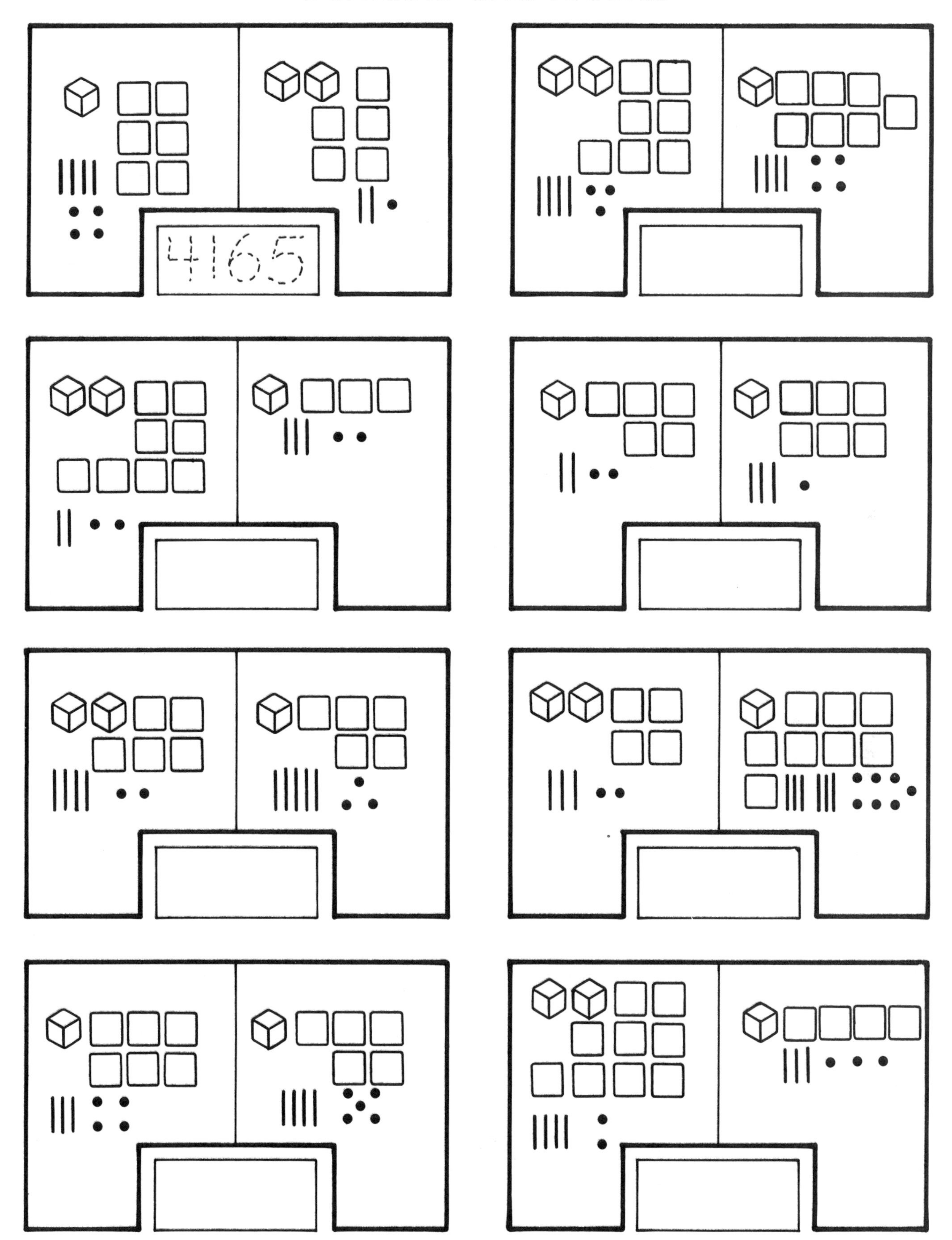

Combine and record.

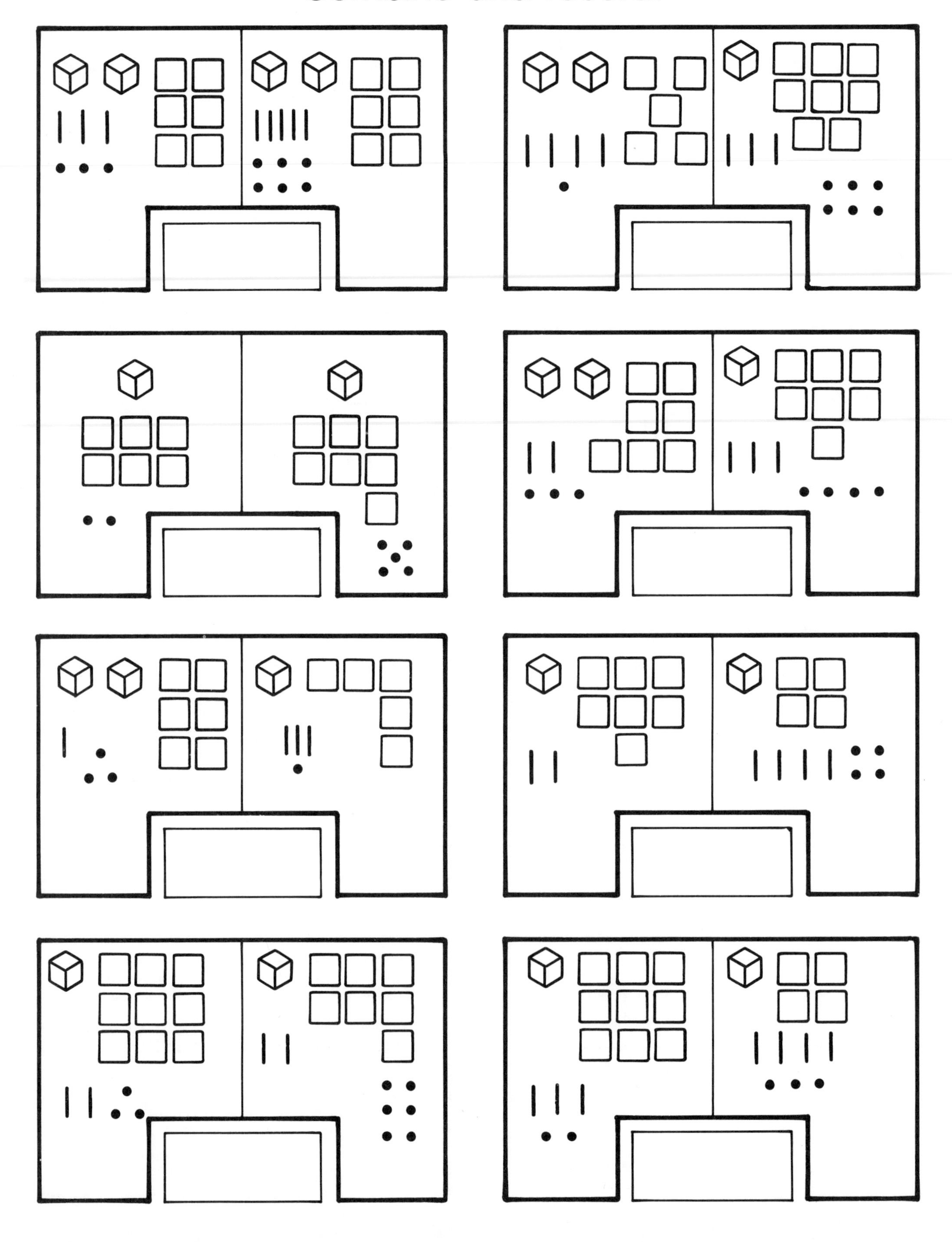

Combine and record.

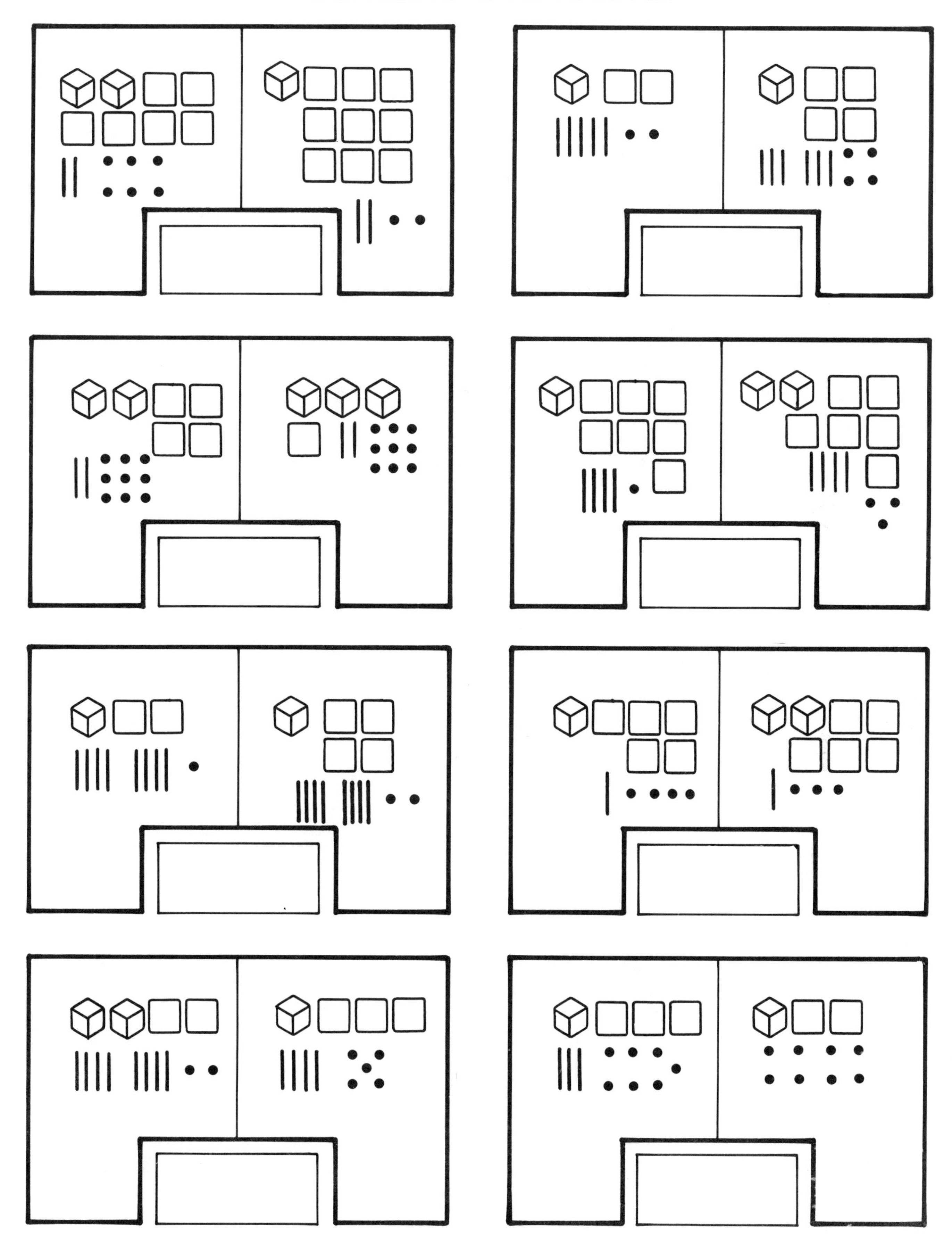

Combine and record.

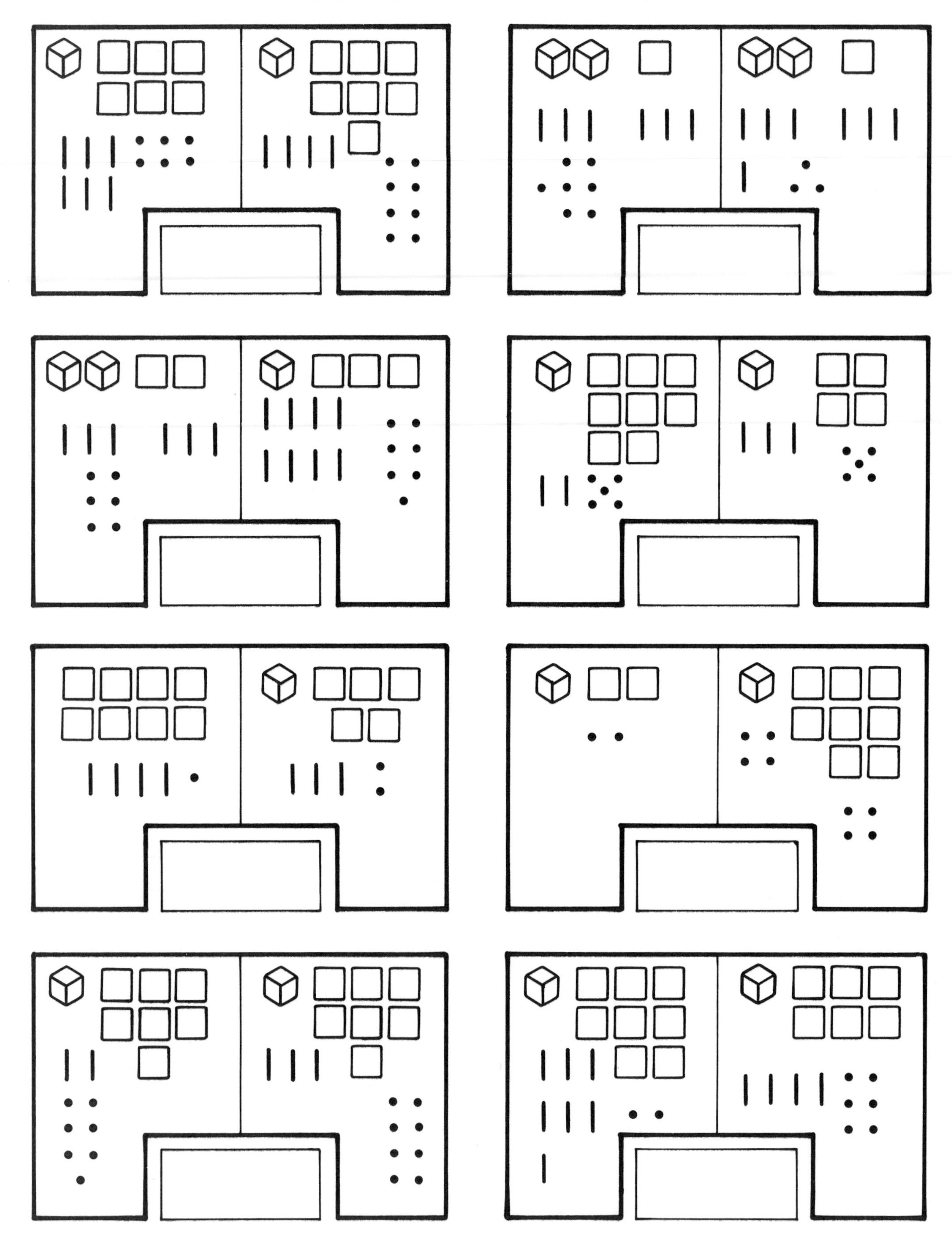

Combine and record.

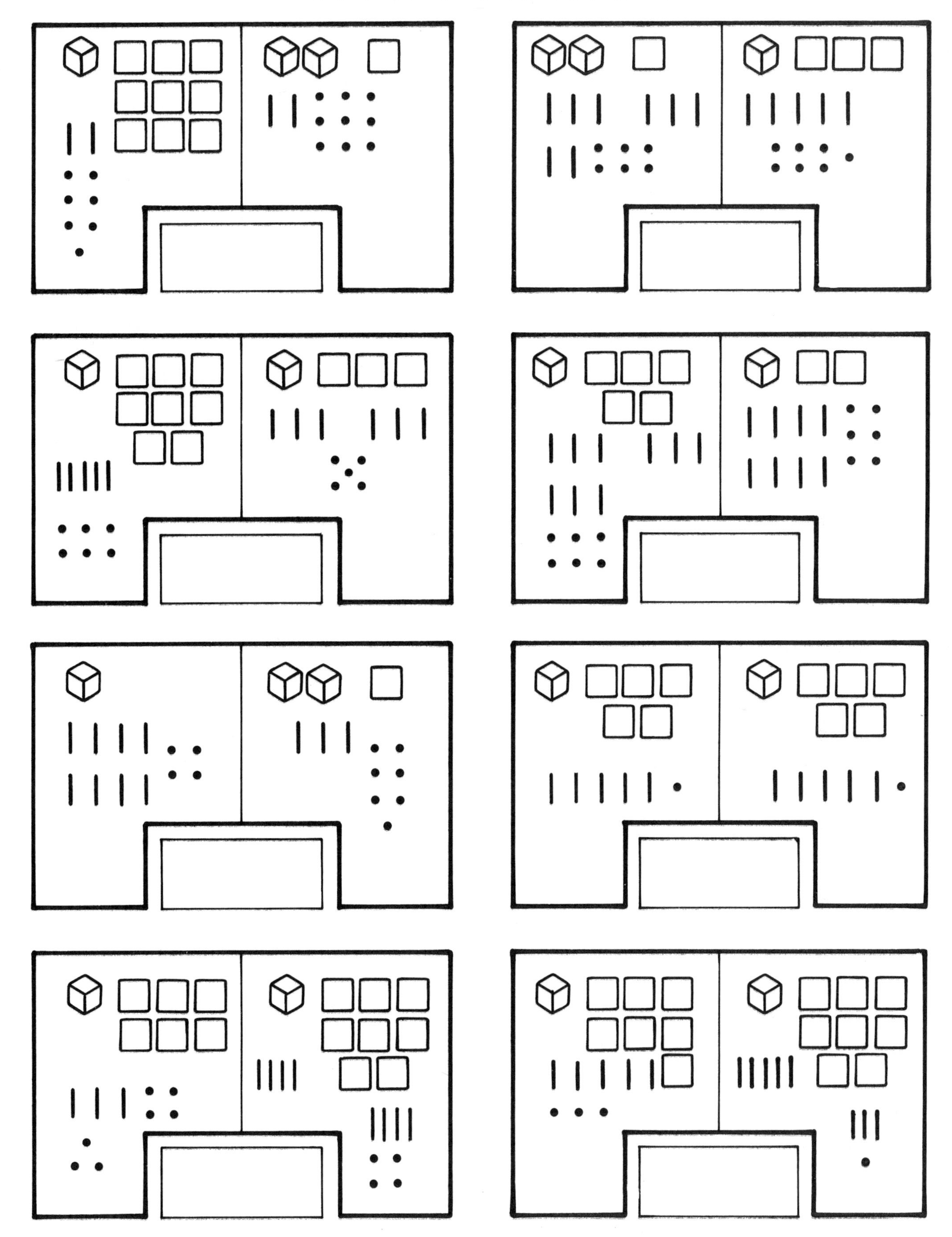

Color the ones, tens, hundreds, and thousands. Add.

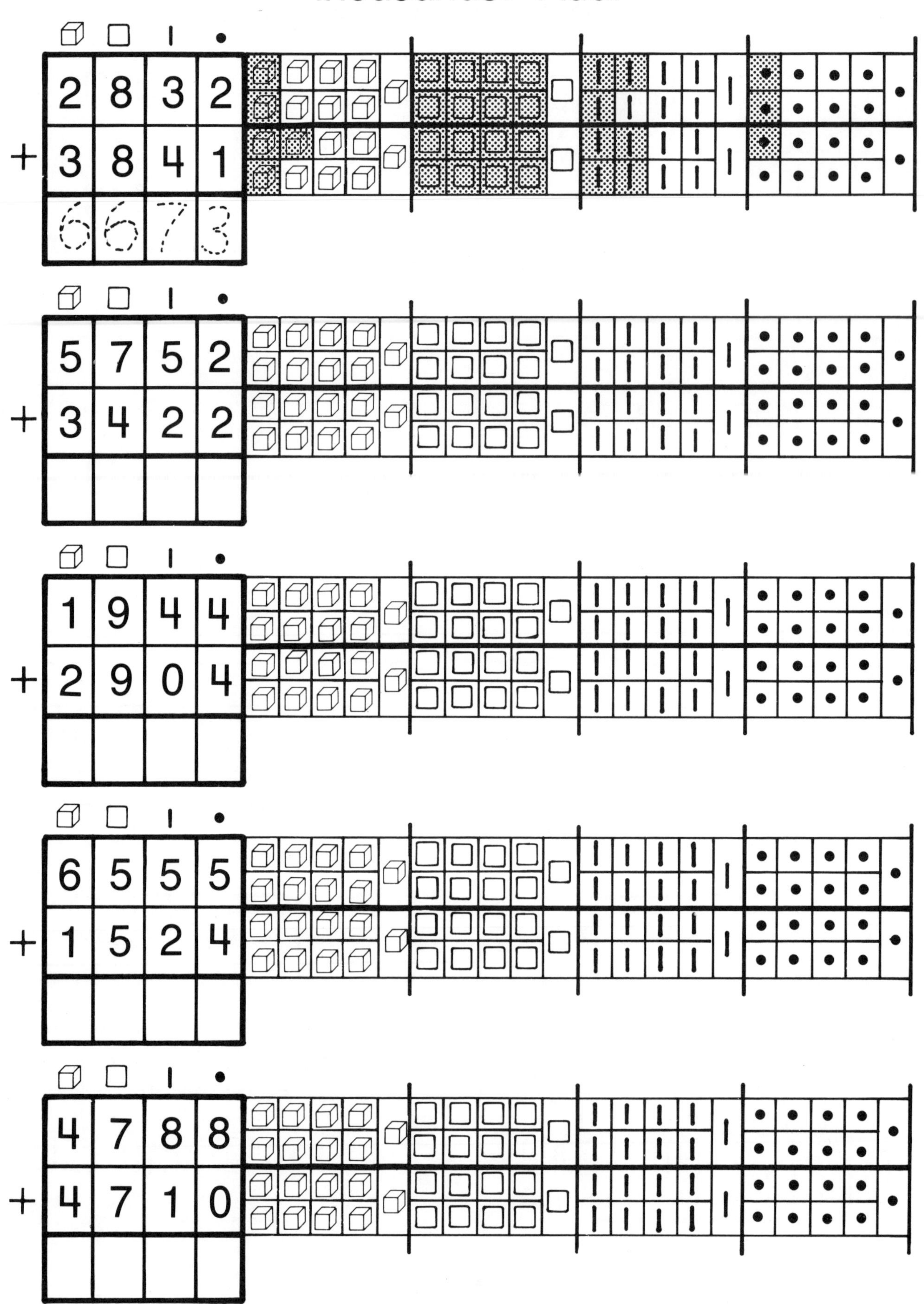

2 8 3 2
+ 3 8 4 1
6 6 7 3
5 7 5 2
+ 3 4 2 2
1 9 4 4
+ 2 9 0 4
6 5 5 5
+ 1 5 2 4
4 7 8 8
+ 4 7 1 0

Color the ones, tens, hundreds, and thousands. Add.

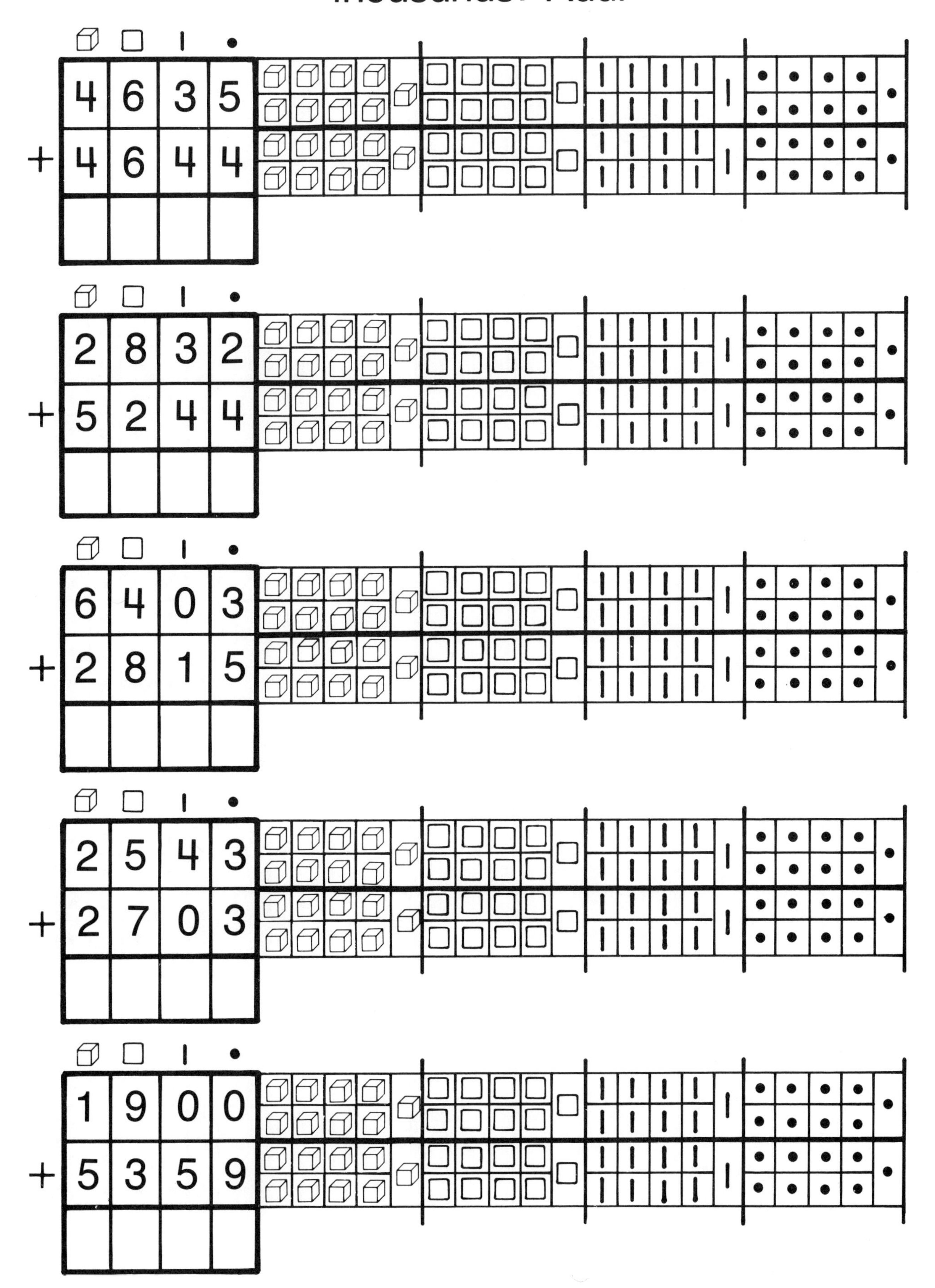

Color the ones, tens, hundreds, and thousands. Add.

H or T or O

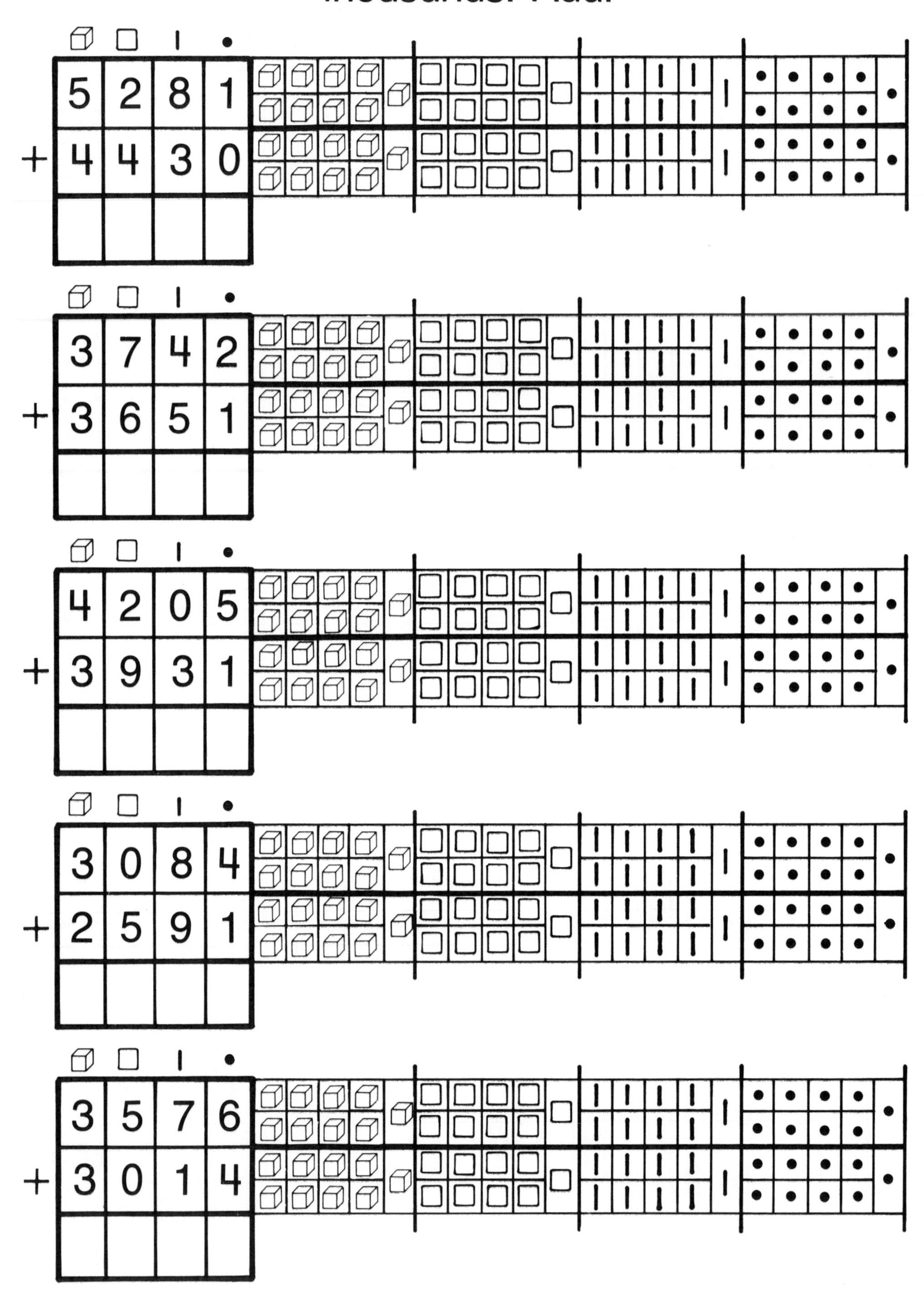

Color the ones, tens, hundreds, and thousands. Add.

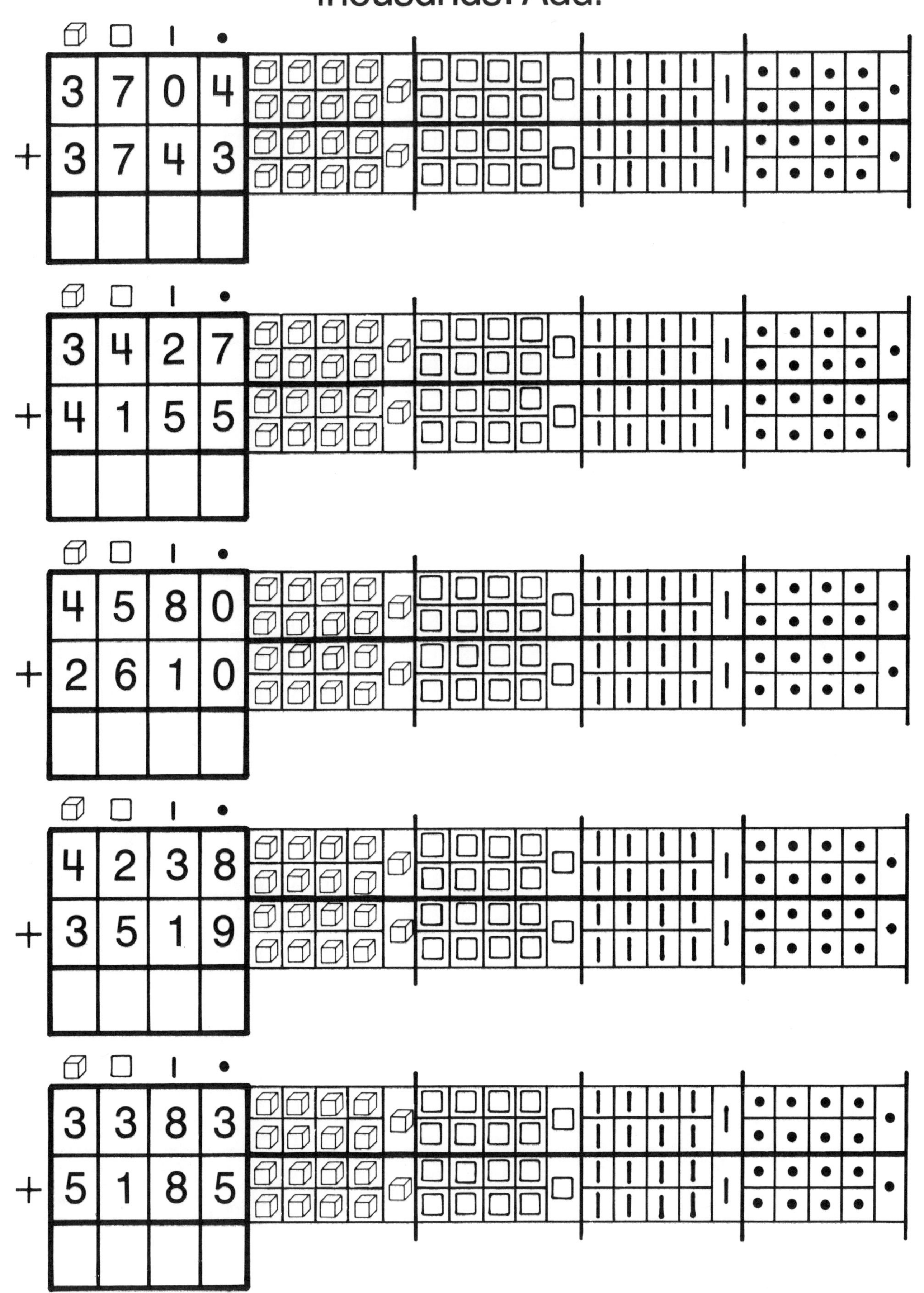

Color the ones, tens, hundreds, and thousands. Add.

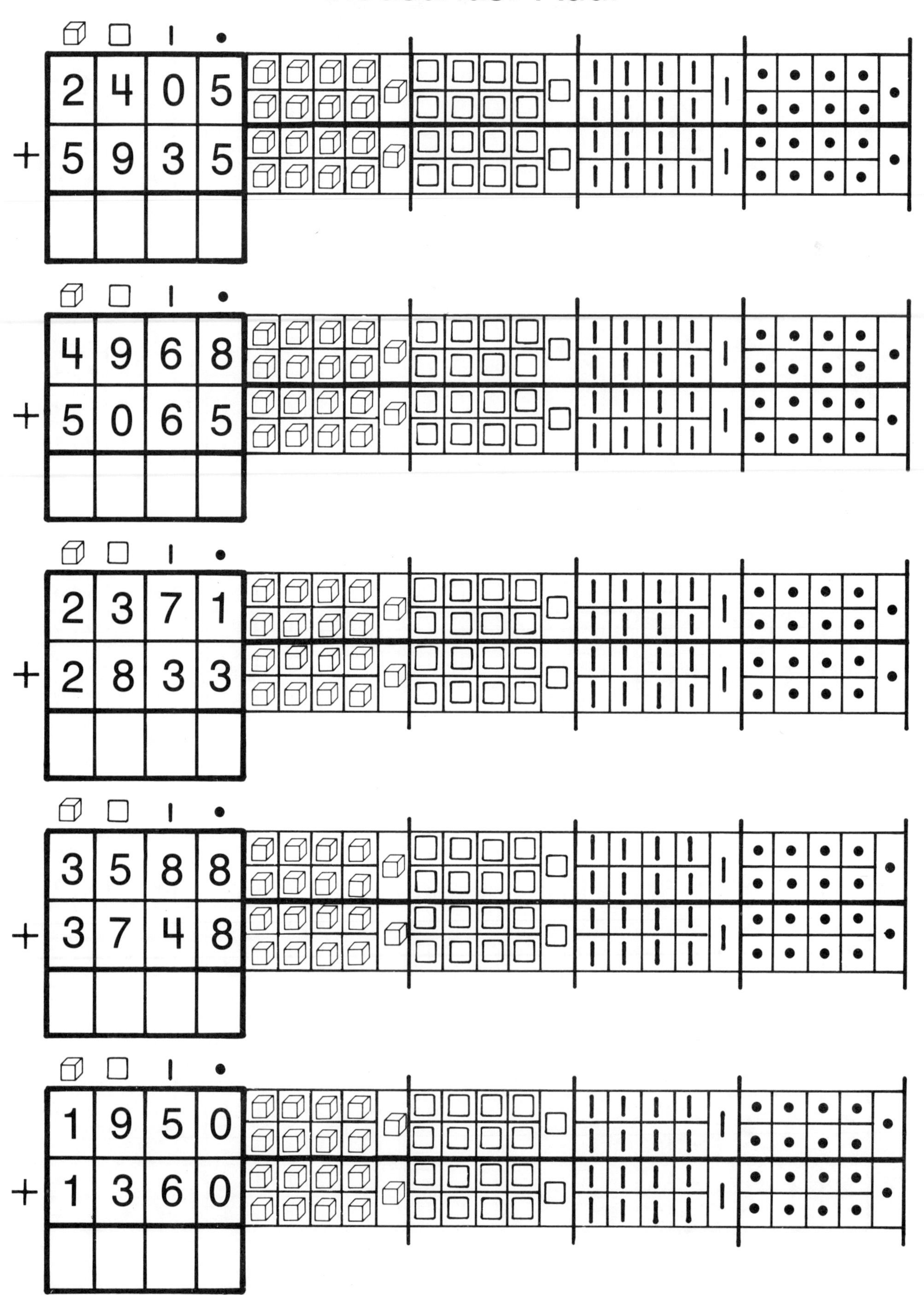

Combine and record.

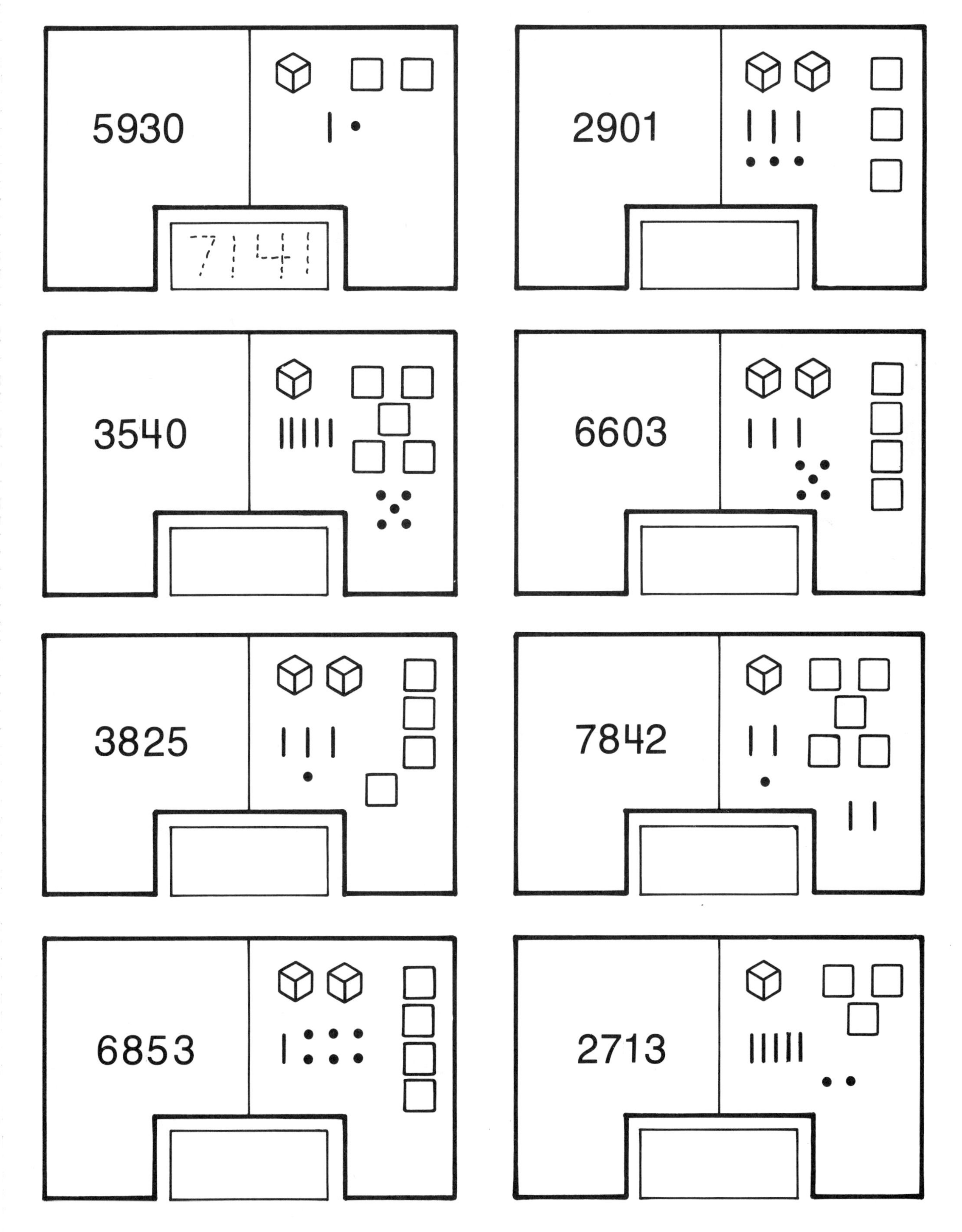

Combine and record.

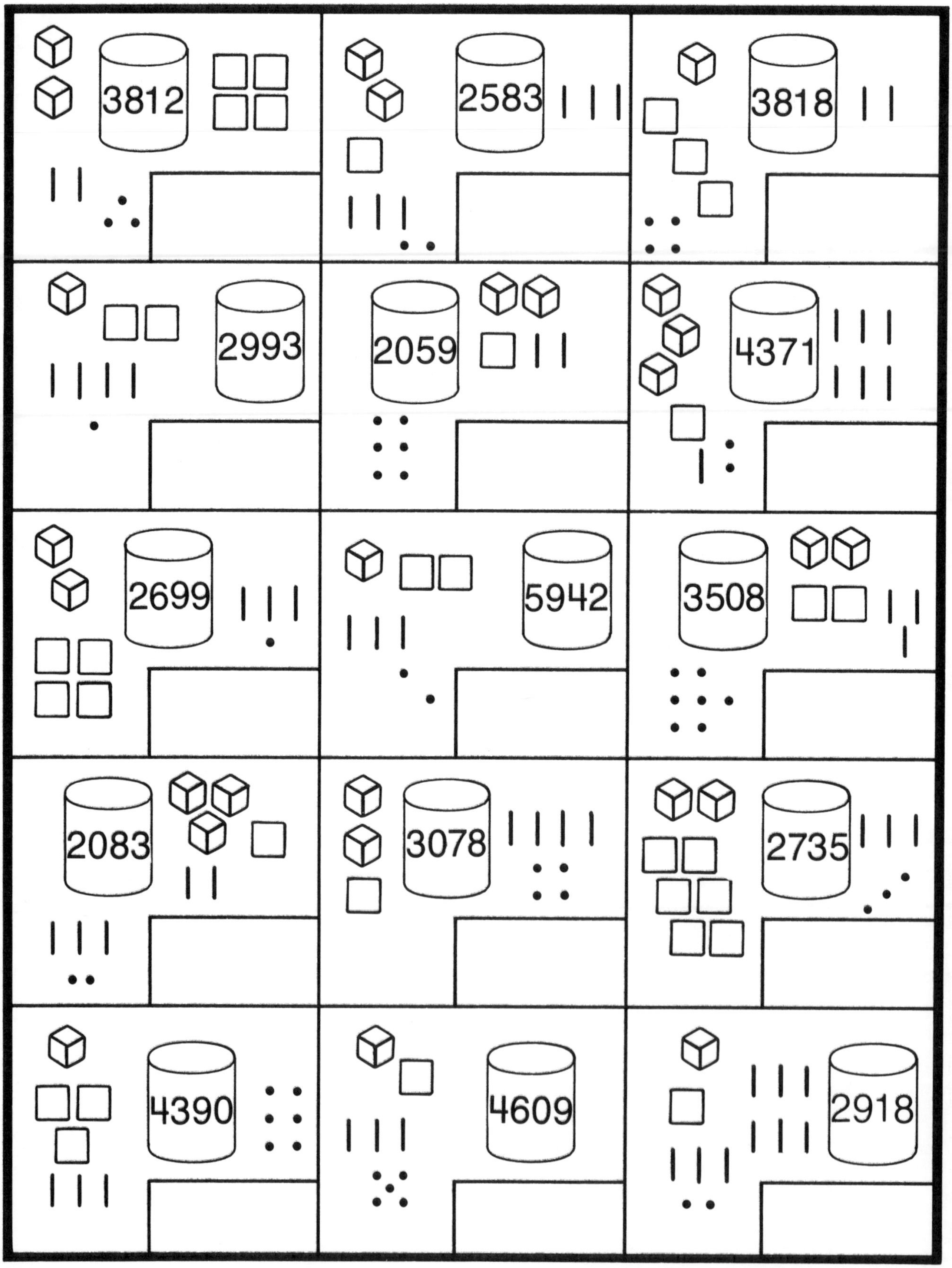

3812	2583	3818
2993	2059	4371
2699	5942	3508
2083	3078	2735
4390	4609	2918

Combine and record. Trade if necessary.

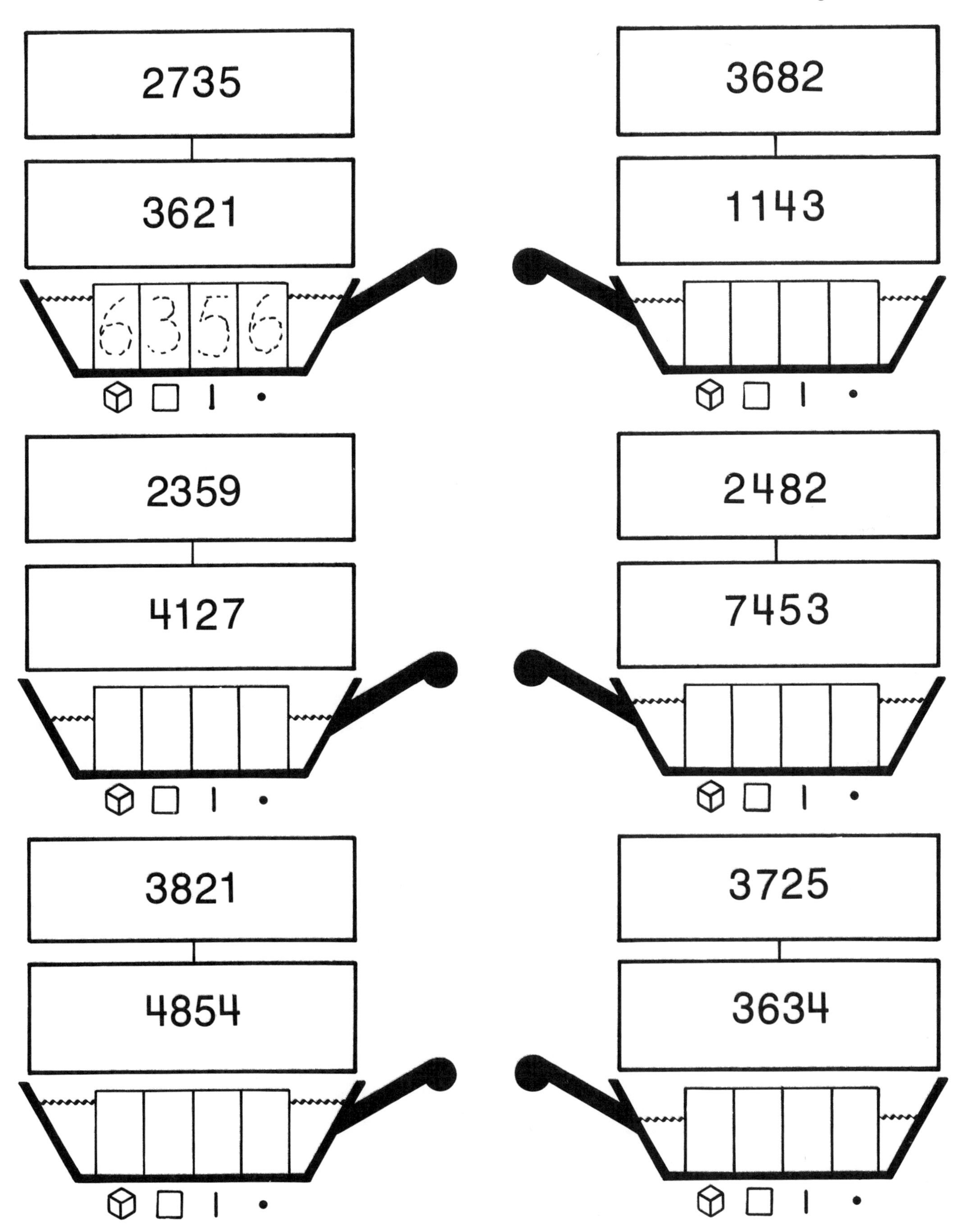

Write the numeral. Trade if necessary.

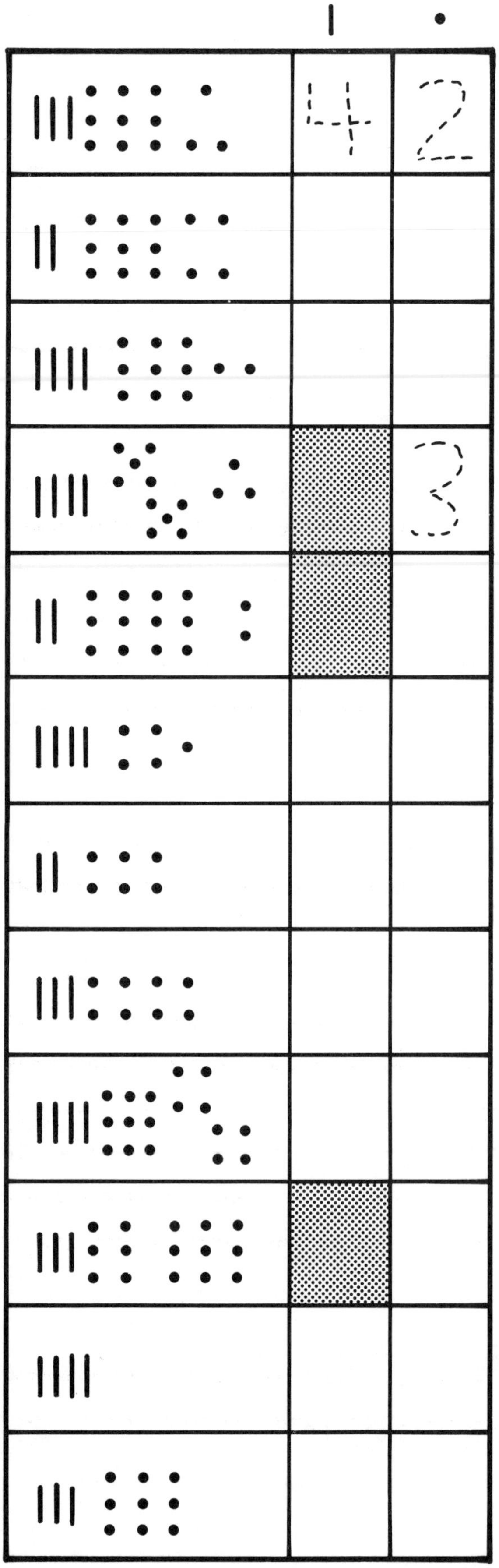

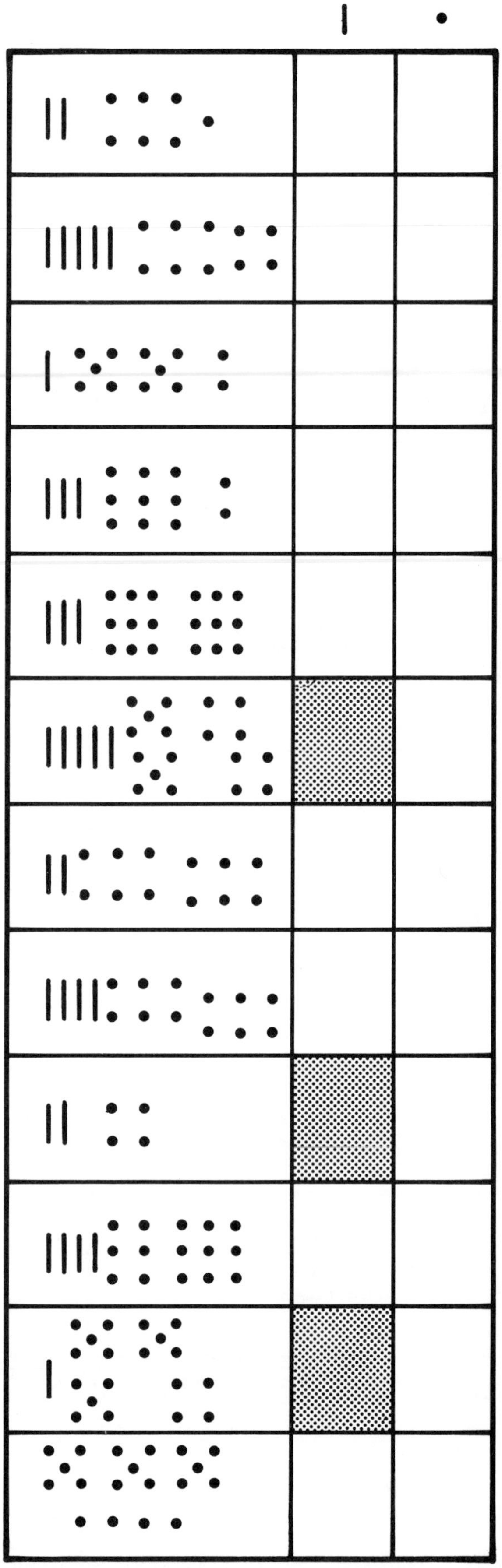

	I	•
III	4	2
II		
IIII		
IIII		3
II		
IIII		
II		
III		
IIII		
III		
IIII		
III		

	I	•
II		
IIIII		
I		
III		
III		
IIIII		
II		
IIII		
II		
IIII		
I		

Write the numeral. Trade if necessary.

Combine and record. Trade if necessary.

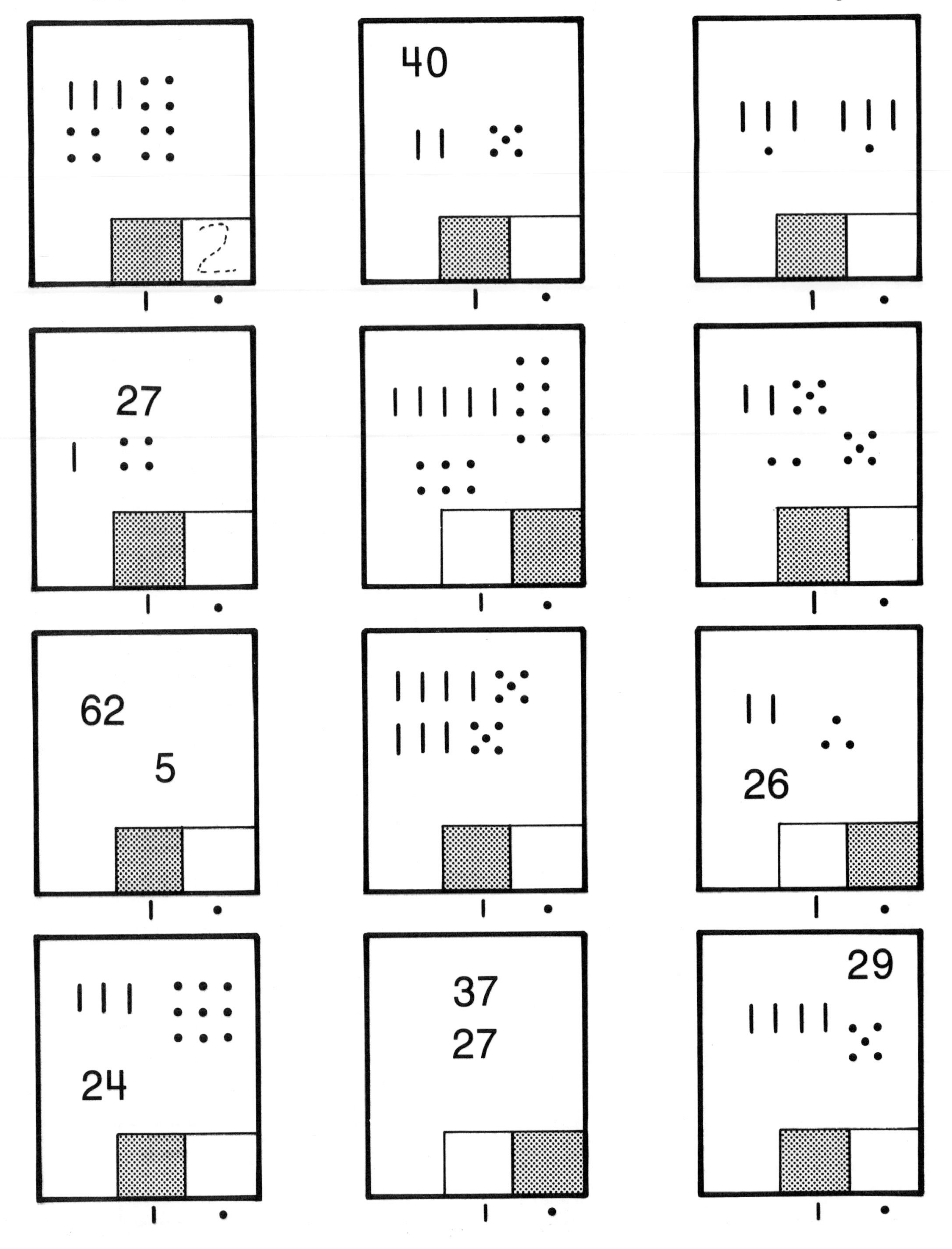

Add. Trade if necessary.

		•
	5	8
	2	3
		1

Add. Trade if necessary.

	|	•
	2	6
	3	6

	|	•
	3	4
	2	7

	|	•
	4	6
	2	9

	|	•
	4	1
	4	2

	|	•
	3	9
	4	7

	|	•
	3	5
	5	8

	|	•
	1	7
	2	1

	|	•
	5	7
	2	8

Add. Trade if necessary.

	I	•
	3	9
	3	4

	I	•
	3	6
	2	8

	I	•
	5	5
	2	7

	I	•
	4	2
	3	3

	I	•
	4	5
	2	2

	I	•
	5	6
	2	5

	I	•
	2	8
	4	9

	I	•
	3	7
	4	7

Add. Trade if necessary.

	|	•		|	•		|	•		|	•
	4	5		5	8		1	6		2	3
+	4	6	+	2	8	+	2	5	+	4	8

	|	•		|	•		|	•		|	•
	3	8		4	1		2	7		3	9
+	2	7	+	2	9	+	3	6	+	3	9

	|	•		|	•		|	•		|	•
	2	3		1	8		3	5		5	6
+	2	9	+	7	5	+	3	1	+	1	6

	|	•		|	•		|	•		|	•
	1	2		6	9		4	7		5	7
+	8	9	+	2	3	+	5	4	+	1	7

Add. Trade if necessary.

	|	•
	4	6
+	3	6

	|	•
	3	7
+	5	2

	|	•
	4	9
+	2	6

	|	•
	4	8
+	2	8

	|	•
	5	1
	1	5
+	2	8

	|	•
	2	7
	2	7
+	4	3

	|	•
	3	9
	3	4
+	2	2

	|	•
	5	1
	2	1
+	1	7

	|	•
	2	1
	4	9
+	1	0

	|	•
	1	5
	1	5
+	3	5

	|	•
	2	3
	2	6
+	2	9

	|	•
	1	3
	2	8
+	2	2

Combine and record. Trade if necessary.

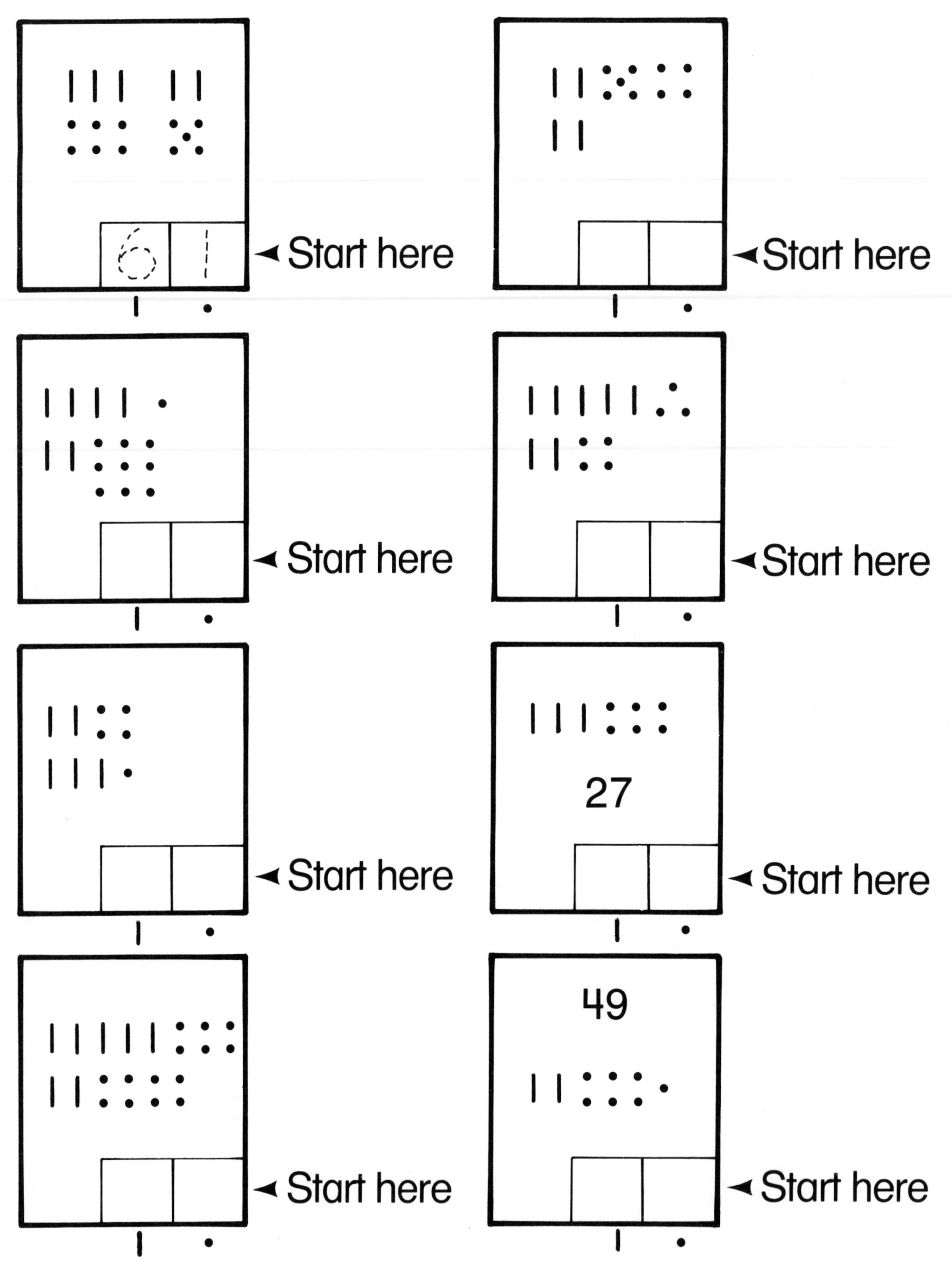

Combine and record. Trade if necessary.

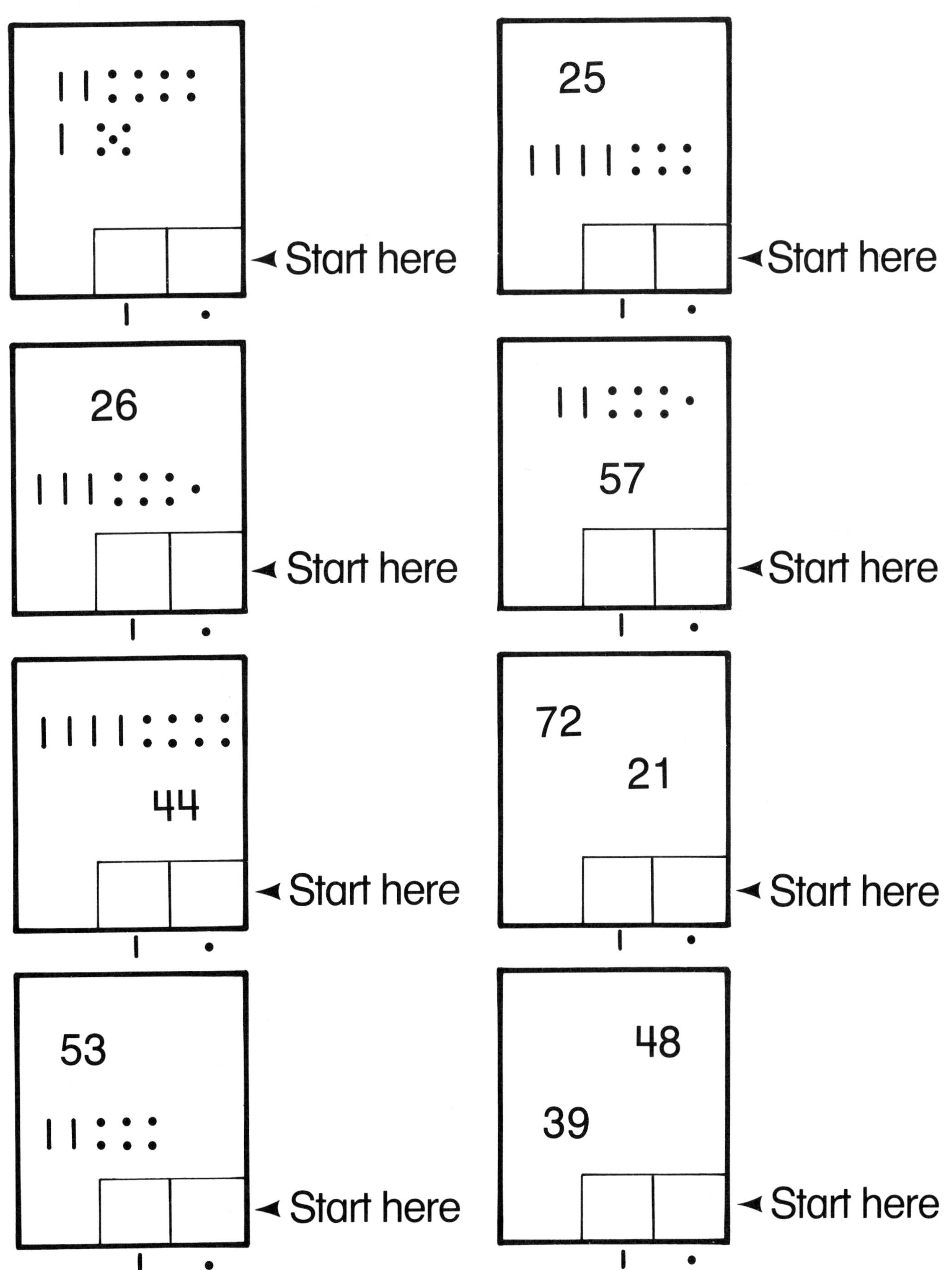

Combine and record. Trade if necessary.

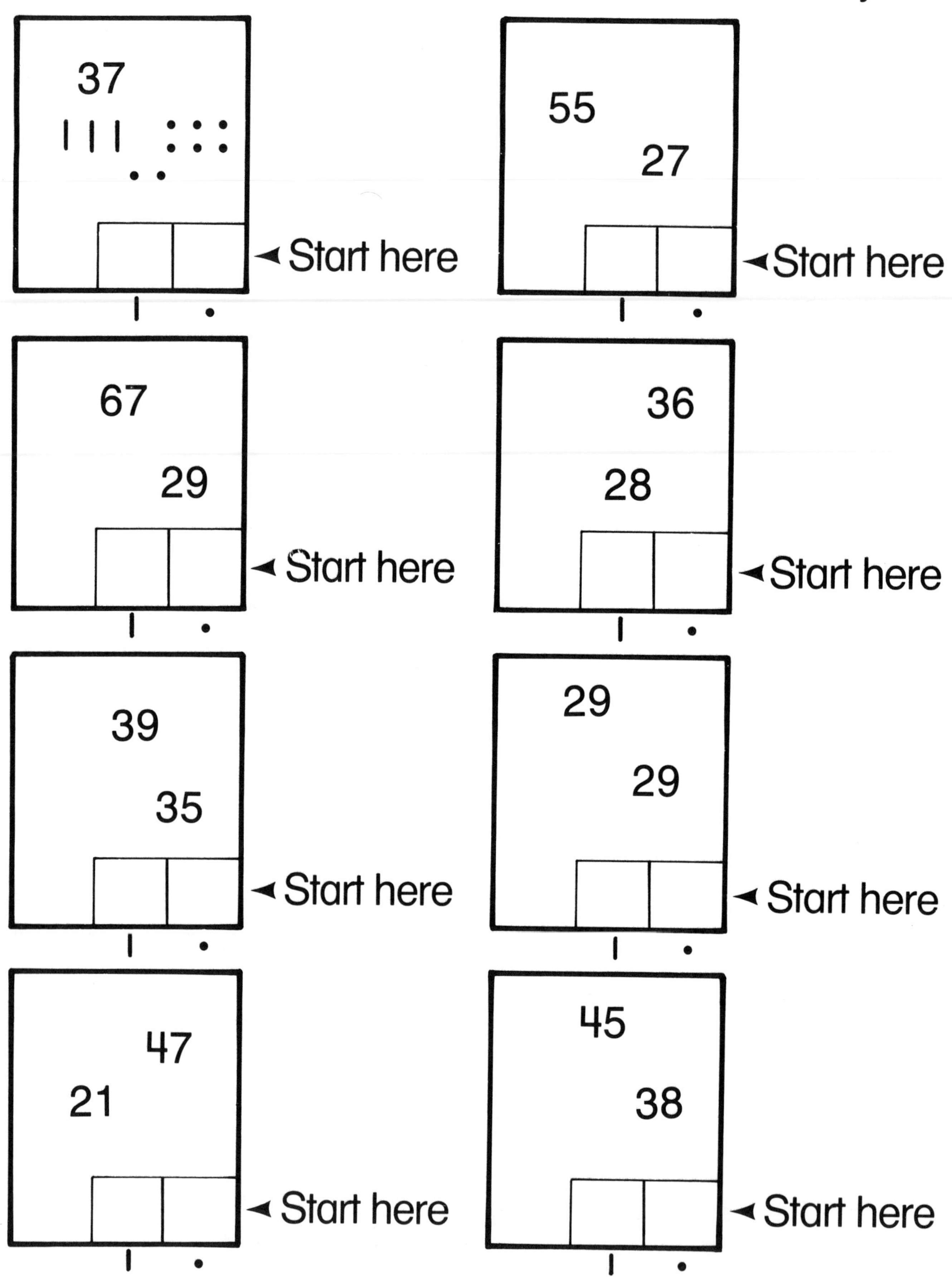

Add. Trade if necessary.

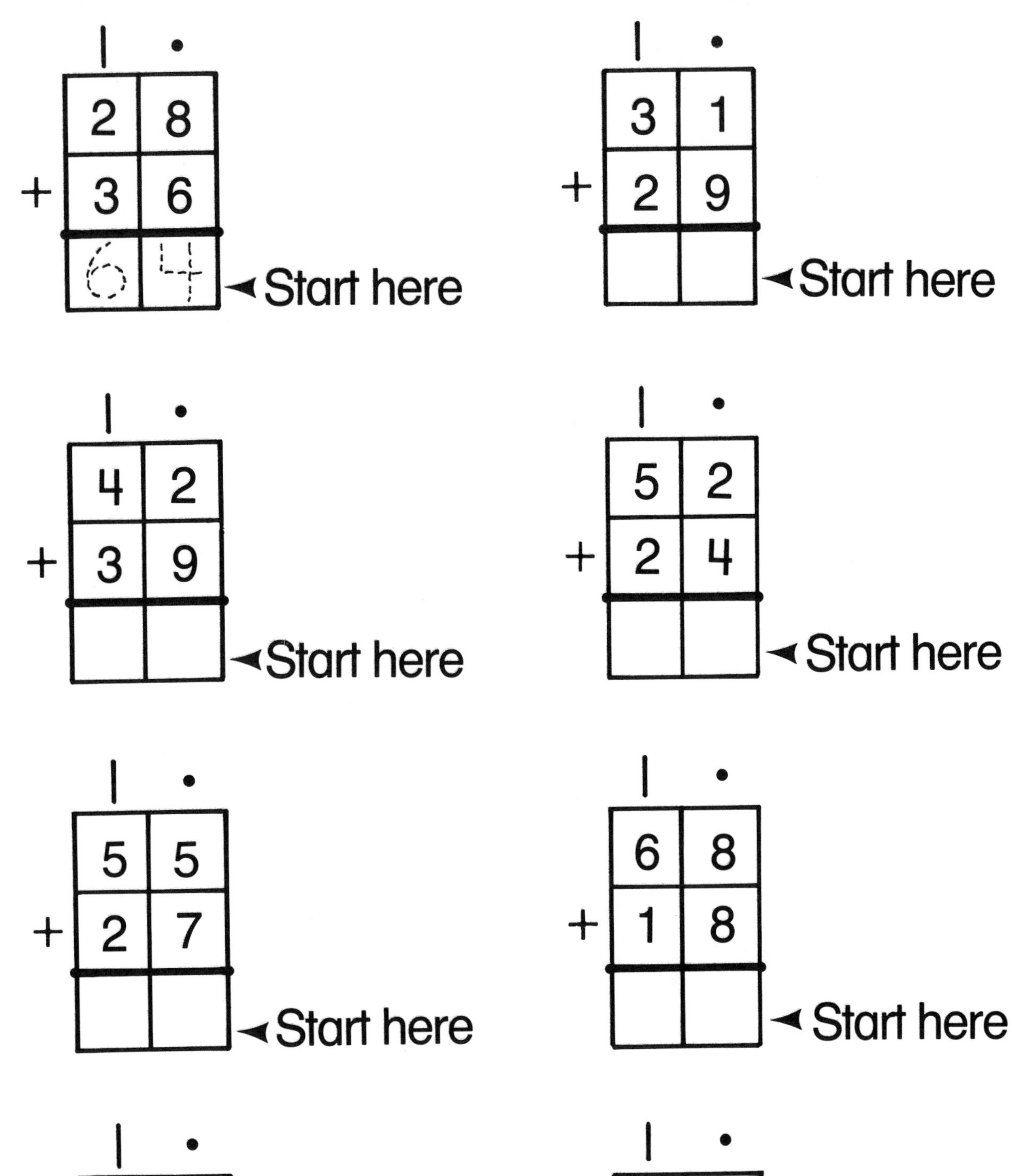

I	•	
	2	8	
+	3	6	
	6	4	◄ Start here

	I	•	
	3	1	
+	2	9	
			◄ Start here

	I	•	
	4	2	
+	3	9	
			◄ Start here

	I	•	
	5	2	
+	2	4	
			◄ Start here

	I	•	
	5	5	
+	2	7	
			◄ Start here

	I	•	
	6	8	
+	1	8	
			◄ Start here

	I	•	
	4	3	
+	2	5	
			◄ Start here

	I	•	
	3	5	
+	4	9	
			◄ Start here

Write the numeral. Trade if necessary.

Combine and record. Trade if necessary.

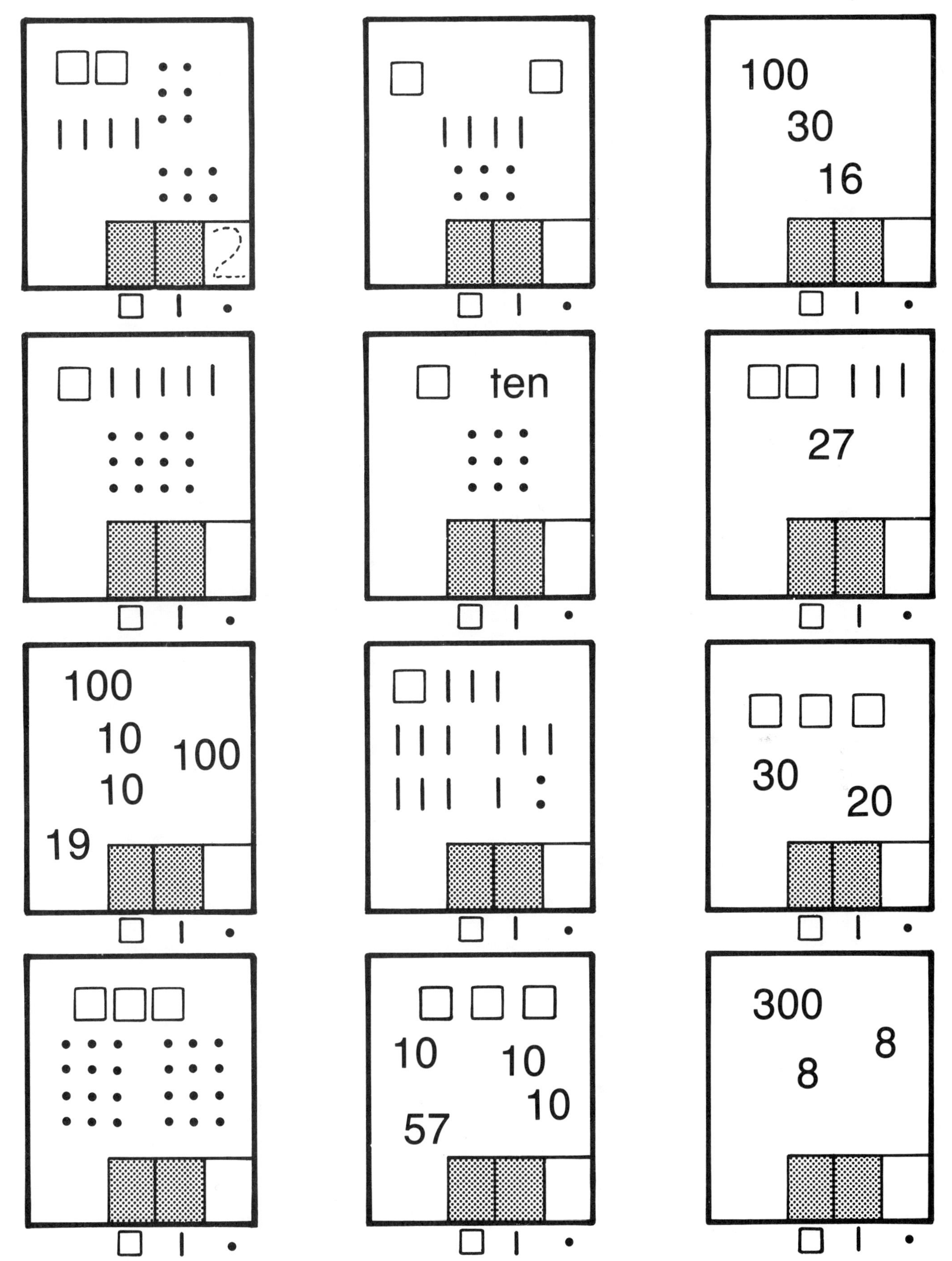

Combine and record. Trade if necessary.

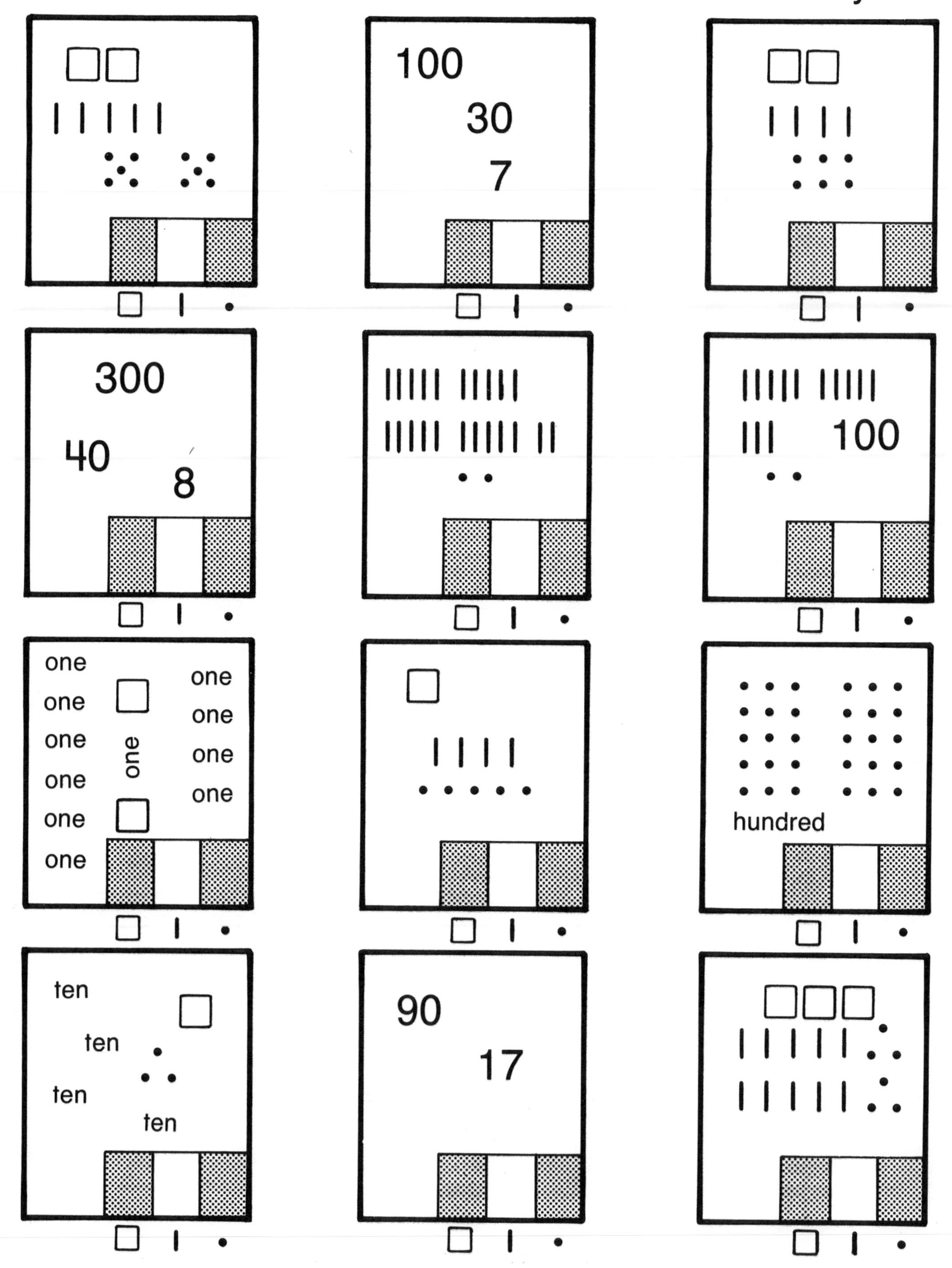

Combine and record. Trade if necessary.

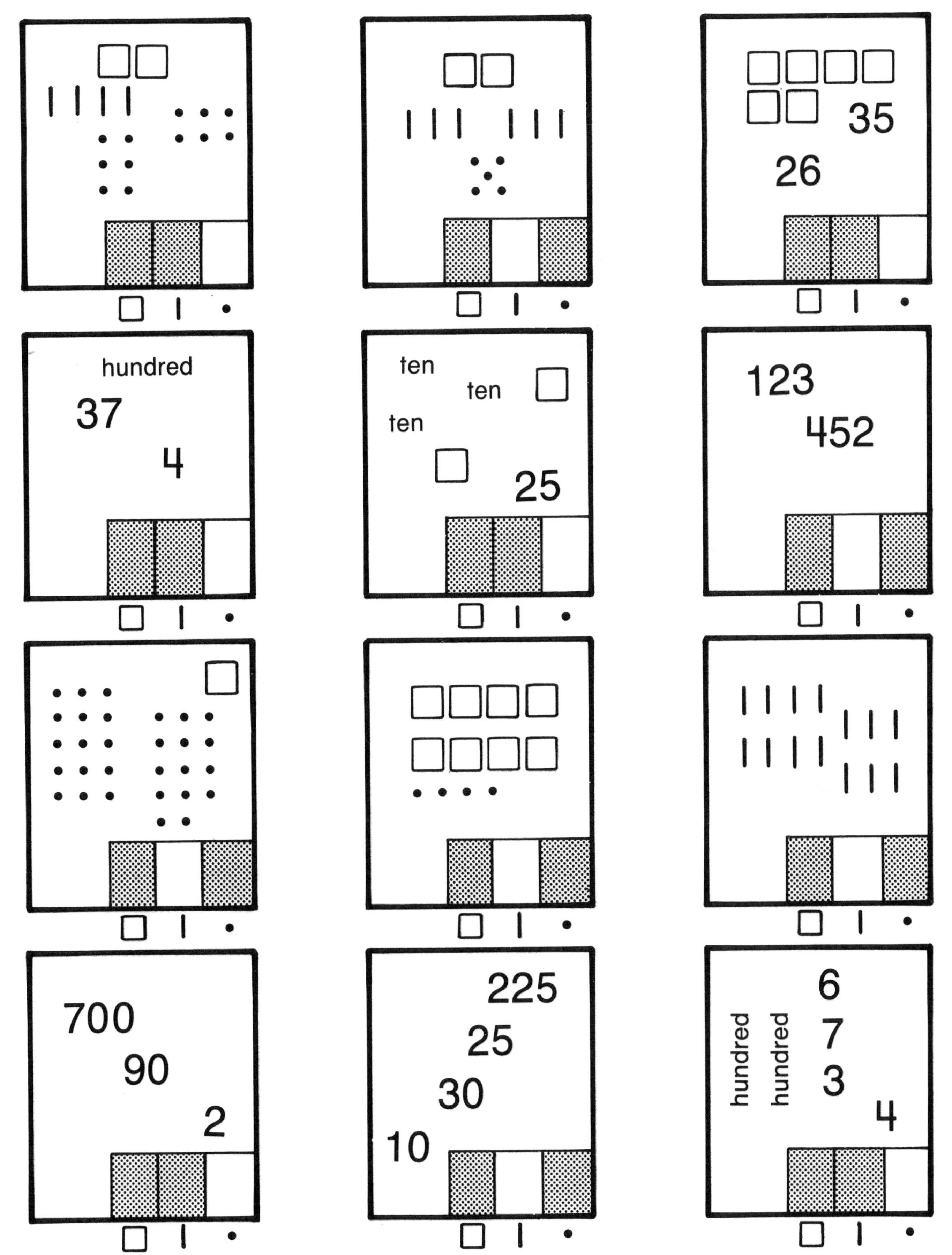

Add. Trade if necessary.

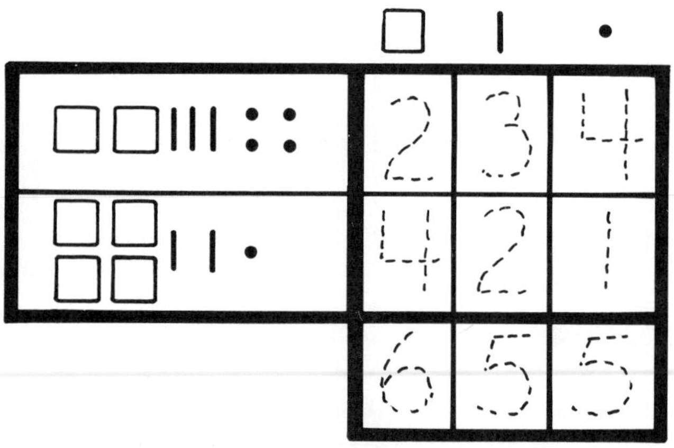

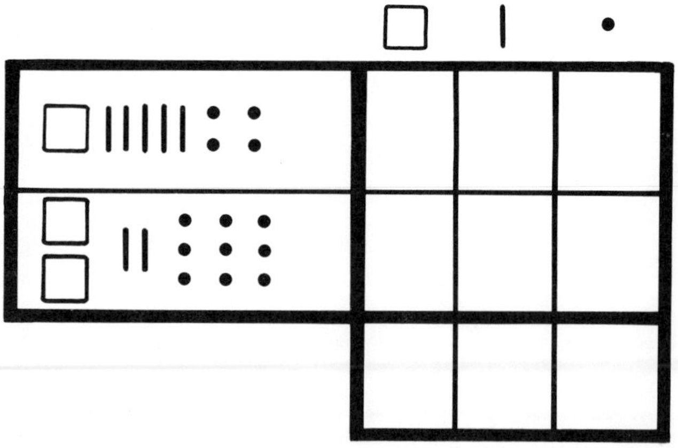

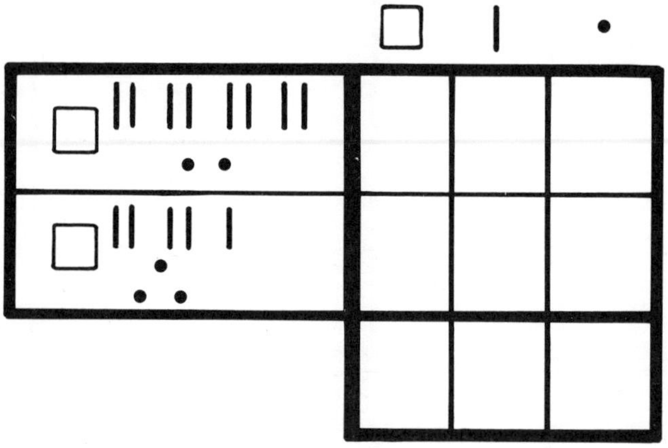

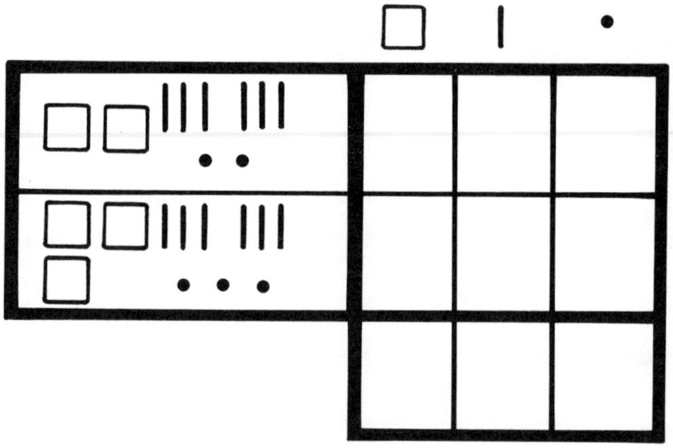

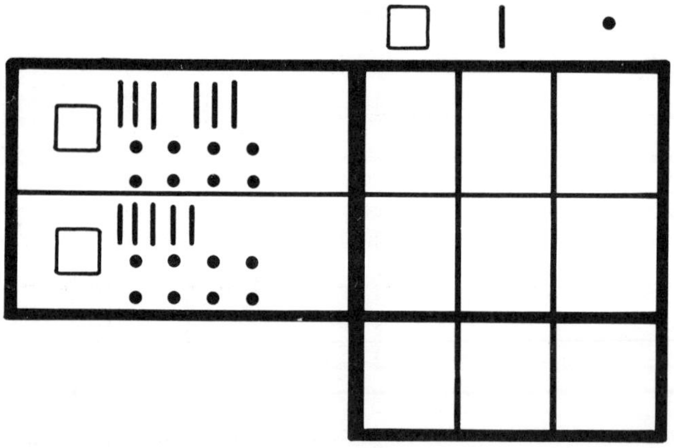

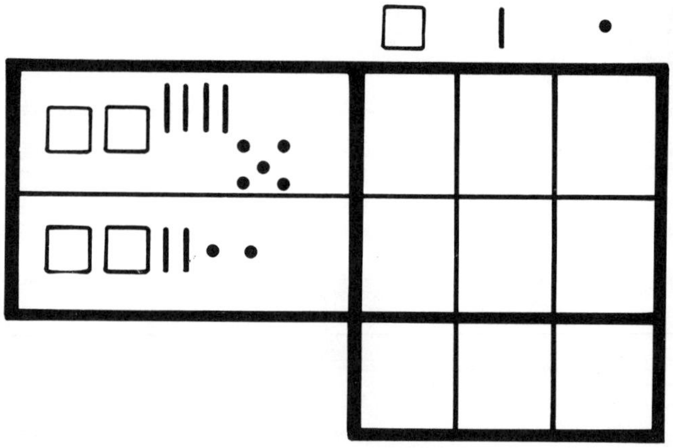

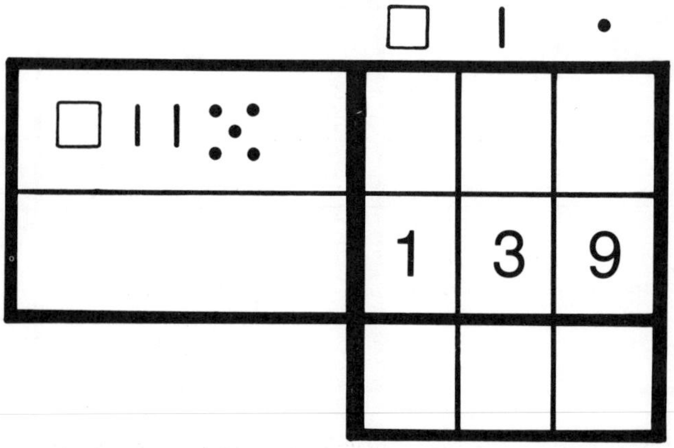

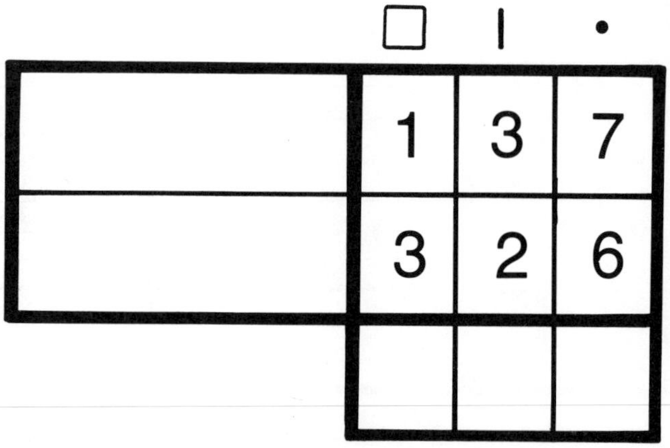

□	I	•
2	3	4
4	2	1
6	5	5

□	I	•
1	3	9

□	I	•
1	3	7
3	2	6

Add. Trade if necessary.

□	|	•
2	3	5
1	2	8

□	|	•
2	4	8
3	2	7

□	|	•
3	8	2
1	9	0

□	|	•
1	7	2
2	9	4

□	|	•
	6	4
3	1	9

□	|	•
3	5	9
	2	2

□	|	•
1	7	1
2	5	2

□	|	•
6	0	8
1	9	4

Add. Work from the right. Trade if necessary.

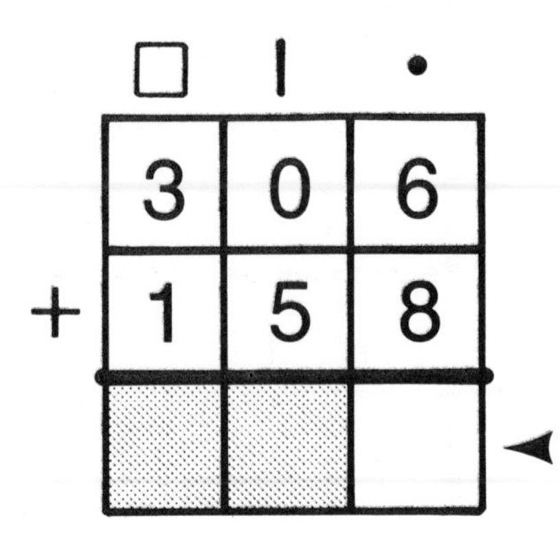

	□	I	•
	3	0	6
+	1	5	8

	□	I	•
	1	4	7
+	2	3	1

	□	I	•
	2	7	1
+	6	8	3

	□	I	•
	3	4	8
	1	9	0
+		6	3

	□	I	•
		5	1
	2	3	7
+	3	0	1

	□	I	•
	1	3	7
	2	3	4
+	2	1	7

	□	I	•
		4	2
	1	5	8
+	3	3	9

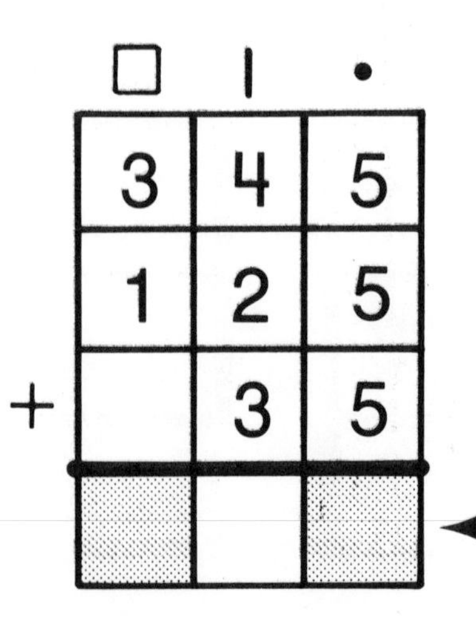

	□	I	•
	3	4	5
	1	2	5
+		3	5

	□	I	•
	1	4	7
	2	0	1
+		3	3

Combine and record. Trade if necessary.

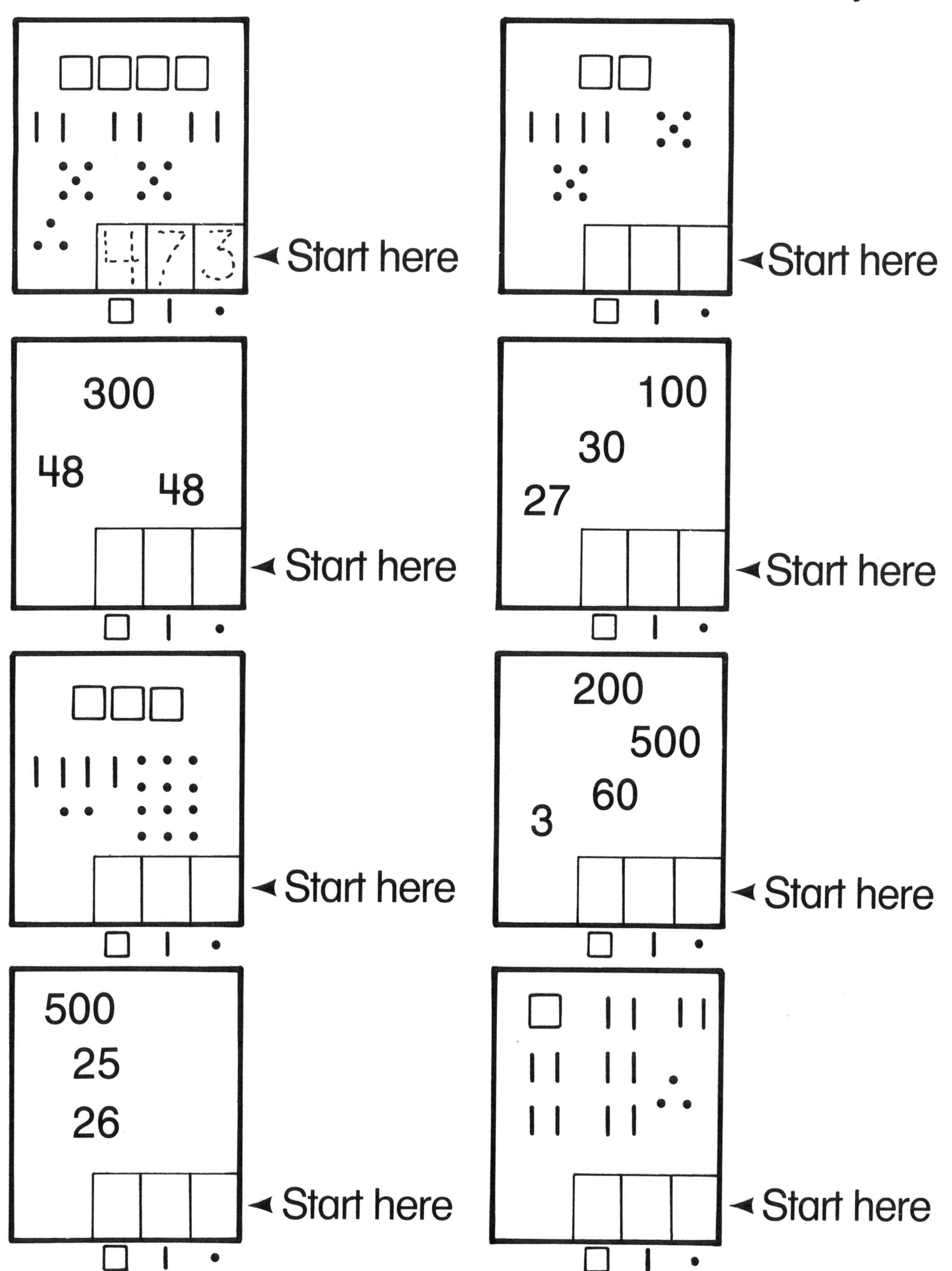

Combine and record. Trade if necessary.

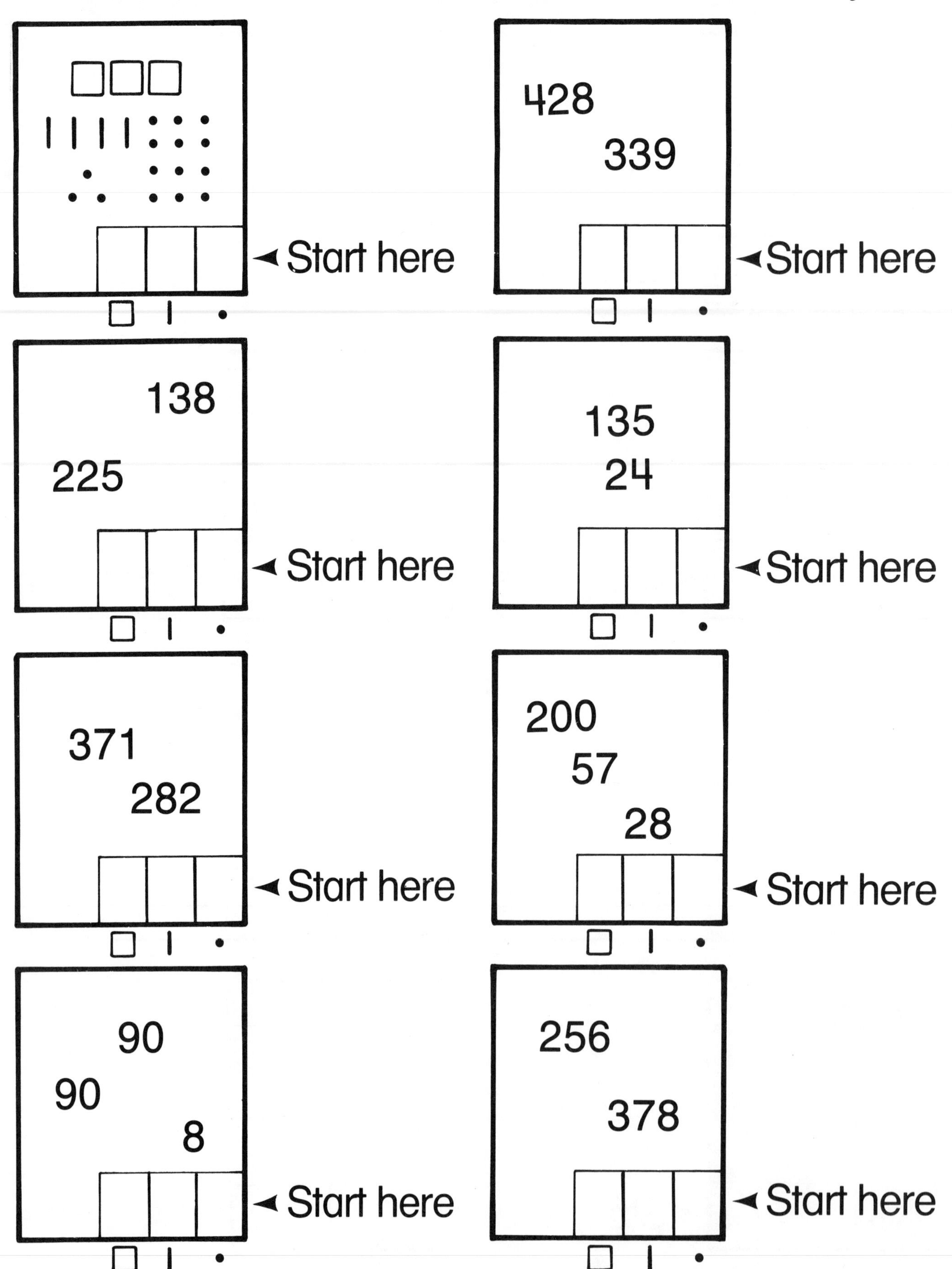

Combine and record. Trade if necessary.

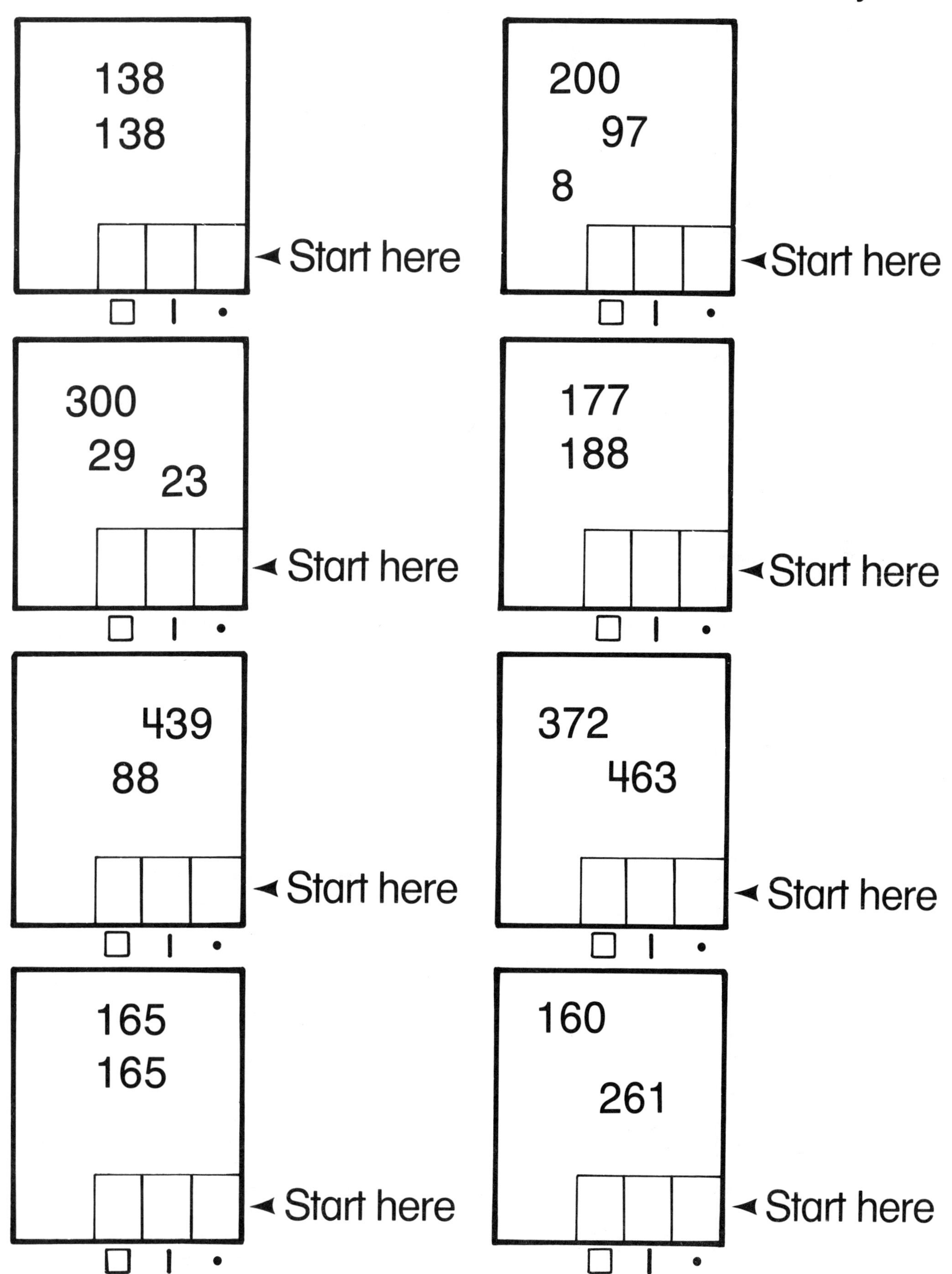

Algorithm 22 179

138
138

◄ Start here

☐ | •

200
97
8

◄ Start here

☐ | •

300
29 23

◄ Start here

☐ | •

177
188

◄ Start here

☐ | •

439
88

◄ Start here

☐ | •

372
463

◄ Start here

☐ | •

165
165

◄ Start here

☐ | •

160
261

◄ Start here

Add. Work from the right. Trade if necessary.

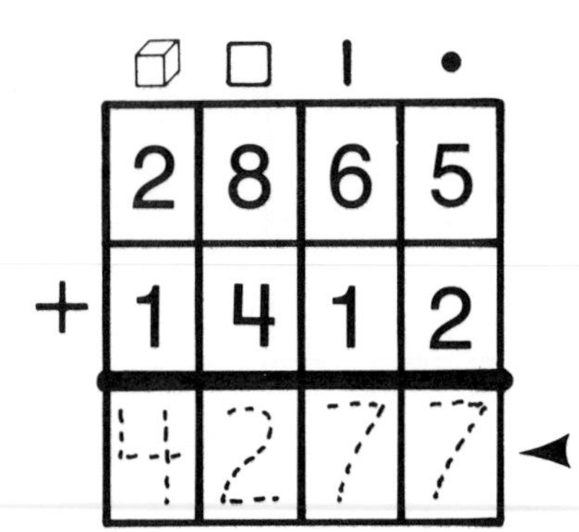

	5	7	3	1
+	2	8	4	2

	3	7	1	2
+	2	9	4	4

	1	4	7	2
+	3	2	7	1

	2	5	8	3
+	3	2	4	1

	2	9	3	5
+	6	9	1	4

	3	2	9	4
+	1	5	8	8

	3	5	2	7
+	4	1	3	8

Add. Work from the right. Trade if necessary.

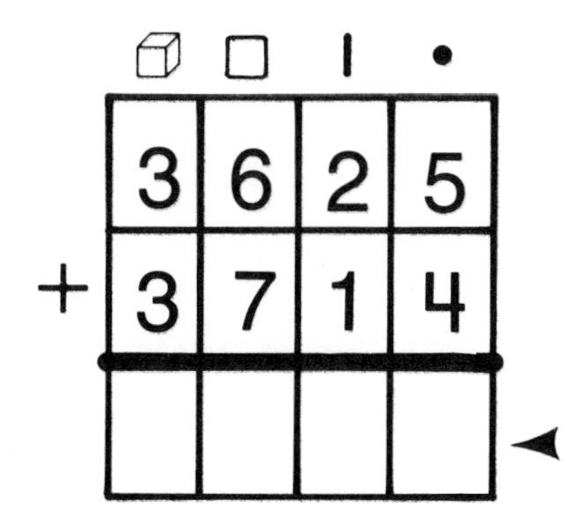

	4	6	8	3
+	2	6	9	1

	2	8	3	6
+	4	4	1	5

	3	5	8	6
+	2	2	4	9

	3	5	7	6
+	5	9	3	7

	4	8	2	2
+	1	7	9	3

	6	8	8	8
+	2	3	4	5

	2	2	8	9
+	1	4	9	9

Combine and record.

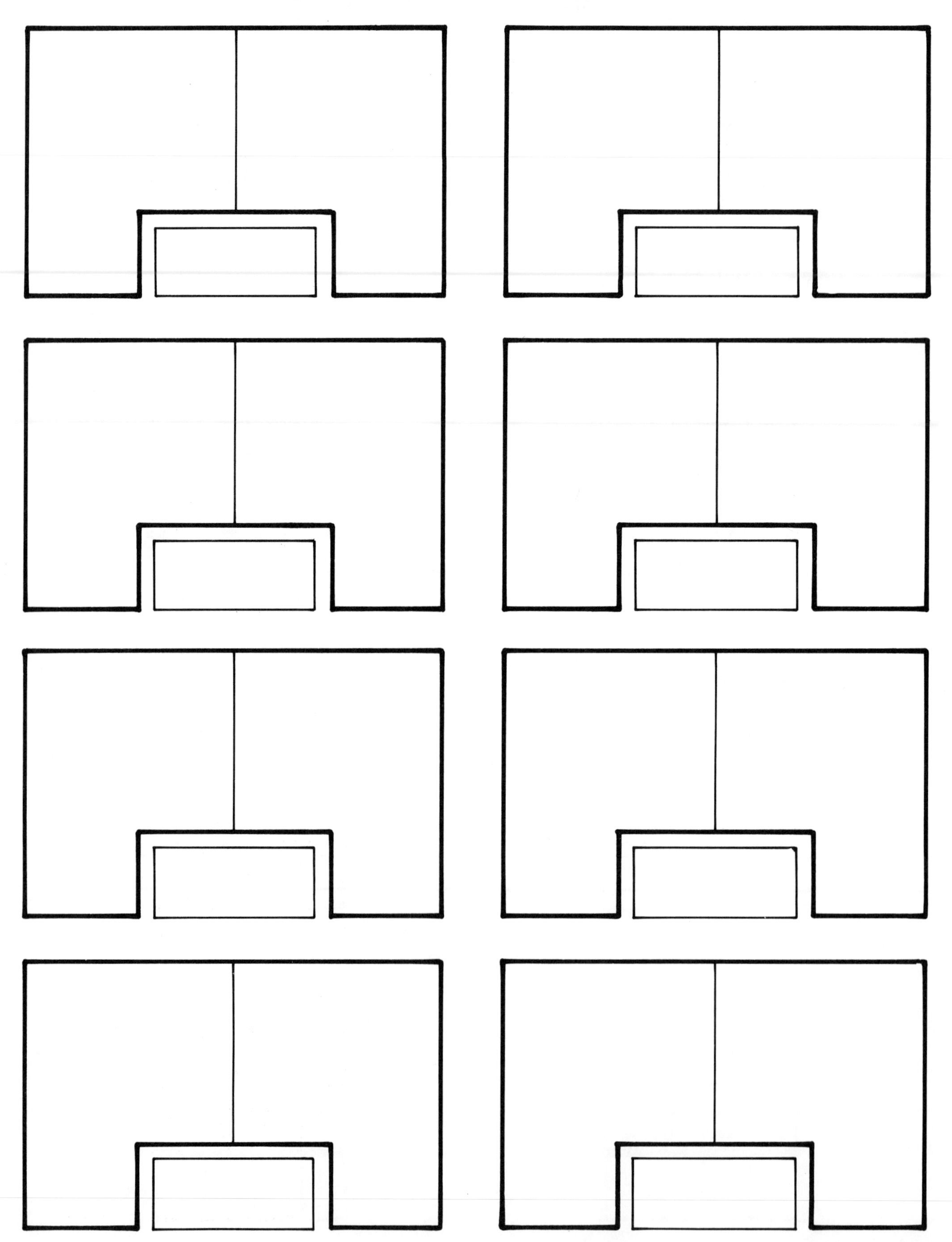

Combine and record. Trade if necessary.

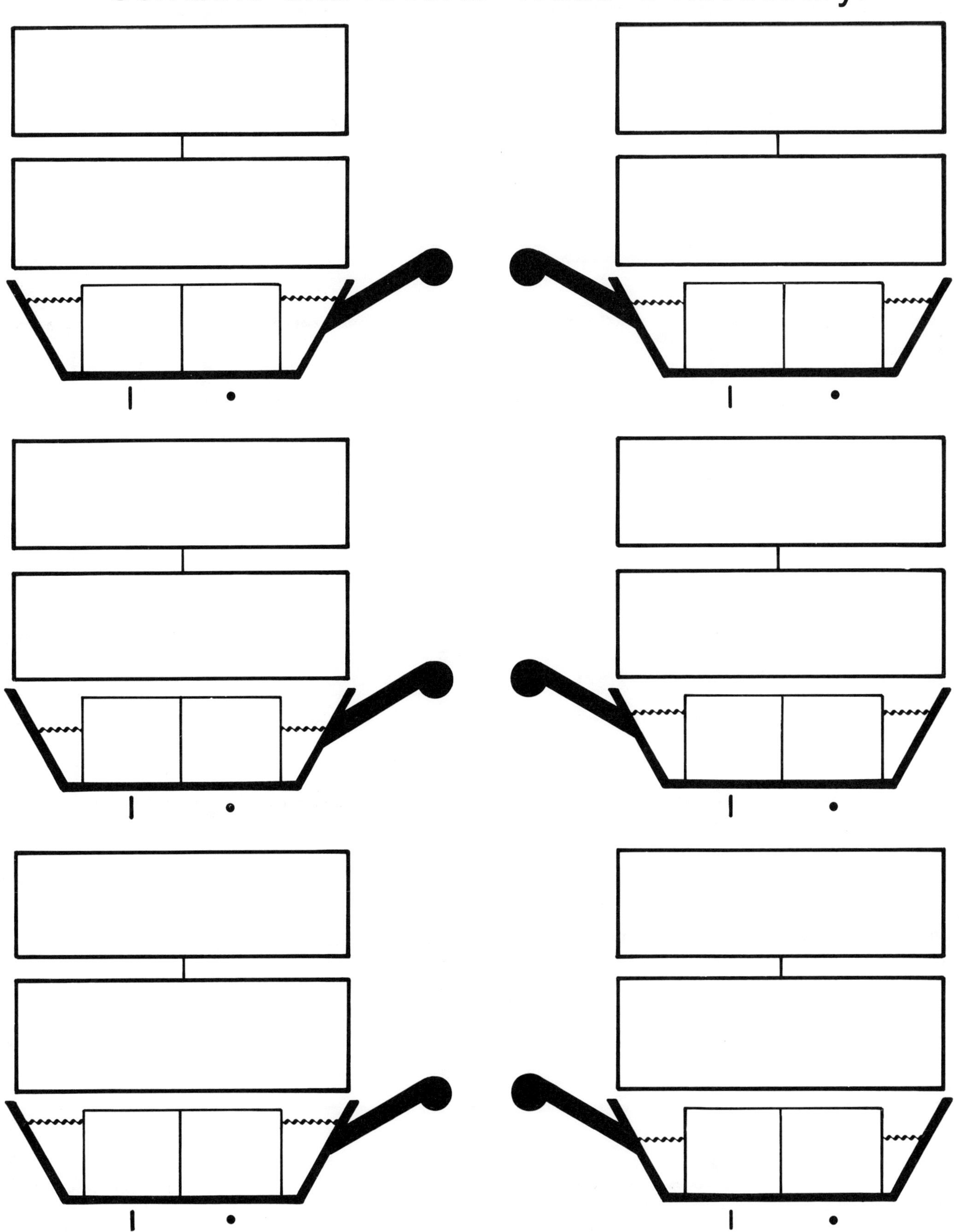

Add. Trade if necessary.

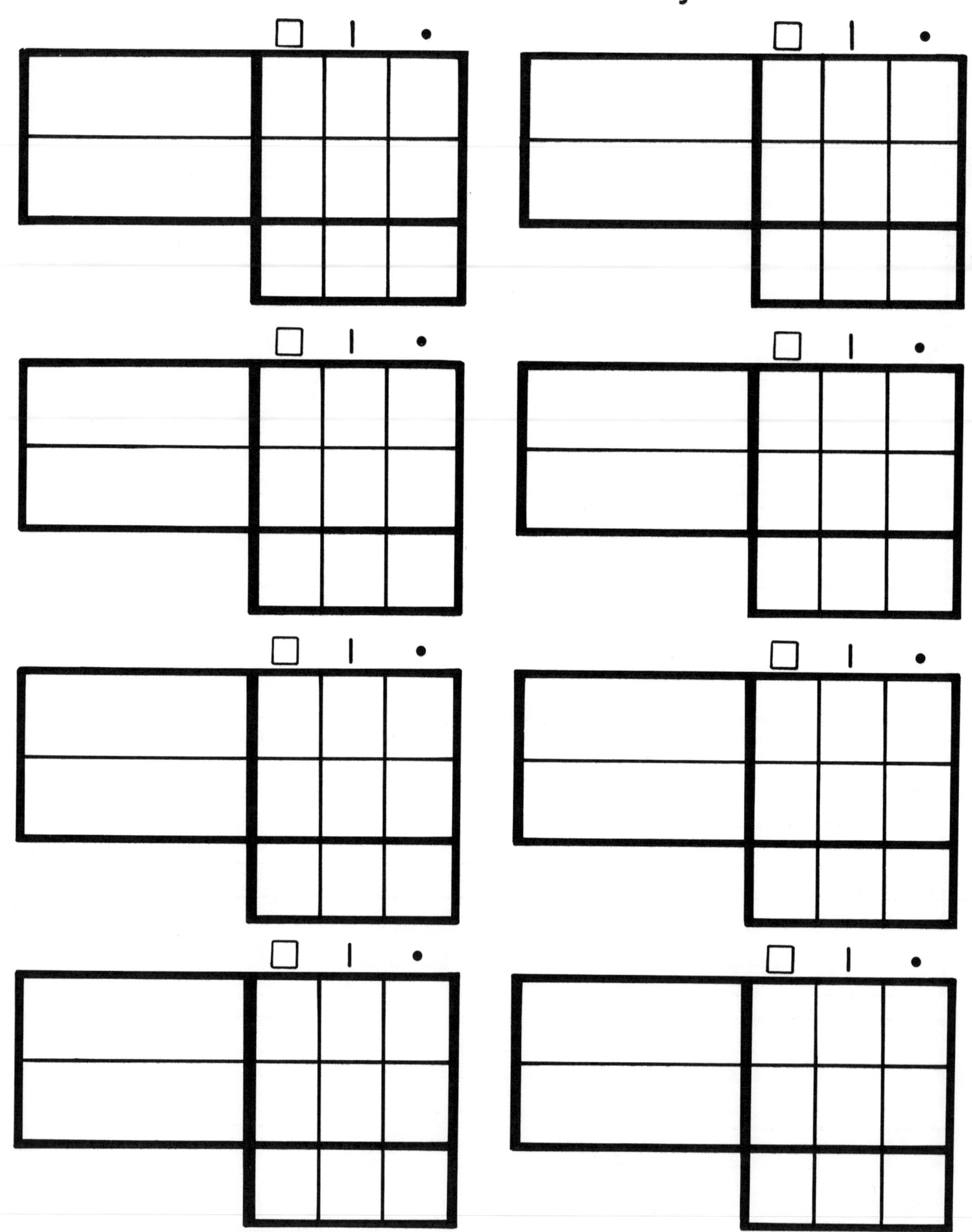

Add. Trade if necessary.

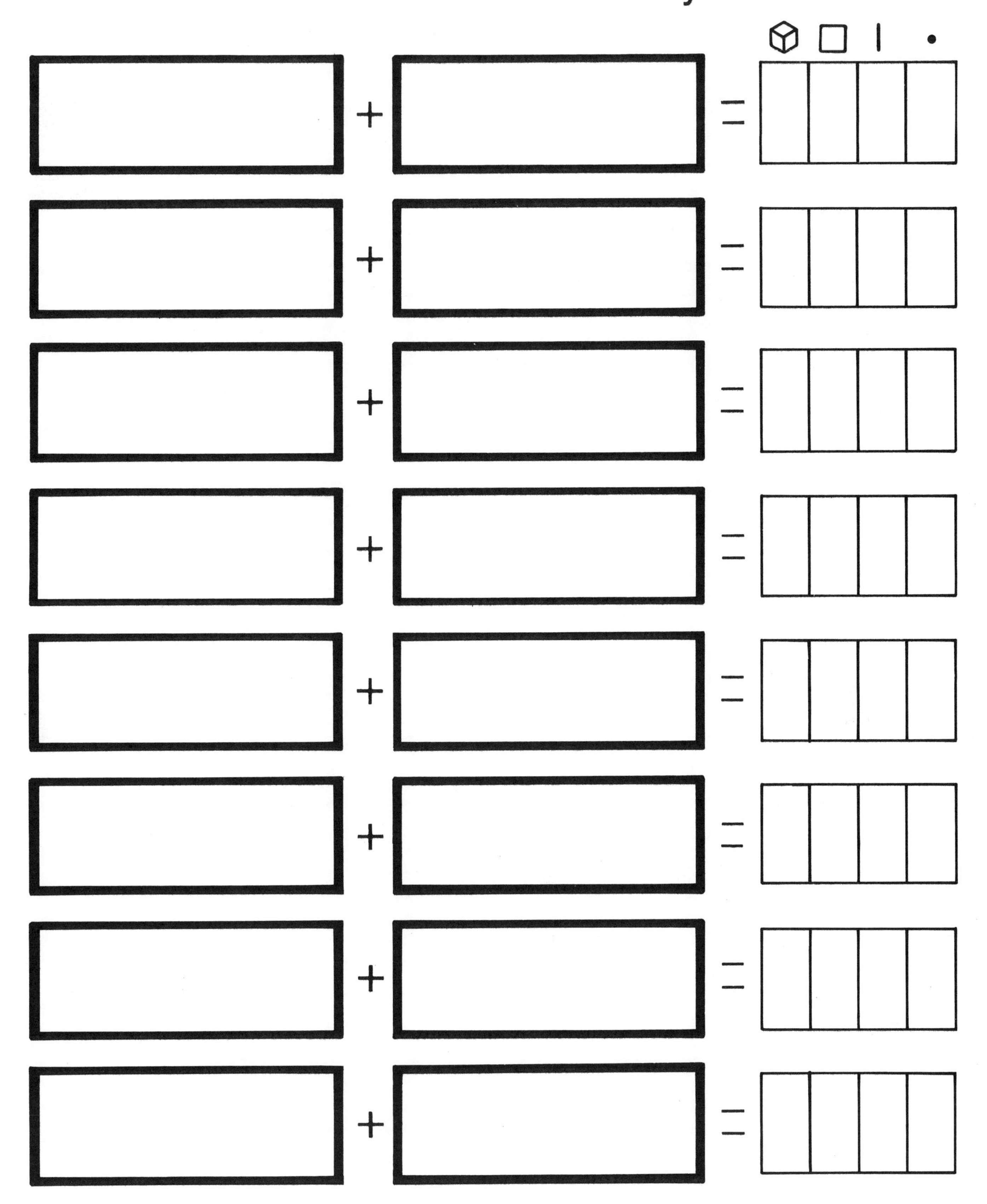

Color the ones and tens. Add.

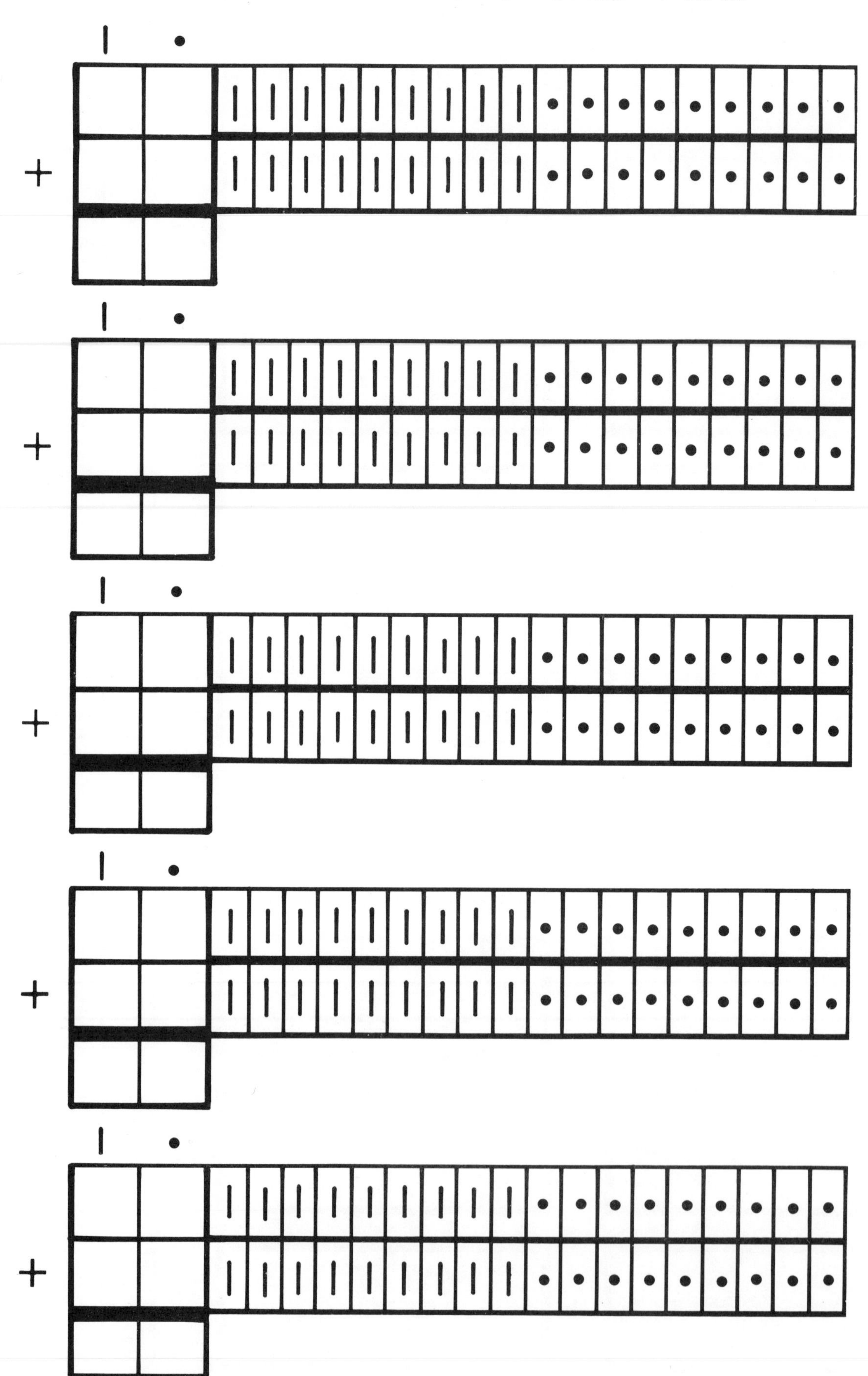

Color the ones, tens, and hundreds.
Add.

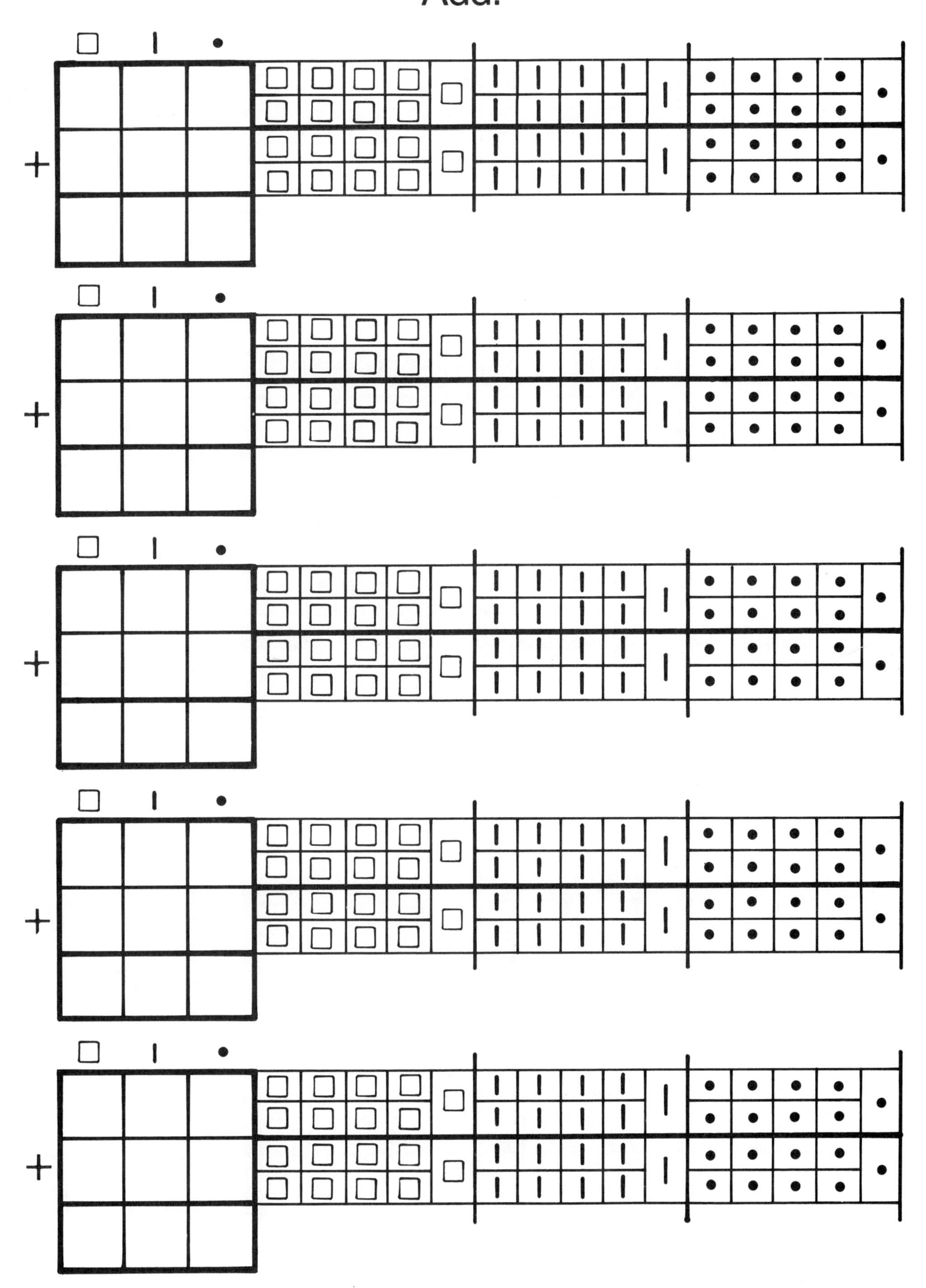

Color the ones, tens, hundreds, and thousands. Add.

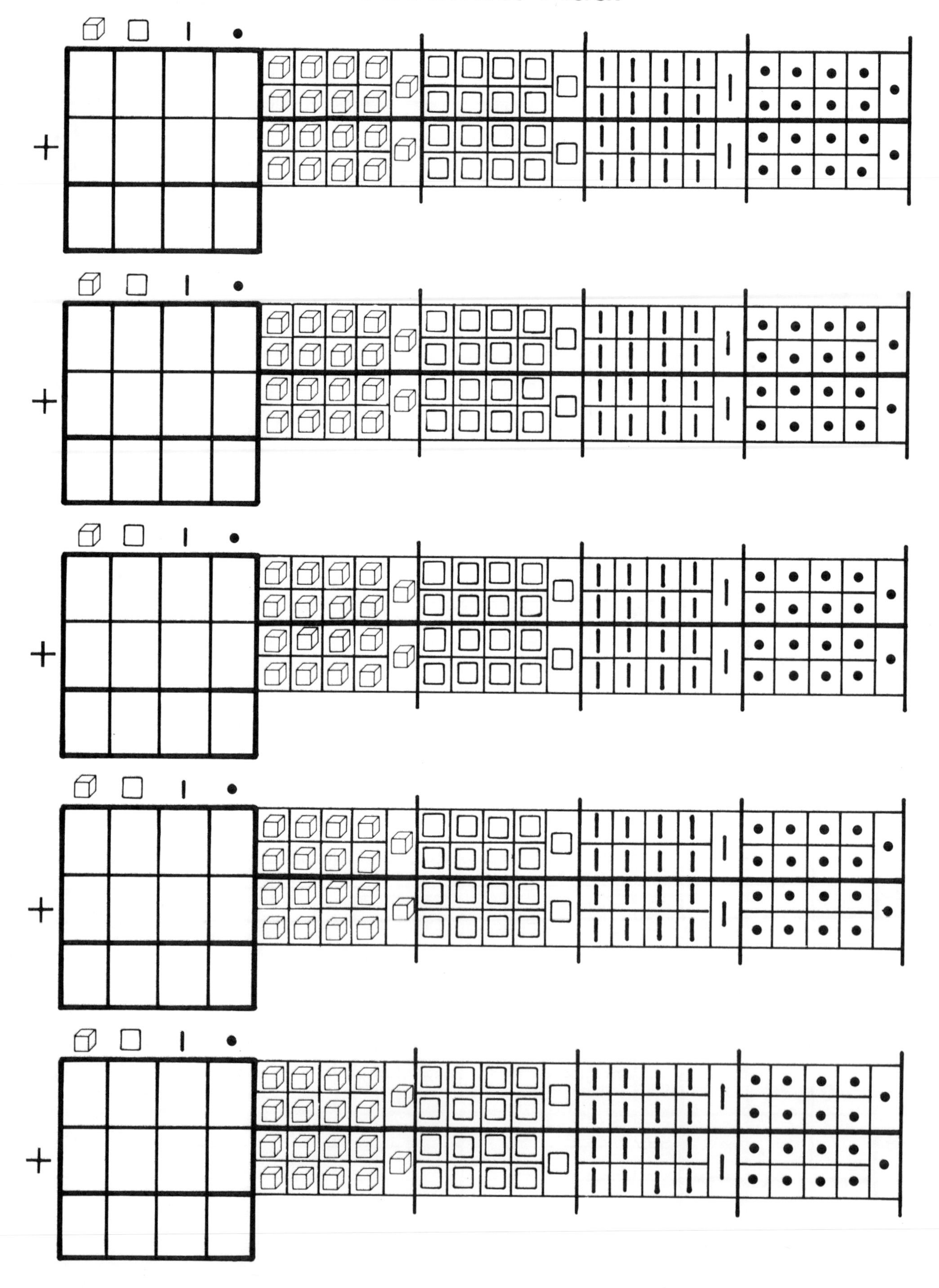